MW00586979

THE SONG OF ASCENTS

TOM HINEY

The Song
of Ascents

Lives of Rage and Stillness

IGNATIUS PRESS   SAN FRANCISCO

Unless otherwise indicated, Scripture quotations are from Revised Standard Version of the Bible—Second Catholic Edition (Ignatius Edition) copyright © 2006 National Council of the Churches of Christ in the United States of America. All rights reserved worldwide.

Unless otherwise indicated, all English translations of papal documents and homilies are taken from the Vatican website.

Cover art by © istock/MriduL Panda

Cover design by Roxanne Mei Lum

© 2022 by Ignatius Press, San Francisco
All rights reserved
ISBN 978-1-62164-509-2 (PB)
ISBN 978-1-64229-222-0 (eBook)
Library of Congress Control Number 2021941907
Printed in the United States of America ∞

Contents

Acknowledgments

Excerpt from "Ambulances", by Philip Larkin, from *Whitsun Weddings*, reproduced by permission of Faber and Faber Ltd.

Excerpts from "Campo dei Fiori" and "Dedication" from Czesław Miłosz, *New and Collected Poems: 1932–2001*, © 1988, 1991, 1995, 2001, by Czesław Miłosz Royalties, Inc. Reproduced by permission of HarperCollins US Publishers and Penguin Books Ltd.

Excerpts from Krystyna Carter's English translation of lines from *Symphony No. 3 OP 36* (Wilhelm Szewczyk/Henryk Górecki/Jerzy Lisowski) © 1992 by Boosey & Hawkes Music Publishers Ltd. Reproduced by permission of Boosey & Hawkes Music Publishers Ltd.

Introduction

Deo Gloria

England has really got into so wrong a state, with its plu-
tocracy and neglected populace and materialistic and ser-
vile morality, that it must take a sharp turn that will be
a sensational turn. No *evolution* into Catholicism will have
that moral effect. Christianity is the religion of repentance;
it stands against modern fatalism and pessimistic futurism
mainly in saying that a man can go back. If we do decidedly go back it will show that religion is alive.[1]

G. K. Chesterton, Letter 1923

It is impossible for me to pretend much detachment in introducing what follows. The world is crazy, and for a long
time working on these stories was my secret treasure trove
and punchbag, as I processed this unpalatable fact. There is
a wonder to them that still sustains me, and a love that I
hope is now mine to share—but let me not deny that each
story was also written in anger, an act of defiance against
chaos, fears, and nonsense, mostly my own.

I am a biographer by instinct, which means that I tend
to hide behind other people's stories, and these portraits are
no exception. However, since Jesus Christ began revealing
more about me than I ever intended to show, memories of
my own have kept popping to the surface, like parts of a

[1] Ian Ker, *G. K. Chesterton: A Biography* (Oxford: Oxford University Press,
2011), p. 488.

crashed aircraft. In the end, I decided to let them speak, for they also have a story to tell, and a hopeful one at that.

The Triune God of Christianity, Father, Son, and Holy Spirit, is referred to using both upper and lower-case pronouns (He/he; You/you, etc.). These have been left unstandardized, for I and others use both. The Creator and Redeemer in whom we believe does not stand on ceremony, but sometimes using a capital letter seems the least one can do.

— TH

PART ONE

How It Feels to Believe

Preface

There is a church on the Somerset Levels, in southwest England, so ancient that it is perched well above the village of Aller it serves. The hill up there is not steep, but all hills were islands in the days before those coastal plains were first drained by the Normans. Until then, they were a marshy maze, which was why King Alfred hid here from the Vikings in the ninth century, and it was back to this fastness that he brought the Viking king Gudrun to be baptised after finally defeating him in battle. Follow the sign to "ANCIENT CHURCH" from the village, and the latter appears from behind hedgerow, sitting next to a dairy farm. Stonework, lead roofing, stained glass, and electricity have transformed it over the ages, but it has not budged, and baptisms still take place here.

The oldest churches in England were annexes to Roman villas or repurposed pagan temples. Others were built in stone from the start out of deference to Catholic basilicas or with timber techniques from northern Europe. Some churches, now invisible to archaeology, began life as mud and wattle. Whatever they were made from, these buildings were celebrating Christmas and Easter long before Alfred was born and centuries before "England" existed as a nation, let alone "The United Kingdom".

In London, on the floor of the central lobby between the House of Lords and the House of Commons, is a verse from the Bible laid out in tiles: NISI DOMINUS AEDIFICAVERIT DO-MUM, IN VANUM LABORAVERUNT QUI AEDIFICANT EAM. "Un-less the LORD builds the house, those who build it labor in vain" (Psalm 127). It dominates the floor, even if few stop to read it. Downriver, in the expansive and ancient legal chambers at Temple, King Alfred's law code is acknowl-edged as a foundation document of a justice system that has been exported around the world. Written in Old English, the code is prefaced by eleven excerpts from Scripture, one of them almost an entire Bible chapter long.

A Fijian once told me that the British soldiers with whom he served in Afghanistan would not go out on patrol until he had prayed for them. Back home, they would probably not have been seen near a church, except perhaps in the equiva-lent "no atheists in foxholes" moments that even suburban life can throw up. I was no different, and being a believer does not mean I want to spend my life arguing with people —quite the opposite. People wanted to argue with Jesus all the time, but he was not interested. This was not cowardice on his part, for Jesus of Nazareth could hardly be accused of that. While on earth, he insulted the religiously power-ful, stood up to crowds, snapped his disciples into line, and stared Roman justice in the face; but it was never what you would call a debate. He was the Truth, and you either be-lieved him or not, and that is still the issue. As the Catholic philosopher Jean-Luc Marion says of the Resurrection, it is not as if we can expect any further information.

Watching a gospel service erupt in an African township or reading the Bible with the growing suspicion that it is true; seeing the atmosphere whiten at a downtown Mass or being immersed in the authority of Orthodox chant; surren-dering to the unity of a chorus of praise or hearing an old preacher's voice catch at what he is talking about; sometimes a wonderful stillness falls. It can fall at four in the morning when you are alone with insomnia, and it can fail to fall when advertised. It seems to have a life of its own and can sometimes fall with a special intensity. The Hebrew word *shekinah* denotes a Glory beyond any other, for God's presence is not to be categorised; it takes people's breath away. Another Hebrew word, *shalach*, means both "to praise" and "to still". I can hardly believe such faith has happened to me; clumsy, cynical, selfish, over-thinking me. Having faith is a miracle that still creeps up on me and takes me by surprise. I am under no illusion that I am perfect, but I believe Christ is, that His Church is alive, and that I am called to proclaim this to my generation.

The challenge is knowing how deep to go, how much to say, without being too intense or equally too casual. Only love and the Holy Spirit can get the measure right, and I am not always full of either. Saint Paul recommends this: "Let your speech always be gracious, seasoned with salt, so that you may know how you ought to answer every one."[1] "Seasoned with salt" is rendered "flavoured with wit" in another translation. Wit springs from honesty, not an easy bedfellow with the natural wish not to offend nor the conviction (prophesied by Scripture and Tradition and felt in the belly) that things are likely to get worse before they get better. That is not many people's idea of a joke but consider this honesty from Saint Paul: "understand this, that in the last days there will come times of stress. For men will be lovers of self, lovers of money, proud, arrogant, abusive, disobedient to their parents, ungrateful, unholy, inhuman,

---

[1] 1 Colossians 4:6.

implacable, slanderers, profligates, fierce, haters of good, treacherous, reckless, swollen with conceit, lovers of plea-sure rather than lovers of God".[2]

It is hard not to think, as successive generations have done, that such scenes are coming to a head in our day, and there have been moments, certainly, when it has felt like blas-phemy to be quiet. Watching insanity descend on society, as consumerism makes fools of us all. Hearing managers lie, know they are lying, and be applauded for the quality of their lying. Listening to endless debates about money as if it were theology. Waiting for artists to say something, only to watch the best ones end up with mortgages and ex-spouses. Seeing churches implode in scandal and mediocrity and knowing that there are wicked spirits in this world, drunk on easy pickings, and even good people staggering about in a daze.

The darkest pages of Isaiah have cheered me at times, the Apocalypse has consoled me, until I recall my own sins and find myself cringing again before God. Has the world always been this insipid? Why do we give way to such a base noth-ing, such a pandering to hell? At times I have to consider Jesus in the Garden of Gethsemane praying for us, urging us with whatever gifts we have to tell the truth better than they tell their lies. But how to convey something as vast, delicate, powerful, simple, and beautiful as faith? That, in a nutshell, has been my quandary for the last two decades. At the end of a work-leaving party not long after returning to church, a colleague asked me: 'What is Christ to you?' It was 2 A.M., and I was far more used to fielding banter about my faith than a serious question. But, since it was I who was leaving and the curiosity seemed genuine, I tried my

[2] 2 Timothy 3:1–4.

best to answer. I doubt either of us remember what I said, but I never forgot the question: *What is Christ to you?* I was meant to be asking such questions, and yet I could barely answer.

What is Christ to my country, once known as an "Evangelist to the Nations"? There is still a Christian cross on our royal crown and an image of the crown on stamps, banknotes, and cap-badges. There are crosses on three out of the four flags we fly, and our national anthem is a prayer. The Christian faith once tied us together, and the lack of it now drives us apart. Yet, like other nations, we still measure time from Christ's birth, and cathedral churches dominate our city centres. I was brought back to faith by Africans in Africa and could not be less interested in a narrow Anglo-Saxon or Celtic revival, but nor do I think for a moment that anyone on these islands has ever forgotten Jesus. I think we have been ignoring Him, which is a different matter altogether. As G. K. Chesterton put it in 1910, in *What's Wrong with the World*: "The Christian ideal has not been tried and found wanting. It has been found difficult; and left untried."

The following stories concern people turning to God in very challenging (sometimes horrendous) situations, with human hearts like mine, and repeatedly finding Him to be faithful, albeit in strange and unexpected ways. These people taught me, even as I read their testimonies and tried to imagine their experiences, how to give a reason for my hope.

I

Northern Lights

Have mercy on me, O God, according to your
merciful love.

Psalm 51:1

There is a graveyard in Hull, on the northeast coast of England, called Springfield Cemetery. One blue morning, snowdrops appearing on the ground, I found myself searching for an old grave I had read about earlier in the town's maritime museum. The section of the cemetery I was looking through was full and no longer taking new entries, its residents largely forgotten according to the testimony of brambles and litter. Some of the more elaborate mausolea had been pushed over and defaced with graffiti.

For a long while, I could not find the one I was after, its elusiveness in sharp contrast to that day in 1867 when half of Hull was said to have lined the streets to watch the body of Captain John Gravill brought out here. The late poet Philip Larkin used to walk around Spring Bank. An atheist, he conveyed as well as anyone the bleakness of living without faith in post-industrial Hull. In his poem "Ambulances", he described a group of children watching a dead body being taken out of a local house: "And sense the solving emptiness / That lies just under all we do, / And for a second get it whole, / So permanent and blank and true."[1]

---

[1] Philip Larkin, *Collected Poems* (London: Faber and Faber, 1988), p. 132.

An old grave is like the back of a paperback, offering a summary of the plot in terms that are perhaps bolder than the lived reality. Here a child who died in infancy ("Thy will be done"); there a couple who lived long enough to find "Strength in Suffering"; here a sailor who shall "Sail the wild seas no more". Finally, I found the one I was after, obscured by branches, standing beside a fire-scorched ring left by a tramp or youngsters: "In memory of John Gravill of Kingston upon Hull, Master Mariner who during a period of forty years was engaged by the Northern Whale and Seal Fishery. He died on board the steam whaler Diana in Davis Straits 26th December 1866 aged 64 years. His death resulted from exposure, anxiety and shortness of provisions during a four-months imprisonment in the ice surrounded by all the dreariness and perils of a cold and desolate Arctic winter."

My interest was in the ship's surgeon who had been on board during the ordeal. Charles Smith was still completing his medical studies at Glasgow University when he applied, against the wishes of his father, to gain experience on the *Diana*. Others at the school had done the same, and Smith, a Quaker by upbringing, wanted likewise to prove himself and taste adventure. There was reason to hope the *Diana*'s voyage that year would be less dangerous than normal, for over the winter she had been fitted with a modern, coal-powered steam engine, which would give her added capacity in the Arctic waters.

Still bearing sails, she had been the first Hull whaler to fit an engine, drawing an especially large crowd on the day of her departure. Smith's brand new journal records, in its entry for 19 February 1866: "Every pier, wharf, ship and 'coign of vantage' was covered by a multitude of well-wishers, who cheered lustily."[2] This novelty apart, the ship was set on a

[2] Charles Edward Smith, *From the Deep of the Sea: An Epic in the Arctic*, ed.

course familiar to any of the whaling crews who ventured from that port. She would first make for Icelandic waters to hunt seals; then to Lerwick on the Shetlands, where she would pick up extra crew and final supplies for the main business. After that, they would head northwest toward Greenland, where each year the endless summer sun would open up otherwise frozen bays of rich whaling.

For meals, Smith joined the senior crew members in the captain's cabin, his own berth barely large enough to store the clothes, instruments, and books he had brought. Smith had never been to sea before, and, despite the strangeness and discomfort, his early journal entries show him eager to learn as much as he could. Among the books he had brought for his private reflection was a biography of John Newton, the converted slave-trader and author of "Amazing Grace". He had also brought a dog with him, a small terrier named Gyp.

The voice of Captain Gravill that appears in Smith's journal clearly enjoyed regaling his enthusiastic surgeon with memories: "Once, when in Greenland, I watched a school of 'Bottlenoses' constantly going backwards and forwards beneath a piece of ice on which there was a seal laid. Every time they went under the ice they struck it with their tails, but whether it was to break the ice or frighten the seal off I don't know, but the seal was frightened enough of 'em, I assure you!" Meanwhile, they were making good initial progress, though all at the captain's table agreed the winter was going on too late to be much good for sealing. As they approached Jan Mayen island, they joined a dozen or so British and Norwegians struggling with too much

Charles Edward Smith Harris (Annapolis, Md.: Naval Institute Press, 1977). All subsequent quotes in this essay are taken from that edition of Smith's journals. The original journals can be viewed in the archives of Hull Maritime Museum.

fog, swell, and floating ice for any of them to be able to hunt.

Gyp had started to suffer from both the cold and seasickness, but for Smith it was still intensely interesting, surrounded as he was by an experienced crew whose professionalism he enjoyed. Sat off where they huddled, the volcanic summit of Jan Mayen glittered with snow, "till one imagined oneself gazing upon some terrestrial similitude of 'the great white throne' in the Revelation". But on Good Friday the fun stopped, as fog and swell separated the *Diana* from the other ships, and huge shards of sharp ice began thudding against her sides. For protection from the growing storm, Gravill anchored in the lee of a solid icepack. Smith records going to bed that night at about 10:30 P.M. and being woken at 2 A.M. by the ship being thrown about. Going on deck in his dressing gown, he could see that the storm had broken up the ice behind which they had anchored and that the men on night watch were using long fenders to hold off the shards again threatening their sides.

He went back to his berth but was unable to sleep, "partly from the motion of the ship, but principally from a feeling of uneasiness". Leaving his berth, still in his dressing gown, he met the captain, fully dressed and looking concerned, while on deck the winds were "like thunder". The first mate grabbed Smith and told him to get dressed in case they had to abandon ship. Smith rushed below and put on several layers of flannel shirts, woollen neck wrappers, and stockings. Back on deck, the moon was illuminating a swell, "thickly covered with massive pieces of ice". They had been struck, and men were working the pumps as the carpenter worked in the keel to patch a puncture. Men were moving up and down with fenders, pushing ice away, while others brought bags of biscuit, cheese, and meats up to be lowered onto the boats if they abandoned. A tot of rum was issued to everyone, and all this activity took place against deafening gales, as the *Diana* rose and fell in the ice-strewn swell.

Smith started to take his turn at the pump, and then fender, for dawn brought no relief. The *Diana* was alone and surrounded by deadly swells. The new engine was running, but it was impossible to steam out of this maelstrom, and they expected to be "stove in" at any moment, the first mate assured him, and "'twould be by a miracle" if they weren't. Smith was tasting the dark side of adventure: "The excitement, the state of mind, was intense. It was one long agony of danger, a protracted mental torture, almost more than I could bear." As the carpenter worked to save them, those with fenders fought off "jagged, cold, cruel monsters, rising, falling, and retreating on the crest of the swell, and then rushing down the slope towards us in lines and columns, abreast, in straggling groups, or dense companies".

Smith was amazed how coolly the crew went about their business:

> There was no skulking; no appearance of fear, faint-heartedness, or despair; no unmanly croaking or prophesying the worst (though all expected it) among them. Every man kept up his own spirits and cheered his fellows. Never in my life did I feel so proud of being an Englishman, so proud of the calm, self-possessed, resolute bearing of my fellow-countrymen, who, with sudden and inevitable death staring them in the face, yet did their duty as though nothing unusual were occurring.

At 2 P.M., all hands were ordered to the captain's cabin, where

> the captain told us in a few words that we had done all that men could do, and that we must put our trust solely now

in the mercy of God. He exhorted us to prepare for the eternal world, and proposed to sing a hymn, "and mind you sing it with all your hearts". We then, with voices choking with emotion, sang those lines:

> Commit thou all thy griefs
> And ways into His hands;
> To His sure truth and tender care,
> Who earth and heaven commands,
> Who points the clouds their course,
> Whom winds and seas obey.
> He shall direct thy wandering feet,
> He shall prepare thy way.

Smith watched as "the captain then, kneeling down, prayed very earnestly to God to have mercy upon us all, to spare us for the sake of our friends and families, or, should He see fit to take our lives, to watch over and comfort them when we were gone." Ice began banging against the ship, and the captain ordered everyone back up and "urged us to offer up mental prayers when on the deck, at the wheel, aloft, wherever we might be." The horizon was full of dark clouds, "like a funeral pall about to descend upon our closing scene". No other ships were in view, but Smith felt different: "Though distressed enough in mind and fearfully uneasy at times, I felt remarkably free from the secret terror of the mysteries of eternity, especially after the service in the cabin. Nay, at times I felt cheerfully resigned and prepared for the worst. I contemplated death without the slightest fear—'twas only a few minutes' struggle in the waves, one of the easiest deaths to die."

At the very pitch of danger, the storm ceased, and four weeks later, shaken and having depleted much of her coal, the *Diana* came into harbour at Lerwick, back in a world of newspapers, post, and a hotel. She had survived her thrash-

ing and remained on schedule to catch up with the rest of
the Greenland fleet, once repairs had been made and extra
crew hired. For ten days, Smith stayed in the hotel: "It is
impossible to describe the exhilarated feelings. . . . [The]
singing of the larks never seemed so sweet to me before,
while the sight of some primroses in a sheltered nook among
the rocks by Gulverwick brought back all manner of home
recollections." He roamed the island, visiting houses made
of stone and thatch, "of one room, with bed cabins ranged
round the sides, a peat fire burning on the middle of the
floor."

The men these homes produced were some of the tough-
est whalers in the world, but the port could not replenish all
the coal they had burned. However, winds were favourable,
and they made good progress as they got going again, up
toward Pond's Bay, some 2,000 miles northwest of Lerwick.
There they caught up with a fleet still being frustrated by
the persistent winter. The *Polynia* was there, and the *Tay*,
Ravenscraig, *Retriever*, and *Intrepid*—ships many of the crew
knew. Though already June, none of them had yet ventured
into the bays, which were still clogged with ice. There was
camaraderie as well as competitiveness between these ships
as they waited, bonded in their shared horror at the conditions: "Captain Gravill is utterly confounded at the unprece-
dented state of matters here. All on board are idle and de-
pressed, and despair of 'getting a voyage' after all our labour
to arrive at this 'promised land' of the whalers. What is
worse than all, should a strong South-East wind set in, the
whole fleet would inevitably be crushed and 600 or so men
turned adrift upon the ice."

Depending on their rank, crew were paid a percentage of
the catch, and nothing else, meaning this was a fleet of 600
men willing to push that risk for as long as necessary. But

as the captains conferred, it was uncertain what the point of the gamble was. Smith visited another ship's surgeon, accompanied by Gyp, who had recovered from his initial shock at life on board. Smith himself was still in buoyant spirits, and, when the fog lifted, Greenland provided a "stupendous" backdrop: lofty, snow-covered mountains, whose summits rose above the clouds, shining purple and crimson. The light was more vivid than anything he had seen. Smith was drawing as well as writing, recording with fascination a small iceberg "which seemed as red as blood, and which evidently had been formed upon and broken away from some ferruginous rock".

Life had become more cramped on board, with the Shetland whalers having doubled the crew size from twenty-five to fifty-one. These included all the harpoonists, ready to take to the water on boats whenever whales were sighted. Seven youngsters had also joined in Lerwick, some of them like Smith having never been to sea before, filling menial tasks for a nominal share in the voyage. Apart from Essex-born Smith and the ship's Dundee-born carpenter, all the original crew had been from Hull. All were now in confined quarters off the southwest coast of Greenland and facing unprofitable inactivity. To their west lay barren ocean, full of pack ice. It was east and north along the bays of Greenland where the whales usually congregated in their thousands.

Perhaps only Smith, who was not doing this for the money, could still enjoy it. On the Greenland coast, he could see how the glaciers crept off the mountains into old valleys, breaking into the icebergs that impeded them. When the fleet finally decided to try its luck, those ships with coal engines piloted the rest into thin clearwater floes. These were narrow, at times needing to be pushed out by fenders. Progress was so slow that men took turns to go ashore and stretch their legs on the mainland, Smith helping collect stones to write "DIANA HULL" on a snowy hill.

On Thursday 14 June 1866, at 7 P.M., "there were seen upon the ice some dark objects which the ship's telescope showed to be Esquimaux. I went with a boat's crew to meet the party, which was in three sledges, driving at great speed towards the ship. The party consisted of three men, who were delighted to see us." The sledges were each drawn by six yellow-white dogs, "remarkably fine animals, the size of a wolf", and were ingeniously made of fir-wood, with runners of walrus tusk fastened to the woodwork with rawhide. Their whale-horn handles were tipped with iron, and the seats had skin cushions stuffed with grass. These visitors were given rum, traded craft for clothing, and stayed the night on deck. The next day, they left, and the *Diana* went on her way, the fog so heavy that at times they could barely see the ship in front of them. Reaching a promontory that had been their target for days, the bay beyond that looked just as bad.

The first whale was sighted on a Sunday, and, although Captain Gravill did not like hunting on a Sabbath, he let the men go after it in deference to their livelihoods, confiding to Smith that he was glad then to see the whale escape. For a while, the fleet scattered, each vessel looking for what catch it could. When the sun broke through, it gave little relief to the deteriorating morale on board: "The heat is so great as to make all on board feel lazy and indisposed for the necessary exertion at the windlasses when warping the ship through the ice." The open water was like steel, refracting and reflecting the scenery into "a thousand grotesque shapes". On Saturday 30 June, the *Diana* caught her first whale, followed by another, allowing Smith to see the factory of hauling and "flinching" that went into business at such times and the mood improve. With blubber valued at £50 a tonne, and whalebone £700 a tonne, that one day's catch had an estimated value of £2,050, the price of a large house in 1866.

At his table, the captain turned back to his stories. Of the sharks that hovered around whaling ships, he told Smith: "They are very tenacious of life. . . . I've seen us cut up a shark into pieces and bury them in the snow. On going to look at them twenty-four hours afterwards the bits were alive and moving about." Some of his stories were darker, of shipwrecks and frozen human corpses. The fleet got as far north as Baffin Bay, but were met with nothing but black cliffs, icepacks, and snow-threatening skies. "The past week has been indescribably dull, gloomy, and cheerless. Everybody is in the blues." The captains conferred, and it was the same on every ship. This was the worst season in memory. The *Intrepid* had had a case of scurvy, owing to the spoiling of the ship's potatoes and the bad quality of her meat: "The men are talking of nothing else but the return home." As acceptance of the season's failure spread, blues gave way to apprehension, since they faced the same icy maze by which they had come and, in the case of the *Diana*, this time with almost no coal left.

Instead of trailing the coast, the fleet decided to sail west for a clearer way back to the Atlantic.[3] "All on board are beginning to look and talk seriously." They reached the coast of Baffinland, but it was no better than the Greenland route, and less assured on the charts. They turned back but were met with "immense amounts of ice" now being blown into their path by a northeast wind and were brought to a stop.

[3] To their north lay the scenes of various treacherous attempts by crews to find a "Northwest passage" over the Arctic circle into the Pacific.

With the short summer disappearing, the first snows fell, and, in thick fog, the fleet began to disperse. When it lifted, most of the ships had gone, with just two remaining, the *Diana* and the *Intrepid*. Then the fog returned, and, when it cleared, they couldn't see the *Intrepid*.

Rapidly, the *Diana* had found herself in the worst of all possible situations. Stuck with little coal, while strengthening winds from the south started to push her against an unfamiliar coastline and encircle her with floating ice. These southerly winds also brought clouds off the Atlantic, waves of sleet now adding to their misery. They had insufficient fuel to exhaust it countering these winds, but the danger was that a weak summer would now be followed by an early winter: "This is the last day of the most miserable fortnight I have experienced since we left Hull. No pleasure, no satisfaction; nothing but crosses and disappointments."

Before dawn on Sunday 26 August, a wind from the northwest finally blew ice away from their escape path, and by breakfast they were making eight or nine knots, through occasional floes of weakening ice. That afternoon, however, they came up against "a neck of very heavy ice" extending across their path and the very winds for which they had been praying were now jamming them against this wall. As the storm broke up the ice around them, they were surrounded by this wall on one side and "floes and loose pieces crushing and forcing each other upwards" on all others. The winds were blowing with "amazing speed", reported Smith, as the ship was pinched, surface ice stacking around her, and deeper thuds to the hull reverberating with a "deafening sound".

As sleet fell, the crew hauled provisions up. "It was with the greatest anxiety I watched these doleful preparations." Smith went below to get as many clothes on as he could, as well as his medicine case, only to be told by the first mate: "It's not much use taking such care of your *crang*, doctor. . . . This sort of weather will soon finish us all!" The captain, with agitation visible in his eyes, confirmed the prognosis. If the ship went, he informed Smith, "our chances of saving our lives at such a distance from other ships or settlements [are] not worth a rush."

When the gales abated, they were left completely imprisoned by ice. A mast sighted through the fog turned out to be the *Intrepid*, whose Captain Deuchars reached them by boat, but with no good news. "The state of the country is frightful and our chances of escape very small indeed." Smith was privy to the discussions being held in the captain's cabin, but one did not need to be there to know the truth: "tales of horrible sufferings and deaths from starvation on board unfortunate whalers that have been beleaguered amongst the ice . . . form the staple conversation amongst our crew."

The *Intrepid* had coal reserves and was separated from the *Diana* by ice-floe thin enough for the latter to break through with a decent wind, or with the very last of her coal. Beyond the further wall of ice that held them both trapped was the tantalising sight of open sea to the south. The *Diana's* hopes, therefore, rested on getting to the *Intrepid* and relying on the latter's engine to break a way through that wall. As well as breaking the ice at the right point, the *Intrepid* needed to time such an attempt at a point when the fog lifted long enough for her to see where she was going. On the night of Friday 31 August, the fog that surrounded them both lifted to reveal the Northern Lights "glaring like a blood-red streak beneath a bank of clouds", and the *Intrepid* began getting up steam. This was the *Diana's* cue to use the last of her coal to get across, but in the plummeting night temperatures, the floe between them had thickened. Three coal-sapping times she failed to break through to where the *Intrepid* lay. The latter, having breached the bigger wall, disappeared without them. Quoting Macbeth, Smith recorded the crew cursing "not loud but deep" as they watched the *Intrepid*'s flight.[4] The *Diana* was now trapped, her fuel finished, and the worst of the winter yet to happen. She retreated to protection of her natural harbour of the night before, a spur of ice, but that night a storm deprived them of even this flimsy solace: "We have nothing left to depend upon but the merciful providence of God."

At this point, Smith's journal changes. Gone are the enthusiastic observations and jokes, as he addresses his family directly, in the chance the journal might one day find them, apologising for being so headstrong to have left his studies and for the anguish his death will cause them: "Hardly can I find the heart to sit down to this journal." The following night, without the spur's protection, they were exposed to the full force and pressure of "miles and miles of heavy floes driving before the wind". The winds pushed her northward, into the glacial waters of the Baffinland coast, until all clearwater had vanished. Pinched between two colliding forces of ice, one from the coast and one from the sea, with thick snow now falling, the *Diana* no longer sat level, but was tilted, her timbers making a nerve-shredding din each time they were squeezed. Preparations for evacuation were made "with the energy of despair".

When the winds abated, the crushed floe ice up against them froze, six or seven feet in thickness. The crew squeezed into the captain's cabin for prayers, as he tried to rouse them again with a hymn:

---

[4] The quote is from act 5, scene 3, of Shakespeare's tragedy: "honour, love, obedience, troops of friends, I must not look to have—but, in their stead, Curses, not loud but deep." Captain Deuchars of the *Intrepid* would later claim he had thought the *Diana* was behind him.

> Give to the winds thy fears;
> Hope and be undismayed.
> God hears thy sighs and counts thy tears;
> God shall lift up thy head.

By the next morning, bay ice had covered the last visible clearwater, nearly an inch thick. In the captain's cabin, they discussed abandoning the ship and wintering in a cave on Baffinland, hoping the ship would survive where it was anchored. There were pros and cons to this, but most attention was now on food, and the captain ordered whatever was left, including any personal stores, to be locked up as the communal reserves. When a dead whale was spotted, men were sent over the bay ice to grab what meat they could, and men shot at any birds they saw. Smith could not help but notice how beautiful everything looked, the mountains "glittering and flashing in the blue heavens", whilst icebergs "seemed transformed into dazzling rocks and thrones of transparent crystal". The "mallie birds", which had become their only companions, deserted them as the cold began to show its teeth. Their only hope of escaping the morbid arithmetic of their situation was a wind from the north, and, on Tuesday 4 September, the barometer indicated approaching winds.

These proved good enough and pushed them and the frozen prison around them southeast. So long as they kept moving, they could dream of escaping the winter. On 9 September, the men used warps and fenders to push the ship through a crack that took them into the first stretch of clearwater they had seen since losing the *Intrepid*:

> Whoever reads this can have no idea of the wonderful relief of mind we all experience at having effected our escape from Scott's Bay. For the last fortnight we have been face to face with death, never knowing for six hours at a time

whether or not we should lose our ship; retiring at night hoping, fearing, and doubting, uncertain whether the morrow's sun would find us homeless and helpless among the floes. . . . "I shall sleep to-night, doctor," said one of the officers to me this afternoon. "And it shall be my first sleep worth mentioning for a fortnight. I never dared close my eyes whilst we were amongst that ice." And this man had spent his whole life from boyhood in the whale-fishing.

The way south was blocked by pack ice, but with sail they headed east and made it through the first of the floes they encountered, before hitting an impenetrable ice wall. They went north to get around it, but that was blocked. If they stayed in open water, they would be too vulnerable to the next storm, but the only option to avoid that was to return west, back through the floe, and to re-enter their former prison: "Our poor old captain is quite done up. He fairly melted to tears when he came down from the crow's nest." The first mate, whom Smith had earlier described as stout-hearted to the core, was "completely overcome, and wept tears of anguish at the tea-table". Some of the Shetland novices, noted the doctor, had turned pale with silent dread at this loss of nerve among the leaders. When it came to morale, Charles Smith was becoming the one those below-decks looked to, and he only being held together by prayer: "We may none of us be living by this time next week. O God, have mercy upon us all!"

On 21 September, Captain Gravill jammed the ship into as good a natural harbour as he could find, thus declaring his decision not to winter on land, but to move south with the ice. All the ice packs would eventually make this migration, to be replaced by fresh ice, but it was barely quick enough to be called travel. They might reach the Atlantic by April if they did not freeze, and, though that would be sooner than if they stayed in caves, it was not yet October. Having resigned themselves to this slow escape, each day both inched them closer and saw the temperature drop and darkness grow more permanent. Everything in Smith's berth froze—towels, sponges, socks. His oils and medicines became "frozen masses of ice". Tectonic masses of ice could split the hull and sink them in two minutes, so each night's creaks and groans kept eyes open, even if the cold allowed sleep: "How one escapes being frozen to death in one's berth is a matter of daily wonder and astonishment to me, and also, I trust, of daily gratitude."

The surface ice was thickening in this cold, meaning pressure on the timbers was getting worse, especially in the darkest hours of the night. This dreadful noise, and the danger it signalled, made sleep impossible: "To attempt to describe the miserable state of anxiety, dread, apprehension, even positive terror . . . is impossible." The captain was talking incoherently in his bed, broken before his ship was; the air was now so cold that the very act of breathing was "like cutting your own throat"; ink had frozen in Smith's pen; poor Gyp was going mad; on deck frost covered every sail and nail; while rationing made their heads light and skies even more beautiful than ever: "The entire horizon is one brilliant purple, blue and crimson flush."

Whales frolicked around them, as if deliberately in taunt, but the sailors were too weak to move. The Northern Lights appeared "in a magnificent arch like a rainbow". There was an ebb and flow of prayer meetings, and, on Tuesday 6 November, a storm blew the *Diana* from her protected spot and pinched the plates of ice so heavily against her that "at about 11 A.M. we were compelled to blast the ice on our port quarter to relieve the opposite side of the ship from the pressure." They had already had so many near misses. One

night, a spot they had tried again and again to harbour in had
been obliterated in a storm that would have crushed them.
On another occasion, pressure looking guaranteed to burst
the ship like an orange, the creaking had ceased without
any change of conditions. On another, the bay ice immediately around them had remained uncrushed, while heavier
ice "was forced up into high ridges" just out of danger's
way. Smith noted and gave thanks for it all.

On Wednesday 7 November, the captain's condition became critical. Smith, who put it down to anxiety, stayed
with him, forming a rota with some of the Shetlanders. His
instruments were frozen, and there was not much more he
could do than hold the captain's hand. At one point, while
this was going on, the *Diana* found herself in the centre
of "a whirling pack of ice, the masses of ice on our star-
board side moving with great rapidity towards the stern of
the ship, then crossing her stern, advancing at great speed
along our port side, then driving across our bows". During
two hours of this upheaval, they were miraculously spared:
"Every separate fragment of ice seemed to be following the
bent of its own inclination, whilst the bergs were pursuing
their usual erratic courses in all directions."

Smith could see that dread was "wearing us out far more
rapidly than cold or want of food". Nerves were so frayed,
he said, that people were leaving the little biscuit they were
issued uneaten as they tried to perform basic functions with
"anxiety and horror" stalking them like wolves. On Saturday 10 November, he was asked to attend a prayer meeting
being held by the men belowdecks, where the Dundee carpenter Donald led them in heartfelt intercession. The next
day the ice slackened, and they were able to sail southward
for a while in the sliver of daylight before reaching an icefield
as it fell dark: "You can hear . . . the shrieking, screaming

and groaning of the immense masses as they are forced and ground together." Pressed on both sides, the *Diana* tilted and sounded "as though she were some living creature struggling in the agonies of dissolution". Without moonlight, it was impossible at night to use the warps and fenders to protect the ship from what might befall her.

On 13 November, the men decided to hold the prayer meetings daily and to start a Bible study. By a visible land-mark they now knew themselves to be by a place called Cumberland Gulf: "Seldom have I seen such a beautiful sunset. . . . The light clouds were tinged with the most bril-liant carmine and lake, fading away into crimson, yellow, and saffron, while the sky continued to glow with light and glory for some time after the sun had disappeared." It was, said Smith, "a matter of astonishment to the captain and his officers that we have been kept in safety so long. . . . The cabin walls are encrusted with ice, which sparkles in the dim lamplight as though one were sitting in a veritable cave of Golconda."

It was still getting darker and colder, and, as the captain's condition worsened, Smith was close to cracking, at one point scrawling the words "WE MUST DIE!" in his journal. Each such brush with death brought a further shedding of spiritual inhibition. "O great and unmerited mercy!"; "Be-hold, what manner of man is this, for even the winds and the sea obey Him?"; "We are humbled in the very dust be-fore Thee." When the hull finally burst, it made a sound "as though every timber in her was being split into firewood". Under the light of two lanterns hanging in the gangway, men threw bedding and clothes onto the ice, where others dragged the boat clear. When all the work was done, "the poor old captain walked along the quivering decks and over the gangway." He climbed in one of the boats, which was sitting on the ice, reclining in the stern sheets, and covered himself in rugs, while others started putting up tents.

They all took turns going back on board to work the pump, giving the carpenter Donald a chance to fix what he could. Smith took his turn with a harpoonist named Magna Nicholson, who groaned with physical disability, but continued to pump "in an agony of exhaustion". Donald eventually emerged satisfied, and some went back on board, while others stayed where they were. Smith went on board but couldn't sleep. Lying awake, he worried he was going mad and tried to remember simple Bible verses he had known since childhood but could not. He went back out, "stumbling about amongst the rugged masses of ice, scarcely conscious of what I was doing. I went to the tent and taking out my opium bottle from my bag I weighed out two grams of opium powder. I returned to the ship, swallowed the opium, and lay down in my berth again. Could not sleep. My brain was wandering. I was becoming delirious."

He gave instructions that if he were to start raving, someone should cut his hair off and apply ice to his head. He then finally fell asleep: "God preserve me from experiencing the like of it ever again! . . . Our only hope is in Thee! We are prostrate at Thy feet!" The captain's condition deteriorated, and, on 22 December, he lay motionless, watched by Smith, crying: "This is death!" On Christmas morning, Joe Mitchell, the Hull cook, put the last of the ship's fruit into a pudding, which was served to everyone. The next day, Gravill died, "his lips moving incessantly, as though in prayer".

With First Mate George Clarke now acting as captain, Smith's responsibility of holding up morale on board also

increased, as he moved about the ship inspecting the weakest
of them ("Myself as weak and feeble as a child"). On examining Gravill's body, he had discovered that the captain had
died of scurvy. He decided to keep the news from the men,
even when others began to show the same tell-tale symp-
toms, for there was no cure on board for this malnutrition.
Instead, he administered gargles and other placebos as en-
couragingly as he could: "it satisfies the poor fellows." But
nine of the Shetlanders and four more of the Hull men died,
their bodies stacked with that of the captain on deck. Any
expendable timber was now being sawn for firewood, and
journal-writing had become a terrible release of pressure:
"The reluctance to sit down to record one's miseries and
privations in black and white, to chronicle the poor events
of each miserable day . . . how can I sit down to this log with
my heart in my mouth?" The "deadening, numbing influence of cold" dominated him like everyone else: "Our daily
prayer meetings have been discontinued. . . . The Bible is a
closed book. We are a miserable company of most miserable
men." Gyp went completely mad, and Smith had to shoot
him.

When Clarke found a food thief among the Shetland boys,
Smith begged him not to hang the child, insisting that the
growing lad's nutrition needs were higher than any adult's:
"I am trying to write myself into a different humour." He
read the parable of the Prodigal Son in his berth, convinced
he had similarly abandoned his father's house for pleasure
and seeing that now he also "would fain have filled his belly
with the husks that the swine did eat: and no man gave unto
him."[5] His handwriting was a scrawl, but there was fight
in what he wrote: " 'Why art thou cast down, O my soul,

[5] Luke 15:16 (King James Version, hereafter abbreviated KJV).

and why art thou disquieted within me?' Hope in God, for something at times bids thee trust that thou shalt be spared yet to praise Him who (with all humility and reverence) is the strength of thy countenance and thy God. At times, things seem very dark, dreary; again, they look brighter and more hopeful. Oh, that I could always say and feel with the Psalmist: 'In Thee, O God, do I put my trust. Let me never be confounded.'"[6]

That February he witnessed "the most beautiful sunset I have seen this year . . . indescribably brilliant and beautiful". The incremental ease in latitude was being amplified by the return of daylight, but all of them were on the edge. "O God, in mercy, bring us speedily out of this awful ice. The men are failing and falling away in strength and appearance daily." At 2 A.M. on the night of 13 March, the *Diana* began to roll in an enormous swell. She had ice stuck to the rudder, which made steering herself away from the floating shards of ice impossible. "As I write she is receiving a succession of severe blows", wrote Smith, who carried on writing "with a pen that trembles in my hand".

At dawn, the man in the crow's nest declared that the swell they were in was "none other than the long regular roll of the *Atlantic Ocean*!" Although they could not steer, were ravaged by scurvy, and were still surrounded by ice, just the sound of this report was enough to put men on their feet. They steered with the sails, trying to clear the final pack. By the morning of Sunday 17 March, they could all see the ocean from the deck, but were still in the thick of the ice. That afternoon, they "ran close up to the ice edge, and then put ship about to weather the point. 'Tis a long point of ice running out from the pack. Had the wind been

[6] Psalm 42:5; cf. Psalm 31:1 and Psalm 71:1 (KJV).

quite fair, we would have shoved the ship straight through it. . . . Am feeling very tired with hauling and pulling at the ropes."

Night came, and they were yet again at the mercy of the black swell: "Such hours of agonising anxiety are never to be forgotten." At ten o'clock that night, "the mate came down from the crow's nest and informed us that there was no more ice ahead, that we were well out of the pack at last, and running with all possible sail set ON OUR PASSAGE HOME!" These are the last words of the journal kept by Smith, who could be forgiven for never keeping another diary. The *Diana* reached Lerwick on 11 April 1867. Having been presumed lost, an eyewitness account of her arrival was printed in *The Scotsman*: "The sight . . . cannot well be told in prose. Dante might have related it in the 'Inferno'. Coleridge's 'Ancient Mariner' might have sailed in such a ghastly ship—battered and ice-crushed, sails and cordage blown away, boats and spars cut up for fuel . . . the main deck a charnel-house not to be described. . . . Most pitiable sights of all were the ship's boys, with their young faces wearing a strange aged look not easily to be described."[7]

Today, beside the place where they came to anchor at Lerwick stands a stone drinking fountain, fallen into disuse but whose text still clear. Erected by Smith's brother, it reads: "In memory of the Providential Return of the Whaler *Diana* of Hull. God is Faithful; Then they cried unto the Lord in their trouble, and he delivered them from their distress." Smith, said one of the survivors to the *Scotsman*'s correspondent, had been "all a man should be" throughout, and when the repaired *Diana* reached Hull, the doctors there held a dinner to honour him. Precisely what damage the experi-

[7] Smith, *From the Deep of the Sea*, p. 263.

ence had wreaked on him was one diagnosis he may have taken to the grave, but he would not live long, being buried in the Quaker burial ground at Coggeshall, Essex, twelve years later. His son, Charles Smith Harris, became a ship's surgeon and found himself anchored in Hull shortly after World War I. Realising that the story of the *Diana* was still remembered there reawakened pride in how his father had conducted himself and "impelled me to take in hand at last my father's old manuscript".[8]

Some people foolishly say that being Christian is the delusion that life is easy, or nice, or that the faith misleads its followers with offers of permanent good fortune. None of these misconceptions survive the experience of actually being a Christian this side of the grave. What is rather true is that, when you do suffer, you know to Whom to go. Sometimes you only go there as a last resort, but eventually you remember to go there, and, when you do, and you utter the words "Jesus" or "Lord", you know you are not talking to the air. You are talking to a Person who has suffered and who watches. A mother praying in a hospital, or a *favela*, or a prison, does not care how prayer works. She prays because it works, because God listens. Smith prayed for deliverance from the ice and was saved, as the fountain at Lerwick testifies. At other moments, he simply prayed that his soul might be made ready for death, and, in the years following his return, I imagine it was that prayer, and the extent to which he had been able to help others, that made him not regret embarking on the *Diana*.

[8] Ibid., p. v.

2

Tears in the Garden

I believe; help my unbelief!

Mark 9:24

In the grounds of Newstead Abbey, ten miles north of Nottingham in the English Midlands, lies a memorial to a dog. The latter, a Newfoundlander known as Boatswain, was the prized companion of the poet Lord Byron, who had inherited the former monastery from his great uncle in 1798. During his time there, he had little respect for Newstead's history, deliberately burying Boatswain underneath the ruins of the high altar and turning the monks' old mortuary chapel into a swimming pool. "The great object of life is Sensation" was Byron's credo, and the scandals and fame that followed him were testimony to his commitment. However, as the words he had engraved on Boatswain's stone memorial infer, it was not an outlook that had brought him much sustained happiness:

> Oh man! Thou feeble tenant of an hour,
> Debas'd by slavery, or corrupt by power,
> Who knows thee well, must quit thee with disgust,
> Degraded mass of animated dust!
> Thy love is lust, thy friendship all a cheat,
> Thy tongue hypocrisy, thy heart deceit. . . .
> Ye! who behold perchance this simple urn,
> Pass on, it honours none you wish to mourn,

43

> To mark a friend's remains these stones arise,
> I never knew but one—and here he lies.

Byron would die in Greece at the age of thirty-six, bloated, beset with gonorrhoea and debt, and doubting his cynicism. He had once intended to be buried next to Boatswain and gone so far as having the vault built with three extra spaces: one for him, one for his daughter Ada, and one for his servant Joe Murray. Murray is said to have responded to the idea with the words: "His Lordship might be buried with dogs, but I will be buried with Christians", but, in the end, not even Byron was buried there.[1]

Newstead Abbey is also known for its association, a generation later, with the Scottish missionary explorer Doctor David Livingstone. Livingstone could hardly have been more different to Byron, in disposition or background. Asked to give a talk in nearby Mansfield, he was once asked what advice he would give to a young man and replied, "Fear God and work hard." Prior to departing on what would be his final expedition, he was staying at Newstead Abbey with his daughter Agnes at the invitation of the current owner, a Mr. William Webb. Far from inheriting an estate, Livingstone had worked his way up from the factory floor of a textile mill near Glasgow to become one of the most recognisable names in the British Empire. Self-taught, despite long hours from the age of ten in the mill, his medical studies had been paid for by a missionary society looking for men practical and robust enough to survive in remote regions of the world. He had none of Byron's natural eloquence, and the first time he ever had to preach, at a chapel near the society's training college in Essex, he had frozen and fled

[1] A. Z. Fraser, *Livingstone and Newstead* (London: John Murray, 1913), pp. 92, 93, 215.

from the pulpit. But what he lacked in that kind of confidence, he made up for in white-hot resolve, and history had conspired to provide him with ample opportunities to show his stubborn and ambitious streak.

In 1997, when I was living under Table Mountain in Cape Town, a suburban train used to run past my house each morning. The singing coming from the cheapest carriages was not in English, but you could tell it was gospel. On my morning walks, I would hope that I would coincide with them as I went past the station, for I had rarely heard anything so exuberant in my life. The sound of unbridled praise can do strange things to you, and theirs unsettled me as much as it delighted me. There were reasons why this might have been the case. Firstly, it was new to me, for I was not local. I was a young British journalist who had moved here to get away from London and write his second book, a gently satirical history of early Protestant missionaries.

There were other possible reasons. I had been born into a church-going family, although I had stopped attending church in my early teens, replacing it with a pantheon of literature, music, film, hedonism, and wit that thus far had worked well for me. Like many of my generation, I probably thought there was "something up there", but I had not spent much time worrying about it. In truth, I was on the sensation-seeking end of the spectrum more than anything down David Livingstone's end of the see-saw. This also was probably not atypical of my peers, but early success in London had brought a lot more scope in which to make mistakes. At my wedding in England a few months earlier, something odd had happened. As I was about to address the guests in the marquee, I had heard a voice inside me, clear as a bell, say the words: "Change your life."

I had had enough champagne in me to carry on and had not substantially changed my life, and the beauty of the singing on the trains was somehow a reminder of this. My bride was lovely, and pregnant, and had some money of her own, which I would do my best to squander in those early days, so convinced was I that I was backing a winning horse. It was intoxicating to be in South Africa, with President Mandela a stone's throw away and me set up with stories for the Sunday papers back home if I kept my powder dry. But I did not keep my powder dry, partly because of that singing train and because I was falling in love with the missionaries I was meant to be mocking. Immersed in their letters and journals, I was becoming a believer at my desk, an ironist in the kitchen, and a lost soul on the sofa. I hoped I could understand their faith without having to do anything as annoying as going to a church or reading a Bible, but the singing made me think all these might not be as annoying as I remembered. The disharmony of all this was becoming an issue because I did not know which register to write from. I blamed city life for the confusion, so we moved to a beautiful, mountainous farming town named Swellendam, two hours east of Cape Town, and rented a peeling colonial bungalow with wooden floors and a swimming pool.

The trouble with being able to do whatever I wanted was that I ran out of things to blame. When my confusion did not improve, I convinced myself that I needed what the magazines were calling a "detox" and spent five days on a nature reserve consuming nothing but water. My first night back, I woke to see a ghost, dressed in a diamond-patterned wedding gown, standing over my wife and infant son, who were both asleep on the other side of the bed. I looked at my watch and then looked back, and it was still there. (Months later, when we moved out, the landlady asked me if I had seen a ghost in the house.) Eventually I fell asleep that night, but the memory was fresh the next morning. Co-incidences and synchronicities began to happen constantly, none of which was helping, and my breathing was starting to deteriorate. I insisted that we move a few minutes away, to a supremely quiet spot under the mountain itself, so idyllic that a locations scout once knocked on our door and asked to use it for a commercial. But all was not well in paradise, and our marriage was in its agony.

The second book was somehow published (after some heavy editorial surgery in London) and did well enough to get me an advance to write a third, which I pitched as a tragic love story about David Livingstone and his wife, Mary, and this was when the wheels really fell off the wagon, for it turned out that writing a novel required having several voices in your head at once, and I was already at capacity in that respect. And even if I was ever capable of such a thing, love stories did not appear to be my genre, in life or on page. Something else was grabbing me about the story, though, because whenever I reached the end of a draft, at the point where Livingstone died, I would get a sense of what his faith had meant to him. It was not enough light to walk by but too bright to ignore, and it became my lifeline as the marriage fell apart and my downfall as far as my ca-reer was concerned. I could not let go of that theme. Our maid used to sing in her church gospel choir, and we would sometimes go up to the township to hear her. Gospel music was everywhere up there, in churches, taxis, shops, schools, and homes, and every time I heard it, my breathing would ease, and I knew I had found the key not just to Livingstone but to myself. But knowing is not the same as acting, as any fool knows.

On Livingstone's first posting as a young missionary, he

found himself on the fringes of the mapped world, in the Kalahari Desert of southern Africa. His supervisor there was Robert Moffat, another tough Scot, who had begun his working life as a gardener. Rejected at his first application to the society for his lack of literacy, Moffat learned to read and write, was accepted for training, and weathered harsh years on the frontier with his wife, Mary. In time, they had befriended outlaws, survived near-starvation, lost a child, been looted, attacked, ignored, threatened, and had finally built a mission, with orchard, smithy, and school, at an oasis called Kuruman. In time, he had won the respect of both African chiefs and Dutch settlers, and the once illiterate gardener had gone on to transcribe the Tswana language for the first time in its history, before translating the New Testament.

I remember standing inside the church Moffat built at Kuruman, with my wife and year-old child, the smooth dung floor keeping us cool beneath the blaze of sun outside. I had nearly killed all of us two days days earlier, after losing concentration on a hot, empty stretch of Northern Cape road and crashing through a farmer's fence. The farmer had come to pull us out and taken us back to his house for lunch with his wife. I could see from a stack of videos by the television that he was Christian. "What is it like to have almost died?" he asked. I do not know what I said.

Before the mission station took root, Mary Moffat had rescued baby girls left in the surrounding country, raising some of them in her own extended family. When the conversions did happen, they were accompanied by wailing, exorcism, and interest so intense that Moffat could not manage, so he wrote to the mission society for assistance; hence, Livingstone's arrival. The country to the south was in upheaval, with tribes being pinched between Zulu armies to the east and white settlers to the west. These were now filing in increasing numbers past Kuruman, on their way into the desert. Unsure how they were surviving, Moffat sent Livingstone to find out where they were going. On colonial maps at the time, the whole interior of Africa was a green-tinged desert stretching from the Kalahari all the way north to the Sahara. Travelling with his African companions in the years that followed, Livingstone would discover rivers, lakes, and snow-capped highlands lying at the heart of the continent.

Whether he was travelling as a missionary or as an explorer would become a moot point in his career, but from the start he carried a magic lantern from which he could project scenes from the life of Jesus. Meanwhile, his ability to cure stomach pains and headaches from his medicine chest meant he was soon able to rely on the hospitality of the Africans he encountered. New horizons opened up, as men like William Webb (wealthy young hunters looking for adventure) accompanied him for stretches and left him with navigational equipment, money, and supplies to continue.

He was instructed by Moffat to build a permanent new mission station some 250 miles north of Kuruman, at a place called Mabotsa, with a former builder named Edwards. Livingstone was attacked by a lion during the construction and had to be carried back by wagon to Kuruman, where Moffat's grown daughter, also called Mary, nursed him. They fell in love, and he proposed to her under a tree in Moffat's garden, much to the horror of Mary's mother, who had a more astute understanding of Livingstone's limitations than most. Livingstone was insistent he could settle down and that he wished to emulate his father-in-law's mission station at Kuruman, but the lure of further discoveries, and the disconcerting arrival of explorers he knew he could out-do, would break his resolve. Mary was African-born and resilient, and for a while they travelled together, taking their young family on long and dangerous journeys, over parched salt pans and around the shores of malarial lakes. But when a newborn baby died after one such journey, Livingstone had to decide where his priorities lay.

Sending Mary and his family back to Scotland, he trekked west to Portuguese Angola, through desert, delta, and rain forest, stunning the British consul when he appeared on the Atlantic coast at Saint Paul de Luanda. Refusing the offer to sail home, since it would involve abandoning his African companions, he traced the Zambezi river all the way east to the Portuguese enclave in Mozambique. Probably no one now knew more about the interior of southern Africa, but the Portuguese knew a lot more than they had been disclosing to the rest of the world. For with the slave markets on the western Atlantic closed by the British and French, the Portuguese were busy transporting slaves to their colony in Brazil from the lesser known and malarial east coast. Livingstone, who realised the size of the trade, was determined to stop them.

His epic journey, including the "discovery" of Victoria Falls, made him a hero back in Britain, where he returned home to rapturous applause. His antislavery message confirmed his hero status. Not all was rosy, for Mary had fallen out with his parents and taken to drinking, his boys had turned either insipid or mutinous, and the directors of the mission society were furious with him for abandoning his mission. But the government congratulated him, the Royal Geographical Society honoured him, the British public were immensely proud of him, and a published account of his travels made him a fortune.

He resigned from the mission society and agreed to go back to Mozambique for the government, with an exploratory riverboat and a team he was authorised to appoint. This was to include a Royal Navy captain, engineer, artist, botanist, and photographer, in which latter capacity he would take his brother Charles, also now a Protestant minister. His passionate speeches about slavery and the need for missionaries in Central Africa had meanwhile prompted the formation of an Anglican mission society, and volunteers, prospective missionaries, and their wives were ready to sail for the east coast when Livingstone called them. Mary was desperate to return, too, and they arranged guardians for the children, but at Cape Town she discovered that she was again pregnant and had to return to England, where the boys were growing old and restless enough to be getting in serious trouble.

The logistics of the expedition went disastrously wrong almost from the start. The steamboat was ill-equipped for the shallows of the Zambezi, the trees on the banks also too quick-burning for the engine, which required a day's chopping for a day's passage. The Portuguese had little reason to help them, which would have mattered less if Livingstone were not having to cope with a blunder he had made while mapping the Zambezi on his solitary descent to the coast. After the glory of the Victoria Falls, he had traced the Zambezi east but had run parallel to the river while exploring highlands on its northern bank. In so doing, he had missed an impassable series of rapids east of the Falls that the Portuguese had not told him about.

This meant that transport into the highlands, where he had envisaged establishing a mission station, was agonisingly complicated, and when the malaria season started on the coastal plains ("Mozambique" means "Land of the Mosquito"), it killed half the Anglican missionaries who had arrived to join him. Livingstone was now in a state of intense frustration, ruthlessly unsympathetic to the widows who were with him, and started to fall out with all members of his party, including his brother. His wrath soon extended to his eldest son, Robert, who had found money to sail to Cape Town with the intention of joining him. By letter to Cape Town, Livingstone ordered him not to proceed east and to either return home or go to his grandparents in Kuruman. Instead, the youngster joined a Unionist recruitment ship that anchored in Simonstown and disappeared to fight in the American Civil War.

All along, the slave trade was being carried shamelessly on under their noses, and with it a hard lesson in the double standards of the British establishment. For, despite all the encouragement Livingstone had been given in London for his campaign against the trade, Portugal was Britain's oldest military ally, and her king was Prince Albert's cousin; whatever conversations had been had, a blind eye had continued to be turned to the flow of traffic to Rio. At one point, in his frustration, Livingstone ended up in a gunfight with slavers off the Zambezi, freeing two prisoners in the process, Chuma and Susi, who would remain with him off and on for the rest of his life.

Resignations began, including that of the boat's captain. The boat herself was now almost a wreck, but, instead of accepting defeat, Livingstone sent designs to England for a new boat, spending his own money in so doing. The boat arrived, and Mary with it, having left her newborn in England. Within weeks, she had contracted malaria and died at an old Portuguese slave station on the Zambezi called Shupanga. It was the apotheosis of Livingstone's agony: "For the first time in my life I feel willing to die."[2] He had a marble gravestone brought up from the port, but still he

---

[2] Tim Jeal, *Livingstone* (London: Yale University Press, 2013), p. 261.

persisted, even when the entire expedition was officially recalled by London and a ship was sent to Mozambique to
bring its remnants back to Britain. Livingstone refused to
get on board, saying it would mean selling his riverboat
to slavers, so the ship sailed home without him. Instead, he
sailed the riverboat across the Indian ocean alone, at the beginning of typhoon season. Miraculously, he reached British
Bombay alive and sold the boat. There, the rest of his capital
had been lost in the collapse of an Indian bank.

Back in Britain, he learned that Robert had died as a
prisoner-of-war in North Carolina. Livingstone was lam-
basted by the newspapers, disowned by the government,
cursed by his mother-in-law, and had become *persona non
grata* with the major missionary societies. His faith was still
there, but his Bible had not been read properly for a long
time. Webb, with whom he went to stay at Newstead, was
one of very few people to have ever seen the Livingstones as
a young and happy family in Africa. Their daughter Agnes
(the best adapted of them all) became his guardian angel,
and Newstead Abbey the place where he licked his wounds
and wrote up his account of the Zambezi expedition, determined that its geographical achievements should be recognised despite its calamity in every other respect.

The president of the Royal Geographical Society, Sir Rod-
erick Murchison, maintained loyalty, as did James Young, a
friend Livingstone had first met as a fellow science student
in Glasgow. Young had gone on to make a fortune from
refining paraffin and was determined to help Livingstone.
With the goodwill of such people, he might have settled
down in a cottage and lived out his days as a doctor and
writer. Already fifty-two, and weakening, it made sense to
stop. But deep down, Livingstone most needed to redeem
himself, and at Newstead the opportunity to do so arose.

Press interest in Africa had switched to finding the source

of the Nile, wealthy British explorers having tried and failed
to do so. Webb, Murchison, and Young all backed Livingstone in his desire to settle the matter, and in 1865 the explorer sailed for Zanzibar, where he set about assembling a
party including Chuma and Susi and no other Europeans.
Travelling along Arab routes into the interior of northern
Central Africa, they effectively vanished. The occasional letter reached the coast, and then rumour, but five years passed,
and no one was sure where Livingstone was or if he was
still alive. World affairs were full of other noise, and relatively few were the voices who called for the government
to send a search party. But the public still possessed curiosity, and some fascination began to build around any mention of Doctor Livingstone. Eventually, the heir and young
owner of an American tabloid, the *New York Herald*, looking
to boost the prestige of his paper, decided to give his best
war reporter a blank cheque to find Livingstone, dead or
alive.

It took Henry Stanley eight months to find him, half-dead
at an Arab outpost on the shores of Lake Tanganyika, at a
place called Ujiji. Despite being the ambitious reporter that
he was, Stanley spent four months befriending Livingstone
before returning to the coast. In that time, wrote both of
them, they became like father and son, not a simile either
was likely to use lightly. Stanley had grown up in a Welsh
orphanage and never known his father. Robert's death was
always on Livingstone's mind, and he asked Stanley to place
a stone over his Carolina grave. They were both self-made
men, and they understood each other—Livingstone now
had supplies to continue, and Stanley had his story. The
night before Stanley left, their porters performed a dance.
"It is a wild dance altogether", wrote the journalist. Of his
last conversation with Livingstone, he wrote: "I have noted

down all he has said to-night; but the reader shall not share it with me. It is mine!"[3]

What might have been said that night? We know Stanley had been trying to persuade Livingstone to come back to the coast, for he was clearly very weak. We also know that Livingstone's reason not to do so, apart from not having found the source of the Nile, was to do with the Arab slave trade. Stanley had asked him how he could hope as one person to change a culture of slavery that was widespread throughout Central Africa, to which Livingstone had replied: "Someone must begin the work. Christ was the beginner of the Christianity that is now spread over a large part of the world. I feel sometimes as if I was the beginner for attacking central Africa."[4] We know also that Livingstone thought he was dying.

When he left, Stanley carried with him Livingstone's account of his expedition thus far, which he had latterly been reduced to writing on scraps of newspaper after running out of paper, as well as letters to his children and supporters. Stanley promised him that he would send more supplies to him when he reached the coast. Since Livingstone intended to continue looking for the Nile's source, it seems reasonable to deduce that he believed this discovery was capable of both vindicating him as an explorer and giving him a mouthpiece to campaign against the East African slave trade, whether Portuguese or Arab, for his experience of criticising the trade farther south had convinced him that if he failed to find the source, no one would listen to him. To what extent pride and altruism were balanced in his resolve to stay is perhaps too neat a biographer's question, for they

---

[3] Henry Morton Stanley, *How I Found Livingstone* (London: Wordsworth Editions, 2010), p. 494 (journal entry for 13 March 1872).

[4] Jeal, *Livingstone*, p. 353.

had become intrinsically bound. Stanley bade him farewell at an Arab outpost called Tabora, gathering his strength before what he knew would be the last big effort of his life. He marked his fifty-ninth birthday by writing a prayer in one of the journals Stanley had left him: "My Jesus, my king, my life, my all; I again dedicate my whole self to Thee."[5]

Livingstone had read his Bible from cover to cover four times in Ujiji, and he was reading it again in Tabora, his thoughts often on God. While his notebooks from previous expeditions had been packed with far more geography than spiritual reflection, this was changing, to the extent that modern historians have presumed that Livingstone was going mad. To a believer, most of what he says in those final journals makes sense, even if he rambles at times, which also seems authentic. You can view his King James Bible today from behind glass in a Glasgow museum, but you can hardly know the heart of the man who read it unless you have read it yourself. Livingstone was not only making me read Scripture but also face the mystery that it contained:

> And this is eternal life, that they know you the only true God, and Jesus Christ whom you have sent. I glorified you on earth, having accomplished the work which you gave me to do; and now, Father, glorify me in your own presence with the glory which I had with you before the world was made.[6]

After more than three years in that mountain town, the marriage had ended, as had my contractual relationship with my publisher and agent in London. Yet, I was so sure that I was onto something that I continued on anyway, without a contract, and it would take months for the extent of the

[5] David Livingstone, *The Last Journals of David Livingstone,* ed. Rev. Waller, vol. 2 (London: John Murray, 1874), entry for 19 March 1872.

[6] John 17:3–5.

calamity to sink in. We had moved separately to a town farther down the coast, where there were more like-minded
people, and I moved into an isolated cabin situated between
some woods and a freshwater, marshy *vlei*. It looked an ideal
place for a writer to go mad, and it very nearly was. Working
as a waiter nearby, I started work on a screenplay version of
the Livingstone story with a Cape Town producer, until I
was living off biscuits. There was no electricity or hot water
in the cabin, and neither was there likely to be at the rate I
was going, but I began reading my Bible with a new hunger
and stuck a newspaper headline I cut out by the door that
read: "THE PARTY'S OVER". But the party was not entirely
over, and for every moment of prayerful reading, there was
a doomed love affair in that cabin and encroaching self-pity.

Someone I knew ran a recording studio whose main
clients were local gospel choirs. During a cultural festival
held on the edge of the Karoo, he rented an old church and
invited these choirs up to perform. I went with my son, who
was now old enough to run around with their children,
as singers turned into audience and back into singers for
hours on end, interrupted only by exclamations of praise and
prayer. I would go outside sometimes to smoke a cigarette
and watch the birds on the church roof fly off and return.
The Gospel was peaceful to be around but promised to be
inconveniently demanding to follow. By now, my sister was
the only person I could think of in England who did not
think I was broken. When I flew over there to try to salvage
my career, the two of us had gone for a drive, and I had noticed that her passenger door kept squeaking. Determined to
do at least one thing right (since the salvaging by that stage
was not going well), I told her to stay in the car while I
got some oil. After applying the oil, it squeaked even louder
than before, and she laughed in the way we all had done as

children. Later, in the pub, when I tried to explain to one
of her friends what I did for a living, she laughed again and
said: "I love you." She was a churchgoer.

Nothing was opening up for me, and after a few months I
decided to use my return ticket to fly back with about three
hundred pounds cash [$400] in my pocket, which did not
promise to go far, even in Africa. At Johannesburg airport,
my connecting flight to the coast was delayed because of
storms, so I went and sat in the prayer room. It was as empty
and lifeless as these places generally are, but I sat down and
tried to pray. After a few minutes, three airport staff came
in on their break and went to the front and started praying.
With deep African voices, they stood there next to each
other and began telling God all the problems of their lives
at the same time. I watched, mesmerized, as they went on,
and then it was as if they all realised at the same time who
they were talking to, as their voices turned to praise. I must
have stood up myself at that moment, for the next thing I
knew they were standing in a circle, praying for me: "Sur-
round him with your fire!" one of them said. I exclaimed
to him: "None of my friends believes any of this!", and he
said, "You will show them!"

Beside my cabin were several felled eucalyptus trees, and
my neighbor chain-sawed some discs off them and lent me
his axe: "Sell firewood", he said. So, I sold firewood for a
few weeks, and on Sunday nights I would go to my neighbor's house for supper, and together with his wife we would
pray afterward. It was the first time I had prayed like that in
front of others, and I prayed from my belly, like I had seen
them pray at the airport. It was a physical as well as spiritual
relief, but, for reasons I cannot adequately give even now, I
passed up an invitation to join them at church.

What I did instead was burn the Livingstone novel in my

stove and break all the computer discs I had it on and begin to write some journalism for the South African newspapers with a photographer living nearby. He had covered much of the violence of the last years of apartheid and experienced the suicide of a friend and fellow photographer. Neither of us had been in print for a while, but for a year we traveled around in his old car selling stories to whoever was interested. It was a relief not to be tinkering with the book anymore, and, at my request, we had begun with a story about township gospel churches and drove one Sunday morning to find an authentic example. It did not take long to find, with its corrugated iron walls and GOD TAKE THE CITY painted over the doorway. The singing had started before the arrival of the pastor, who listened to what I had to say and handed me the keys to his car. "We are going somewhere else today. Bring some of them with you."

We drove together in convoy up into the hills, the pastor driving a taxi minibus he had requisitioned that Sunday. Finally, we entered a state-owned pine plantation, where I could see rows of dilapidated wooden cottages and a hall in similar condition. The residents of these cottages, I learned, were about to lose their homes and have to move into the township. They had little hope in politicians of any shade to help them and had been meeting each evening in the hall to pray. The men stood outside, and for the first time in my life, I wished that I had dressed smarter, for they were all impeccable in suits despite facing redundancy. The women were inside, on all fours, facing each other in pairs, whispering into each other's ears. The worship started with an exorcism of the elders, an image that would be on a front page of a Johannesburg newspaper shortly afterward. At one point, a man began to walk around the hall, giving his testimony. There were no seats, and we were all standing around the sides as he walked. When he came past us, he broke into English: "When I was a young man and made soup, I thought I was the vegetables!" I understood exactly what he meant.

A few days later, I interviewed the preacher back at his church. "How do you know if the Holy Spirit is in the room?" I asked him. "The atmosphere kind of thickens", he smiled. "Have you ever seen an angel?" He laughed at that: "You only see angels when you are *really* in trouble!" The atmosphere was not particularly thick that evening as we sat there, and I suspected that I was asking the wrong questions. After we ended the interview, I stopped to talk with him while he locked the door. "Will you bless me?" I asked. Without saying anything, he unlocked the door again, and we went back inside. I knelt as he placed his hands on my head and started to pray into the struggles of my life that he had no earthly reason to know about. I knew he worked in a furniture factory, and the thought occurred to me (even as I knelt there) that here was this working man giving up his free time for me, praying for me in my language, and what was I? A useless educated observer? In my soul I crossed a line that night, out of gratitude to him as much as to God. I would cross back over it plenty of times in the months that followed, but that night I planted both feet on the ground of faith as a resident. It felt very normal; no heavenly choirs became audible, but it marked the beginning of a reliability in my faith by which I could live each day and return to when I strayed. Weeks later, as we drove back from a story along the coast, I spotted some graffiti in a surfers' café: "LIVE AN ORDINARY LIFE SO THAT YOUR WORK MAY BE VIOLENTLY ORIGINAL".

And he came out, and went, as was his custom, to the Mount of Olives; and the disciples followed him. And when he came to the place he said to them, "Pray that you may not enter into temptation." And he withdrew from them about a stone's throw, and knelt down and prayed, "Father, if you are willing, remove this chalice from me; nevertheless not my will, but yours, be done." And there appeared to him an angel from heaven, strengthening him. And being in an agony he prayed more earnestly; and his sweat became like great drops of blood falling down upon the ground. And when he rose from prayer, he came to the disciples and found them sleeping for sorrow, and he said to them, "Why do you sleep? Rise and pray that you may not enter into temptation."[7]

Livingstone was not used to inactivity. In Tabora, while waiting for Stanley's supplies to arrive, he became his own doctor and patient as he prepared himself for his final push. Aside from the physical disabilities he carried, including old, bone-deep wounds, he was aware that madness was prowling him, as accumulated fevers took their toll on his reason and frailer state. One day in his journal he wrote: "It must be a sore affliction to be bereft of one's reason, and the more so if the insanity takes the form of uttering thoughts which in a sound state we drive from us as impure." The next entry is three days later and six words long: "A touch of fever from exposure".[8] He knew that the best season for travel was quickly disappearing and that they would be setting out in the rain once the goods arrived.

His journal became increasingly religious: "What is the atonement of Christ? It is Himself: it is the inherent and everlasting mercy of God made apparent to human eyes and

[7] Luke 22:39–46.

[8] Livingstone, *Last Journals*, entries for 23–26 April 1872.

ears. The everlasting love was disclosed by our Lord's life and death. It showed that God forgives, because He loves to forgive. He works by smiles if possible, if not by frowns; pain is only a means of enforcing love."[9]

The Arabs at Tabora thought he was mad to be even thinking of setting off in the rains, but he was resolved to go as soon as the supplies arrived. He also did not want to stay at Tabora a day longer than he had to for he knew that while he did, he was the beneficiary of a slave network. Seven years before, at the start of this expedition, his strategy had been to use whatever means he could to find the source of the Nile. He had always known the Arabs were moving slaves out of the interior but had got on well with some of the Omanis, men such as Dugumbe, who had looked after him when he fell sick. Their caravans were driven by armed African converts to Islam, wearing white "dishdashi" robes and rifles. They all thought him eccentric, calling him "Rishi" (Holy Man), and he had tolerated their business, knowing that if he could find the source of the Nile the world would listen to what was going on. Which was a year-by-year escalation of the slave trade to put Mozambique in the shade.

But slavery on any scale was no longer tolerable for a man who had witnessed more of the "awful traffic" up and down Africa than he could bear—it was, he said, "congenial only to the Devil and his angels".[10] In the Zambezi, he had seen trees covered with men and women hanging from them. His wife had died in a slave station; his son had died trying to fight slavery. It was personal, and an incident shortly before Stanley found him had ended his ability to

[9] Ibid., entry for 5 August 1872.

[10] David Livingstone to Horace Waller, letter, 5 February 1871, livingstone online.org.

accept any Arabs' hospitality for a day longer than he had to. Travelling with Dugumbe deeper and deeper into the interior of Central Africa, they had entered a country that practised cannibalism, something Livingstone had never encountered before. This had provoked a visceral response of both disgust and bloodlust within the caravans. At times, when trading or negotiating the right to pass over a chief's territory, Livingstone had had to restrain even his own men from turning vicious.

Matters had reached a climax at a village called Nyangwe, on the banks of the Upper Congo. It was market day, and the creeks below had been full of the canoes of those who had come to trade. There were hundreds of men, women, and children in the village square, including Livingstone, when some of Dugumbe's men entered the bazaar with their rifles aggressively obvious. Livingstone was fifty yards away and had watched as, following an argument over the cost of chickens, they started to fire indiscriminately. As the people rushed to the canoes, another group appeared on the bank and started firing both into the fleeing crowd and on those who had already got down to the canoes. Within minutes, bodies were everywhere, on the ground and floating down the Congo. In the detailed description he sent back with Stanley, Livingstone reckoned as many as six hundred people had been killed in the massacre.

For a day Livingstone was immobile. "[T]he depression the bloodshed made,—it filled me with unspeakable horror."[11] Now, as he waited for Stanley's supplies, the whole thing was recurring in dreams "that come back unbidden, and make me start up at dead of night". The only thing that

[11] Livingstone, *Last Journals*, entry for 18 July 1871.

kept him sane was his Bible. Prior to leaving Britain, he had learned of a Rabbinic tradition concerning Moses during his time in Africa. It was said that when he was working for the pharaohs, Moses had once led an Egyptian military campaign against a king at a place called Saba, later renaming it Meroë.[12] Livingstone dreamed that he might see Meroë, and that God would grant him the opportunity to end slavery in Central Africa, as Moses had once ended the slavery of the ancient Israelites.

> And they all said, "Are you the Son of God, then?" And he said to them, "You say that I am." And they said, "What further testimony do we need? We have heard it ourselves from his own lips." Then the whole company of them arose, and brought him before Pilate.[13]

When the stories dried up for us, I found myself sitting one day in a broken-down car beside a broken bridge, whose collapse had temporarily cut my friends off from the outside world. They lived in a wooden house they had built on what was an island between a river and mountain foothills. Jewish (they preferred the term "Hebrew"), they home-schooled their children in their language and lived off the sale, at the various times I visited them, of bird-tables, swings, drumming lessons, and mosaic commissions. In his late forties, my friend had been a potter and barkeeper in Israel and here had made himself a kiln out of two oil drums, while building the house, which was in the shape of the Star of David. Before that house was finished, they had lived in their campervan,

[12] Meroë and its pyramids were in fact situated on the eastern bank of the Nile in the Sudan.

[13] Luke 22:70—23:1.

and my son would play with his children as I sat listening to his stories. Their water supply came down a long pipe from one of the pools in the hills behind them, and seeing them had always been a solace and education and the most delicious food I had tasted in my life.

It was a hot day, and I was turning over the ignition, while he clamped the fuel line under the bonnet. He had fixed my car so many times that it was not an opportunity for learning for either of us anymore. Money was as tight for him as it was for me, and I had been there two weeks, straining their hospitality and wondering what on earth I was meant to do with my car. Just at that moment, the man from the municipality arrived to inspect the bridge and offered to tow me to the top of the river track where I could jump-start. I said yes and left my friend muttering to himself and his daughter as they made their way back across the river by canoe. The car would not start at the top of the track, but the man offered to tow me into the nearby village, where he had some work. After that he would be driving into town and could take me to the garage. My shoes and wallet were still on the island, but I agreed, desperate to fix the car and not to give my friends any more trouble. I guessed that whatever was wrong with the car would not be fixed quickly, but I could at least leave it at the garage and hitchhike back. It was a sleepy old mission village where I waited, especially sleepy on such a hot day, and I sat in the shade, persuading the owner of the village store to give me a cold drink on credit.

After half an hour, the man returned, and we tied up my car and started on the ten-mile journey to the town where my marriage had died. The driver was either extremely confident or annoyed because he flew over those winding back roads faster than I would have done driving alone. I am not a confident driver, and anxiety almost choked me, but I could not afford to panic, so I prayed. At the T-junction by the town, he pulled out so quickly that the rope snapped. He came back, definitely starting to lose patience now. It broke again, edging me into what was in fact a stretch of highway. Again the rope snapped, before we hobbled into the town to which I had moved with my wife and child seven years previously. Of all the places, I thought, for this day to be happening.

He dropped me at the garage. I remembered meeting the owner of that garage when I arrived in the town and how he had told me about his German family history. He was a big man and less interested in me now.

"Aren't you meant to be living here?"

"I used to."

I began telling him about my marriage until I realised how pathetic I sounded, trying to get his sympathy so he would magically fix my car. I was sick of charming my way out of trouble. It was not Christian, and something had to change, whatever it took. He took the keys and told me to come back the next day. It was scorching underfoot as I left, and I had to jump on someone's front lawn to cool my feet down. The highway was a mile away, and there was no way I was going to make it up there with skin left on my soles, so I went back to the garage and asked if they could give me a lift back to the village if I paid for fuel.

"No", said the German. "The car's out." He walked away.

I wanted to weep. There was so much good I could do if I could stop worrying about the next five minutes. There was a stream in the mountain I knew, and I decided to head for it, thinking it would be easier to walk on dirt track and that I could weep there and cool down. I did not want to go back to the river like this anyway. They had their own headaches, and I knew I was now one of them. I could sleep overnight on the mountain and go back to the garage the next morning. I started hobbling, past the golf club where I had once played with my brother-in-law and the dirt track where I used to walk the dog.

The track was full of stones. A car drove past, and people who had once been my neighbours whizzed by. I could hardly blame them for not stopping, for there was little difference between me and a tramp. I remembered working in a restaurant when I was in London where the only person who seemed to be on my wavelength was the man selling *The Big Issue* outside. When I reached the stream, I cooled down and tried to cry but failed. I tried to sleep but could not do that either. I tried to have a big conversation with God, but it was getting chilly as the sun started to disappear up the face of the mountain. No angels came.

I thought about my sister, who had died that summer, and her funeral, where I had given the eulogy. Why had I stopped going to church? I remember lying on my back on a stranger's patio after a heavy night out, my heart palpitating as people cackled at each other inside. It did not feel like freedom, as I stared up at the stars and prayed to the Virgin Mary to help me. Had I ever stopped believing? I was praying now, but no angels came. When it was dark, I walked into the town and to the police station. They drove me back to the village, where I waded across the river. They had been out looking for me:

"I'm sorry, I'm stupid."

"Not stupid, just self-important."

But he looked relieved to see me, and, in his search for me, he had come across someone even more crazy. "Papa

Jew" was in his 60s or 70s with a grey goatee beard and a psychedelic T-shirt. He had been hiding on a farm from people in Cape Town who wanted to kill him. Now he was being evicted from the cottage there ("I saw red, but I didn't do anything!") and was heading back to the city, hoping things there had cooled down. He had been coming to say goodbye—I cannot think they had many normal friends. As he spoke, he grew freshly agitated and asked if he could stay with them. The answer was no. The party was over.

"But they'll take me out!"

"No one is going to take you out! You'll be driving a Rolls Royce next time I see you!"

Papa Jew cheered up when I told him about my day.

"You've got a comedy, there! Trust me, I used to make movies."

"What kind of movies did you make?"

"Don't ask."

"I didn't realise it was a comedy."

"It is! Just make sure you don't become the character."

We drove Papa Jew back to his cottage, along miles of track, into a moon-lit settlers' valley, where he proudly showed off the vegetables and flowers he had brought to life. He certainly had green fingers. As we stood breathing in the baked *fynbos* air, I knew things had changed. The next morning, my friend's wife came back from the river as we were drinking coffee: "Did you hear that? I thought it was someone imitating a bird, but it was actually a bird!"

A bird pretending to be a man pretending to be a bird. I needed to do whatever I had to do to sort myself out, however humiliating. I needed to start going to church.

So the band of soldiers and their captain and the officers of the Jews seized Jesus and bound him. First they led him to Annas; for he was the father-in-law of Caiaphas, who was high priest that year.[14]

When the extra men and supplies arrived in Tabora, Livingstone set off. He had everything he needed—flour, sugar, coffee, tea, tinned food, muskets, gunpowder and rounds, dried milk, two donkeys, and cloth for trading. It was torrid, the heat that comes before the rain, but he had waited long enough and marched at the head of what was a party of fifty. They looked little different to the slave caravans, this resemblance serving to scare villagers around the lake away. This was particularly unwelcome for Livingstone, who, with so few teeth left, was struggling to eat the maize staple his men ate. He wanted to be able to buy livestock, and he also wanted to ask villagers about the river basins. On the higher ground, the rains had clearly already begun, for the shores of the lake were swelling into marshes. Livingstone shot dead a three-foot adder, which the men considered a good omen: "It would have been a bad sign . . . had one trodden on it", he commented in the journal.[15]

On Christmas Day, 1872, he wrote: "I thank the good Lord for the good gift of His Son Christ Jesus our Lord. Slaughtered an ox and gave a *fundo* and a half to each of the party. This is our great day, so we rest. It is cold and wet, day and night. The headman is gracious and generous, which is very pleasant compared with awe, awe, and refusing to sell, or stop to speak, or show the way."[16] Despite the reassuring tick of the chronometer, Livingstone was not

[14] John 18:12-13.
[15] Livingstone, *Last Journals*, entry for 4 September 1872.
[16] Ibid., entry for 25 December 1872.

entirely sure of his position. They were moving clockwise around Tanganyika, and he had mapped this part of the lake by boat with Stanley, but the map he had sketched then did not match the readings he was taking now. So good a celestial navigator had Livingstone been as a young missionary that, on reading his notes, the Royal Astronomer at Cape Town had declared him a genius. But the rainclouds were so thick at night that he could not see the stars and presumed (incorrectly, it turned out) that the chronometer was wrong. He began to lead them in a long, torturous circle.

Livingstone's initial objective was to confirm whether any of the outlets from Tanganyika's western shore could flow north to begin the Nile, and to do this he needed to keep as close to the perimeter of the shore as he could. But the edges of the lake were blurring in the floods, and when the torrential rains began, the shore became a quagmire, quite impossible to take bearings from or navigate over. Some of his party deserted, taking with them the goods they carried. They took shelter on islands in the swamp, wading chin deep through the water between them. The donkeys died, one after the other, as ticks, mosquitoes, and leeches took their toll on the party, which shrank further still: "So many obstacles have arisen. Let not Satan prevail over me. Oh! my good Lord Jesus."[17]

Finally, they obtained canoes: "We punted six hours to a little islet without a tree, and no sooner did we land than a pitiless pelting rain came on."[18] They turned the canoes upside down for shelter, and still this weary, half-dead man kept writing: "Nothing earthly will make me give up my work in despair. I encourage myself in the Lord my God,

[17] Ibid., entry for 19 March 1873.
[18] Ibid., entry for 24 March 1873.

and go forward."[19] When the season's downpours eventually petered out, the chill went, too: "A blanket is scarcely needed till the early hours of the morning, and here, after the turtle doves and cocks give out their warning calls to the watchful, the fish-eagle lifts up his remarkable voice. It is pitched in a high falsetto key, very loud, and seems as if he were calling to some one in the other world. Once heard, his weird unearthly voice can never be forgotten—it sticks to one through life."[20]

Now being carried for stretches, Livingstone was still doing what he did best, noting natural phenomena as calmly as if he were at the zoo in Regent's Park: "One species of fish has the lower jaw turned down into a hook, which enables the animal to hold its mouth close to the plant, as it glides up or down, sucking in all the soft pulpy food. The superabundance of gelatinous nutriment makes these swarmers increase in bulk with extraordinary rapidity, and the food supply of the people is plenteous in consequence."[21] Villagers grew friendlier the farther they went from the lake, but, frustratingly, none of them knew anything about the mountain spring Livingstone believed he was looking for. He was dejected at this, and days passed with no journal entry. Then they reached a village belonging to a man named Kalunganjovu, dressed in Arab clothes and willing to trade: "Knocked up quite, and remain—recover—sent to buy milch goats. We are on the banks of the Molilamo."[22]

Next stop was the village of a man named Chitambo, who had heard good things of Livingstone and allowed his men to stay in the booths that the villagers had erected to protect

[19] Ibid., entry for 25 March 1873.
[20] Ibid., entry for 13 April 1873.
[21] Ibid.
[22] Ibid., entry for 27 April 1873.

their crops from the buffalo. Too weak to move, Livingstone was lifted onto a grass bed in one of them. His companions later told Webb: "Many of the people approached the spot where he lay whose praises had reached them in previous years, and in silent wonder they stood round him resting on their bows."[23] The men took turns to sit with him, for they had never seen him this weak. On the night he died, he called out for Susi, who was in the neighbouring booth. There had been some shouting, and Livingstone wanted to know whether it was their men causing the ruckus. No, Susi replied, it was villagers pushing buffalo away. "Is this the Luapula?" asked Livingstone of the tributary they were beside.[24] When told it was not, he asked how far off it was, and Susi told him three days. An hour later, he called for Susi again and asked him to boil some water and pass him his medicine chest, from which he pointed out some calomel. Then he said: "All right, you can go out now."[25]

At about 4 A.M., the man on watch woke with a start and ran to get the others: "Come to Bwana, I am afraid; I don't know if he is alive!" Susi, Chuma, and a man Stanley had sent from the coast named Jacob went in together. They said Livingstone was kneeling on the floor against the bed, as if in prayer. Not wanting to incur local superstitions regarding dead bodies, they quickly opened him up with his own instruments, disembowelled him, and buried his insides in a tin under an *mvula* tree, Jacob reading the burial service from Livingstone's *Book of Common Prayer*. They folded the corpse over, surrounded it with cloth, and poured tar to waterproof it. Then they set off on the 1,500 miles back to

---

[23] David Livingstone, *The Last Journals of David Livingstone* (Gloucester, Eng.: Dodo Press, 2005), p. 254.

[24] Ibid.

[25] Ibid., p. 255.

Zanzibar, from where his body was transported home for a national burial at Westminster Abbey, Stanley and Moffat among the pallbearers.

The description of his death and the condition of his body when his African companions opened it have invited autopsy by proxy in the years since. From a summary of Livingstone's own notes, it has been surmised that he was suffering from "fever, malnutrition, tropical ulcers and chronic loss of blood from haemorrhoids", as well as suspected delirium and coma.[26] Because of the fist-sized blood-clot they found on opening him, it has been suggested that he was seeking relief from abdominal pain at the moment of death, rather than praying. He of course may have been doing both, but it is common for Western historians to ignore African opinion when it comes to evaluating missionaries. In contrast to secular Britain, Africa still remembers Livingstone fondly. When almost all other colonial names were removed from the streets and buildings of 1960s Africa, his was untouched. Zambia's first independent leader, Kenneth Kuanda, described Livingstone as "Africa's first freedom fighter",[27] and the second largest city in Malawi is still named Blantyre, after the town on the Clyde where he was born.

While even modern historians agree that Livingstone's Christian faith "permeated [his] every thought and deed",[28] few of them really show much understanding of what that means. Modern Africa is less ashamed of a heavenly perspective, and, if Livingstone's deepest prayer had been to stop slavery, it was remarkably answered. For by the time

[26] Sarah Worden, *David Livingstone: Man, Myth and Legacy* (Edinburgh: NMS Enterprises, 2012), p. 71.
[27] Friday Mufuzi, in ibid., p. 141.
[28] Harrison, in ibid., p. 77.

Chuma, Susi, and the others were heading to the coast, his account of the massacre at Nyangwe was being read out in London's Parliament. The British government responded to the response by ordering the governor of Bombay, Sir Bartle Frere, to impose a naval blockade on the Sultan of Zanzibar unless he agreed to close the slave market there. The sultan complied with this on 5 June 1873. The Portuguese had by then also been pressured into stopping, although an illegal trade continued to operate until Brazil gained independence in 1888, when the slave market in Rio closed for good.

Perhaps Livingstone's greatest gift to Africa was this. He had spent so much time alone with Africans that he could not but see the truth of the matter, a truth he expressed in one of the letters he sent back with Stanley as simply as he could: "They are just fellow-men."[29] He may have failed in more enterprises than he succeeded, including finding the source of the Nile, but he carried the Gospel for the first time into the deep interior of Africa, an interior that is not desert but very alive—a gift still treasured daily by millions there today.

> A bowl full of vinegar stood there; so they put a sponge full of the vinegar on hyssop and held it to his mouth. When Jesus had received the vinegar, he said, "It is finished"; and he bowed his head and gave up his spirit.[30]

Years later, I visited Ujiji almost by mistake, having never managed to get there while working on the Livingstone story. I was visiting an Anglican diocese in the northwest corner of Tanzania with a working group, and when I mentioned my previous interest in the Livingstone story, our African host insisted on me going, sending his assistant and

[29] Jeal, *Livingstone*, p. 354.
[30] John 19:29–30.

personal driver on a four-day round trip to take me there. Few tourists visited the lake since the Rwandan war had filled its eastern shores with refugees and vehicles were sometimes held up by bandits. We stopped for the night at a motel in a grim, gold-mining town, a rat running around the restaurant where we ate.

Along with the driver, the other man to come with me was named Arthur, one of the most delightful Christians I have met. In his early sixties, he was the son of two Tanzanian schoolteachers and, as an undergraduate, had excelled at science to the point of winning a scholarship to go to Switzerland to study textile chemistry, followed by a Masters in Manchester. He was then appointed to a dyeing plant in the interior, at a city called Musoma, where he became good friends with the bishop, whose diocese was growing so rapidly that he was struggling to keep pace with the new schools and churches that were opening. The bishop asked him if he would consider giving up his job to come and work for him. Arthur knew it would involve taking a 90 percent pay cut and spoke to his wife, who told him to do what he thought right. He said he then spoke to his mother, "my second God on earth", who told him he would never regret doing anything for Jesus, so he handed in his notice. That was twenty years ago, and he could hardly look more content. When we reached Ujiji, he found it amusing that I went to get a haircut in preparation for seeing this place I had imagined for years.

The next morning, we went to the spot where Livingstone and Stanley had met and were shown around by an old Muslim man, who ran the adjacent slavery museum. He suggested we drive out to the spot from which the old slave route to Zanzibar had once started. He said we would recognise it by the avenue of mango trees the Omanis had planted on the edge of town. Following his directions, we passed a school in what had once been the cantonment pen where the slaves were kept. Just beyond it, we saw the two rows of mango trees. A few faces peered out from breezeblock bungalows and washing lines, but it was a friendly and un-expectedly peaceful place, despite its ghosts. The three of us walked up and down. Neither of my companions had been to Ujiji before, and many of the details in the museum we had just visited were news to them, for slavery had not figured large in their post-independence schooling. As we started back on the long road out, children were screaming with laughter behind the school walls.

When I had reached the end of my time living in Africa a few years previously, my neighbour had driven me to my Jewish friends on the river, who had offered to take me to the airport the next day. As it approached dusk, we all walked up to the pools on the mountainside to watch the sunset. Everyone was in good spirits, which was a relief to me, since I was still conscious of what a burden I had been over the last couple of years. When we were ready to de-scend, my Jewish friend told me to lead the way down. I bounded ahead, excited now to be going back, and instead of following the path at the bottom, took a shortcut through long grass. I suddenly felt a burning sensation on my foot. Nine years in Africa, and I had been bitten by a snake on my last night.

Having examined the puncture marks, a number of thoughts crossed my mind. Firstly, I did not have enough money to go to the hospital—my health insurance had run out about half a decade earlier, and I had not seen the snake, so I had no idea which antivenom they would need and could not afford them all. Secondly, my friends were having fun at my beck, rather than having to help me. Thirdly,

I was not going to miss my flight. By this time, music and cooking had gone on, and I went outside and stood by the river.

When I came back, I think everyone presumed I was emotional because I was leaving my son behind, which I was, but I could also feel a burning sensation travelling up my calf. They were playing all my favourite music and cooking my favourite food. Was this how the comedy ended? By the time we had finished eating, the burning had risen farther. Since praying by the river, I had been still, but what would happen if it rose farther? Instantly, my heart constricted in panic. At that precise moment, my neighbour stood up to say goodbye. After I stood, he gave me the warmest of hugs, and my heart leapt in gratitude, for he was one of many from whom I sought forgiveness. When I sat down, I could feel the poison tingling out through my fingertips and felt an enormous relief. I am not a toxicologist, but I will always believe that that hug saved my life.

The whole evening encapsulated my conversion. Chaotic, permanently out of my depth, and not deserving any of the graces that kept finding me. Converting had not been falling over a finishing line so much as picking a fight, and often I felt more like the battleground than a soldier. But there was solidarity, often from unlikely sources, and a heavenly commander I trusted. Christianity is not neat, but it is a possibility, and two months after returning to England, I sat in Worcester Cathedral with my brother and parents waiting for Midnight Mass to start. The service was being filmed for television, and the cathedral was filling up with congregation and cables. Nervous-looking clergy occasionally made announcements, and no one seemed to pay them the slightest notice. Then a television producer stood up, and everyone went silent. I wondered, for the only time since

my conversion, whether my faith was going to survive being in such a low-faith environment.

But the undeserved graces continued, and even that service encouraged me, receiving Communion in particular. A
few months later, when in the line to receive Communion
at an Anglican monastery, I saw what looked like a human
face, the size of a car, high up in the corner of the nave
ceiling, like a children's-book depiction of God, with eyes
piercing, patient, and kind. Even now, I have no idea what
such an experience constitutes or how common it is, and it
appeared to bring to an end my career of "seeing things",
which does not grieve me. But I treasure the memory, for it
was unsought (I nearly fainted) and remains so vivid, fifteen
years later. If it was a delusion, I beg the Lord to rid me
of it, for it is Jesus Christ I want to follow rather than nice
feelings. It seemed as real as love and causes to this day a
longing to make those eyes proud of me. Livingstone has
been called contradictory, for his published writings are so
emotionless that, even for a sympathetic reader, they are hard
to square with some of the impulsive, brave, and reckless
things he did. But in those years between Mary's death and
his own, we have glimpses of something more honest, and
it was in those raw, childlike pages that I rediscovered the
story that changes lives:

> As she wept she stooped to look into the tomb; and she saw two
> angels in white, sitting where the body of Jesus had lain, one at the
> head and one at the feet. They said to her, "Woman, why are you
> weeping?" She said to them, "Because they have taken away my
> Lord, and I do not know where they have laid him." Saying this,
> she turned round and saw Jesus standing, but she did not know
> that it was Jesus. Jesus said to her, "Woman, why are you weep-
> ing? Whom do you seek?"[31]

[31] John 20:11b–15a.

3

Sammy

God chose what is foolish in the world to shame the wise,
God chose what is weak in the world to shame the strong,
God chose what is low and despised in the world, even
things that are not, to bring to nothing things that are, so
that no flesh might boast in the presence of God.

1 Corinthians 1:27–28

One of the stories I brought back with me from Africa had
come to me in a city called George, four hours east of Cape
Town, at a flea market that had been opening as I came out of
the bank opposite. It was a beautiful out-of-season morning
on the Indian Ocean, but there was nothing in my account,
and I was having to steel myself for the prospect of my
humiliating return to England. The woman at the market
looked like the women on the singing train, solemn but exuberant, and I bought two paperback books from her. The
first was the 1970 New Age bestseller *Jonathan Livingston
Seagull*, which I read in a couple of hours and forgot. The
second was called *Samuel Morris and the March of Faith* and
had been written in the 1940s by someone named Lindley
Baldwin.[1] It concerned a converted African prince who had
travelled to America in the 1890s.

---

[1] Published in 1942, the book was in its twenty-ninth printing by the
1970s: Lindley Baldwin, *Samuel Morris and the March of Faith* (Minneapolis:
Dimension Books, 1971).

The book had the sort of ugly cover Protestant publishers used before they discovered taste but told an utterly beguiling story. The book began with these words: "Dr. Thaddeus C. Reade, who penned the first biographical sketch of Samuel Morris, once requested me to write a fuller and franker account of his life and work. Now, in my seventy-ninth year of a busy life, I have found time." By franker, I soon realised, the author meant miraculous, for to read his book was to be transported into a world in which prayers were routinely answered and God was the main character of everyone's life, whether they knew it or not. Lindley had known Morris and witnessed some of the events himself, and the book was so disarming that I bought copies to give away, but no one else seemed as stirred by it as I was. Back in England, between shifts at an airport newsstand and as a care-worker, I tried to tell the story in a fresher way, less dated in language as perhaps Baldwin's account was. But it did not seem to help.

One evening, I was helping at my church's youth club, an event that often involved as much riot control as evangelism. When delivery of the ever-hopeful "God Slot" fell on my shoulders, I told them the story of Sammy from memory, using poetic license to bring alive the scenes I knew so well. They sat and listened quietly (a novelty) and clapped at the end (a revelation). You take your compliments where you can as an out-of-luck writer, but I knew they were clapping for Sammy, and I understood that, for I had not stopped thanking God for him since reading his story. This is what I told them that evening.

Let us imagine we are in New York City, 1895, where ships in harbor still have sails, taxis are horse-driven, and houses and shops burn coal through the winter. Clutching a blue cap in his hand, wooden floorboards shrieking be-

neath him, a ship's captain marches along a corridor chased
by an elderly woman. At the end of the hall, he rips the
door open with the air of a man for whom door handles
are a nuisance and pretense. From behind a desk, a neatly
bearded man stands up, at the sight of whom the captain
halts, allowing the woman to duck under his arm and apol-
ogize. Rev. Merritt takes in the situation, forgives his secretary, and comes around to take his visitor's cap, but the
offer is either misunderstood or declined (it is hard to tell
which, for the man's voice, when it comes, is a foghorn).

"It's the negro Samuel Morris. Have you seen him?"

"Will you not sit down, Captain?"

He would not.

"I asked you a question!"

Rev. Merritt was not entirely new to such situations and
went over to the stove, knelt, opened the grill, and picked
out two pieces of coal to throw in.

"Sammy's dead, I'm afraid, Captain."

The man's hands strangled his cap, but his voice was qui-
eter.

"I wanted to see him."

Outside, smoke from the stove was losing itself over the
rooftops. It would have been a good day for sailing, but in
their minds the two men, though both now seated, were
already on the other side of the Atlantic.

"His name was Kaboo, Captain. He was the son of a
chief, an unhappy lot as it happened, since Kaboo's father
had been losing a war with a neighboring chieftain for most
of his boyhood. We were partly to blame. Our ships, as
you well know, have been trading off those coasts for a
while, and this neighboring chieftain had acquired a taste
for rum. Nothing, it seems, could stop his determination
to buy more, with ivory and rubber he seized through war.

When Kaboo's people could pay no more ransom, Kaboo was held as prisoner and tortured until they did, and he spent years in and out of captivity. One day, an ultimatum was sent to Kaboo's father: pay today or he dies. In desperation, his father brought his daughter as payment. On seeing her, Kaboo begged his father to take her away and allow him to be killed. So, they left, and preparations began for his execution.

"Kaboo was tied to a tree in the center of the village, in front of which they began to dig a hole.[2] They planned to bury him upright, to his neck, pour a sweet concoction on his head, and entice flesh-eating ants to devour what was left of his poor head. He said he wanted to die by this point, so awful was his lot. A fire was built, and drums drew the tribe in to watch the evening's entertainment. When it was dark, the signal was given, but no sooner had they untied Kaboo from the tree when a heavenly light flooded the scene and he heard a voice telling him, *Run!*[3]

"His cords freed, Kaboo's strength, which had been non-existent for weeks, was restored in that instant, and he ran into the jungle as the light went ahead of him. All night he kept running. When daylight came, he hid in the hollow of a tree and fell asleep. When he awoke, it was dusk, and the forest was full of invisible chirruping insects and screeching

[2] Baldwin writes: "Kaboo's wounds did not have time to heal. The flesh of his back hung in shreds. Soon he became so exhausted from the loss of blood and the fever induced by the poison vine that he could no longer stand or even sit up. A cross-tree was then erected and he was carried out and thrown over it while he was beaten again over his raw back." Ibid., p. 10.

[3] Baldwin writes: "Then, suddenly, something very strange happened. A great light like a flash of lightning broke over him. The light blinded all about him. An audible voice that seemed to come from above commanded him to rise and flee. All heard the voice and saw the light but saw no man." Ibid., p. 11.

monkeys. He had never been in the jungle at night, for it was known as a lair of leopards, snakes, strange people, and evil spirits. But he could not go back home. Then the strange light appeared again, and he got up and followed it. Only the sensation of the roots and leaves beneath his feet convinced him that he was not dead or dreaming. When dawn came, he would look for a hiding place, and each evening for six nights in a row that strange light returned. He drank from the streams and river that ran through the forest and ate fruit from the trees. Finally, one morning, the light left him near a clearing where he could see rectangular white houses and plantations planted in front of them. As he watched, a young man dressed in mission clothes came to work, first kneeling to pray. Kaboo stepped out and asked him:

—What are you doing?
—I am talking to God.
—What God?
—Our Father.

"It was a Friday, a day on which Kaboo would always fast thereafter. He would also always call praying 'talking to my Father'. He was taken to meet the Americans who ran the place, but they didn't rightly know what to make of Kaboo's story. He was given a bed in the dormitory and assigned to a teacher named Miss Knolls. Kaboo wasn't sure what to make of his story, either, but he kept talking to his heavenly Father until, one night, the light returned and filled the dormitory. His cries woke the others, who could not see the light this time and who shouted at him to go outside to pray. But Miss Knolls began to notice something about him. 'Maybe his story is true?' she asked the others. Miss Knolls hadn't been there as long as the others, and there were plenty of things for her to be getting on with. 'But maybe God brought him to us for a reason!?'

"Mission life was not as simple as that, so Miss Knolls settled for getting to know Sammy, which proved a revelation to them both. He was an enthusiastic student, and she chose the name Samuel for him at his baptism, after the boy God speaks to in the Bible. He was inquisitive, too, and when she spoke to him of the Gospel, it was the Holy Spirit that Sammy wanted to know most about. Where did the Holy Spirit live? What did it look like? His questions on this subject grew more persistent, for he was sure it was this Holy Spirit that had saved him and brought him here. Eventually, Miss Knoll said:

—Sammy, I have told you everything I know about the Holy Spirit.

—Who can tell me more, Miss Knolls?

—Reverend Smirl in Monrovia. You could go to him, I suppose.

"As soon as she said it, Sammy was preparing to leave. So, she wrote him a letter of introduction to Reverend Smirl, packed him some food and clothes, and reluctantly said goodbye to him. If it took Sammy a day or two to take in the sights of a modern harbour, it took Reverend Smirl far longer to get his head around Samuel Morris. Weeks later, he was still scratching his head at Sammy's questions. After reading Miss Knolls' letter, he got him house-painting work, but teaching him was another matter. The more Sammy learned, the more he wanted to know about the Holy Spirit.[4] Reverend Smirl might have grown frustrated were it not for the effect Sammy was having on his congregation. Some of the ladies who belonged to Smirl's Methodist church in Monrovia had been praying for revival before Sammy ar-

[4] As with most readers of the King James Version of the Bible, the terms "Holy Ghost" and "Holy Spirit" were used interchangeably by Baldwin, and they would have been by Sammy's teachers.

rived, and when he had walked in the door during one of their prayer meetings, they could not see him but as a direct answer to prayer. His radiance when he prayed drew people in, and Reverend Smirl found himself gazing at a full church.[5]

"Other clergymen and missionaries came through the port, and Sammy begged them to tell him more about the Holy Spirit. They usually showed him the fourteenth chapter of John's Gospel, but this had become his constant study under Smirl: 'And I will ask the Father, and he shall give you another Counselor, to be with you for ever, even the Spirit of truth, whom the world cannot receive, because it neither sees him nor knows him; you know him, for he dwells with you and will be in you.'[6] One day, one of them said:

—Sammy, I have told you everything I was ever taught about the Holy Spirit.

—Who taught you?

—Reverend Stephen Merritt.

—Where is he?

—He's in New York.

—I will go see him!

—How will you ever do that, Sammy?

—My Father will show me the way!

[5] Baldwin writes: "Not long after his own conversion he led another young boy to accept Christ as his Saviour. By a remarkable coincidence this African was an escaped slave who had been held by the same cruel chieftain to whom Samuel had been last in pawn. The slave had been present at the final torture of Kaboo, and had seen the mysterious flash of light and heard the voice commanding Kaboo to flee. [An] ordinary slave was of little value compared to a chief's pawn. Hence, it had been comparatively easy for him to escape, and to travel safely by day along a conventional route. He was baptised under the name Henry O'Neil. He confirmed the testimony of Kaboo regarding his miraculous escape from pawn. Their joint testimony made a great impression upon people of Monrovia." Baldwin, *Samuel Morris*, p. 22.

[6] John 14:16–17.

"With that, he walked to the mouth of the river where the ships anchor. There was nothing in port, but he stayed the night there. The next morning, you came into harbour, Captain. On coming ashore, you ignored him at first, walking past him on your way to town."

"He told you that?"

"You weren't headed to New York, anyway, were you? You'd only just arrived and still had your trading to do. You intended to leave the next morning, but that night two of your crew jumped ship, and you came ashore to look for them. Sammy hadn't moved and said to you: 'My Father told me you would take me to New York to see Stephen Merritt.' You asked him where his father was, and Sammy replied: 'In heaven'. You asked who his father was, and when Sammy replied: 'My Father in heaven', you scoffed and left him, but, when you couldn't find your men, you took him on board anyway. It was a Friday, and he got a tough reception, for your crew were bad drunk, and worse sober, and made him eat his meals off the floor. He was put to scrubbing the decks, and when he got seasick, you hit him so hard you knocked him out and ordered him to be carried up the mast and tied to a spur so he could feel what real seasickness felt like."

"We never took negros."

"Sammy said he prayed when he was up there: 'Father, I am not afraid, for I know that you will take care of me. But I don't like to be up here. Won't you please make it so that I won't have to come up here and can work for this man as I promised.' Your cabin boy befriended him after they cut him down, sharing his food with him. He had a limp, and Sammy prayed for him and healed him of an injury. It was the first of many miracles on board your ship, but you had a Malay among your crew, a giant of a man with a cutlass at his side, who particularly loathed Africans, and who had vowed to the rest of the crew that he would kill him. Your cabin boy exchanged chores with Sammy so as to get him away from the Malay, and that was how he began to clean your cabin."

"He told me the Holy Spirit wouldn't bear filth, and I liked what he sang. My mother had sung some of them once. We hit doldrums out at sea, no wind at all, and I issued rum and let the crew laze about. Sammy went on deck to join them, and, on seeing him, the Malay took objection to him being there and went at him with his cutlass up, cheered on by the others. I heard the noise in my cabin and came out to see the Malay standing over him, frozen, his blade still in the air. They said Sammy had just held out his hand and he'd become like a statue. The Malay was so shocked he fell ill, and it was Sammy who nursed him back to health. Soon, everyone liked to hear him sing."[7]

"He said you later came to a village with no inhabitants."

"It was a bay, and I rowed ashore with some of the others to have a look. Then they ambushed us, darting out from the trees with canoes, a white man with them, firing muskets at us."[8]

"You got back to the ship just in time, but there was still no wind, and the villagers were swarming around the ship and starting to climb on board."

[7] Baldwin writes: "Captain and crew when off duty would sit for hours and listen to him sing those beautiful, soul-stirring religious songs which never lose their power and charm. As Sammy would sing, voice after voice would catch up the melody of the chorus until all would come under the spell of the tender passion of man's eternal quest for God, and sense the wonder of His answering grace." Baldwin, *Samuel Morris*, p. 35.

[8] Baldwin's book says that the crew later learned that this man had led the villagers in a successful attack weeks earlier, when a ship laden with rum had been taken and all its crew butchered.

"We were being bludgeoned, Reverend. I told Sammy to get below, lock himself in the cabin, and start praying."

"A swell started, didn't it? Rocking the ship?"

"They couldn't climb on anymore. The man in the crow's nest shot the white man, and we cornered the others who were on board. Then the sails filled, and we got out. It was a miracle, I know that."

"You threw your dead overboard, and he nursed the injured. He wasn't eating off the floor after that, was he? He said you began to lead daily prayers?"

"I would begin them; Sammy would finish them. He came here?"

"Yes, he did. It was a Friday when you landed at Pike Street docks. Your men had made a collection of clothes for him, and how he found me was a miracle in itself. There are hundreds of churches in this city, Captain, but we run a hostel downstairs, and the very first person he saw at the docks was a tramp who comes here. Sammy asked him where I was, and he told Sammy he'd bring him to me for a dollar. So, they walked across New York City, that tramp and the African prince—he would change my life, too, Captain. I was locking up to go to a meeting when they arrived and heard a voice from the street behind me."

—I have come from Africa to talk with you about the Holy Spirit.

"I asked him if he had any letters of introduction. He didn't. Then the tramp came over the street to join us.

—Hey, where is my dollar?

—Stephen Merritt pays all my bills now.

"I paid the dollar, showed them both into the hostel, and told Sammy to wait there until I returned. The meeting I was off to concerned the biggest funeral I had ever taken, one of the biggest this city has seen, and, by the time I had completed the preparations that day, I had forgotten about Sammy and was halfway home to Hoboken when I remembered. It was already dark, but I told the driver to turn the horses around. Now, Captain, I know that hostel like the back of my hand, set it up and kept it going, but that evening it was like entering a place I had never seen before. Some of the men were weeping, some praising God with their arms raised. In the midst of them was Sammy. A radiance filled the room I had never seen before.

"I finally got him into the carriage, and we headed home, me blabbing on about the opera house, the bridge, and so on, but all the sights clearly meant little to Sammy. Other than asking me about the Holy Spirit, the only thing he expressed any interest in were the horses, which he had never seen before. My wife was taken aback at me arriving late with Sammy. 'We have an angel in ebony!' I greeted her. 'We'll put him in the Bishop's room!'

—The Bishop's room!?

"The next morning, I couldn't find Sammy anywhere. He was out in the stables, helping my driver brush the horses. Mrs. Merritt still looked unimpressed as I brought him in for breakfast, and I will admit to you that for a moment I wondered if I had got a little over-excited at the hostel the evening before, imagining things. But I asked Sammy to say grace for us, and I thank God I did, for, when he prayed, we both saw that holy radiance. By the time he had finished saying grace, he had acquired a second mother.

"I decided he would accompany me to the funeral and that I would buy him clothes in town. Two other Methodist ministers were to accompany me to the service, and I had offered to pick them up on the way. As they climbed on and saw an African, still dressed in his cast-offs, there was an uncertain silence. Once we were going again, Sammy said:

—Do you ever pray in your carriage, Reverend Merritt?

"I told him I had known many blessed moments while travelling, but that I didn't think I had ever formally prayed on board before.

—We will pray.

"He knelt down, and I followed suit. The other two blew out their cheeks and joined us. Then Sammy began to pray: 'Father, I have been months coming to see Stephen Merritt so that I could talk to him about the Holy Spirit. Now that I am here, he shows me the harbour, the churches, the banks, and other buildings, but does not say a word about this Holy Spirit I am so anxious to know more about. Fill him with Thyself so that he will not think, or write, or preach about anything but Thee and the Holy Spirit.'

"After that, the two ministers happily took him off to Fifth Avenue to buy the best clothes. What followed later that morning was more a powerfully anointed service than the commissioning of missionaries, ordination of ministers, or anything we had ever experienced before. The three of us preached as we had never done before, with a burning need to share the glory of God; and the words to do so poured out of us. That Sunday, dressed in his new clothes, he came to my church. The children loved him, of course. They have been raising thousands for the African missions ever since.

"I was now worried, for he kept saying that he had come to see me, but what did I know about the Holy Spirit that Sammy did not already know? If God had brought him to me, it was not to learn that from me. To whom, then, could I send him? There was only one man who came to mind. Dr. Thaddeus Reade was in Indiana, where he ran Taylor

College in Fort Wayne, and I sent him a telegram, asking if he would consider taking on a new student, explaining very briefly the circumstances. He told me to put Sammy on a train for the Midwest, which I did. That was the last I saw him. He had only been here a week and had affected everything I am and do, Captain. My ministry is unrecognizable, but in Indiana a bigger miracle was about to happen.

"We all thought of Reade as holy, but Reade just thought of himself as old and tired. He was running the college out there on a shoestring, and the responsibility was running him into the ground more than any of us realised. Most of his students' parents were modest farmers who wanted a Christian education for their children. They were not rich people, and few of them could afford more than they were paying, but it was not enough to run a college. Reade's staff were already working for almost nothing, and the kitchens were so bare of food by the end of each term that it would be soup for days. In fact, the college was on the verge of closure, for with Reade and his trustees unable to renew the lease on an increased rent, the landlords wanted the site back. Had I known how bad it was, I would not have sent Sammy there at all.

"To make matters worse, most of Reade's students were resistant to their parents' piety. They were mostly hungry for modern things and were not much interested in Dr. Reade or his sermons. As he stood waiting for Sammy at Fort Wayne station, the energy to answer all these problems was more than Dr. Reade felt he possessed. He told me that when they got back to the college on his trap, he lifted Sammy's suitcase out of the trap and said to him:

—Let's see which room you would like.

"To which Sammy replied:

—If there is a room that nobody wants, give that to me.

"Certainly, no one had said that before. It was a Friday. In the town, there was a church for former slaves, and that Sunday Sammy headed there. None of the congregation noticed him enter Berry Street Methodist Church, since the service was already underway, but they noticed when he walked to the front and told them all that he had come from Africa and had a message for them from the Father. The minister told me that he did not hear all of Sammy's message, because he was instantly seized with an overwhelming desire to pray. He said that church had never received such an outpouring of the Holy Spirit as it did that day.

"It was the same at the college. Reade taught him about the Bible, while Sammy taught Reade and everyone else about faith. One evening, a notorious atheist among the student body came to Sammy's room to challenge the effect he was having on the entire college. When this young man marched in, he saw Sammy studying the Bible and announced, 'I don't read that thing anymore! It's full of old lies and tales!' Instead of arguing, Sammy simply knelt down and began to pray for him. Disgusted, the student walked out, but at the doorway he looked back, and saw Sammy still deep in prayer about him. He walked back into the room and knelt beside him.[9]

"One weekend, Reade had agreed to travel by train to preach at another town. On the Sunday night, he told the congregation there about Sammy. The next morning, on his way back to Fort Wayne, he was met by a butcher who had not been in church the night before but who had heard what he had been talking about. He said he wanted to give Dr. Reade five dollars toward his 'Faith Fund'. Reade had not mentioned any 'Faith Fund' but accepted the money. Back

[9] Baldwin tells us that this student went on to become a bishop.

in Fort Wayne, as the bitter winter set in, Sammy was often out speaking at the revivalist meetings that were springing up there, inspired by his story. People were travelling in from other towns to see him, newspapers were reporting on the effect, and Reade's 'Faith Fund' started to grow. When the first snow came, Sammy was overwhelmed by its beauty.

"Inspired by all that was happening, one of the college's trustees, a man named Mr. Lindley Baldwin, sought permission from the rest of the board to look for an alternative site for the campus. He went to the nearby district of Upland and, within a day, had been offered a gift of land and $10,000 to build a new college there. As religious as he was, Reade could hardly believe what was happening. Spring arrived, building began on the new campus, and every one of his hopes and prayers seemed to be blossoming at once. Such was the excitement that no one at first could take it seriously when Sammy fell ill. Even Sammy seemed a little confused, as he lay in his room in the college infirmary. Visitors to his bedside, including Dr. Reade, were lost for words when they realised that he was fading. Then, as Sammy continued to weaken, joy returned. The next time Reade visited him there, he was met with a radiant smile:

—I am so happy. I have seen the angels. They are coming for me soon. The light my Father in heaven sent to save me when I was hanging on that cross was for a purpose. Now I have fulfilled that purpose. My work here on earth has been finished.[10]

—But, Sammy, what about your work among your own

---

[10] Baldwin mentions a parallel case from the heydays of the American missions in China, from the "unimpeachable witness" of F. R. Burroughs: "A Christian youth named Ging-Hua, like Kaboo, was his father's eldest son, and was similarly carried off and held for ransom by a band of men who were in the habit of torturing their captives in order to extract ransom money from

people? You always believed that God wished you to return to Africa.

—It isn't my work. It is Christ's work. He must choose His own workers. Others can do it better.

"A few days later, the college doctor, Dr. Stemen, was working in his garden when Sammy called out and waved at him from his window in the infirmary: "Don't work too hard Dr. Stemen!" Stemen waved back and carried on gardening, but a few minutes later the nurse came out to fetch him. Sammy had passed away. It was a Friday. The body was kept in the college chapel until the day of his funeral, when the coffin was carried by students to Berry Street Methodist Church. Fort Wayne lined the streets to watch it pass, and many of those who couldn't fit in the church massed around it and sang Sammy's favourite hymns with those inside:

> Fade, fade, each earthly joy,
> Jesus is mine.
> Break every tender tie,
> Jesus is mine!
> Dark is the wilderness,
> Earth has no resting place,
> Jesus alone can bless.
> Jesus is mine!

"Sammy isn't dead, Captain. He's more alive than you and me, and I'll come and tell the crew that myself if you like."

---

their families. Ging-Hua was lying bound with ropes and surrounded by his captors when, suddenly, a golden light shone around him, and he recognized that it was of heavenly origin." The light, reported Burroughs, had enabled the youth to untie himself and escape and had then formed itself into "a long beam" and led him "step by step, straight to his family and safety".

The above conversation between Reverend Stephen Merritt and the captain took place, though its details are not recorded. Of Sammy's effect on Merritt, Baldwin later wrote: "Sammy had spent only a week with him; yet the strong faith of the 'angel in ebony' continued to work miracles as long as Merritt lived. After Sammy's departure, Merritt went to the hospitals for the insane and prayed for them, and many were restored to reason; he visited hospitals for the ill and prayed for them, and many were healed. Before the end of Stephen Merritt's pastorate, ten thousand persons had been brought to the Cross."

In 1928, twenty-five years after Sammy's death, his body was moved to a hill that separated the black and white sections of Fort Wayne cemetery. The gravestone, paid for by students, is there to this day, with the inscription: SAMUEL MORRIS, 1872–1893, PRINCE KABOO NATIVE OF WEST AFRICA. FAMOUS CHRISTIAN MYSTIC. APOSTLE OF SIMPLE FAITH. EXPONENT OF THE SPIRIT-FILLED LIFE. When Lindley wrote his book in the 1940s, people were still going to the grave to pray. He tells the story of one woman, at wit's end after visiting the grave of her husband, whose death had left her bereft and penniless: "Something led her to follow a group visiting the nearby grave of Sammy, where she thought to herself: 'If the Lord could save him when he had nothing, he can save me.' She seemed to hear Sammy's voice saying: 'Pray to my Father: He will save you. He will send the Holy Ghost to lead you!' She felt the presence of the Spirit of God. Her prayers were answered!"

A building at the new campus was named after Sammy, and the "Faith Fund" grew and ended up paying for about a hundred Africans and Americans to be trained for mission work in West Africa. A link between Taylor College and the region in Liberia where Kaboo was from continues to this day, as do messages from people around the world who have been touched by Sammy's story. When he had completed his manuscript, Baldwin asked Sammy's former tutor, Dr. Harriet Stemen MacBeth, daughter of his doctor, to read it over: "That reading was followed by one of those endless miracles of grace that still attend the footsteps of Samuel Morris. Though bedridden for weeks and nearly blind, she immediately arose, restored to health and strength."

Baldwin ascribed the lack of miracles in our modern age to a lack of faith. Sammy, he said, reminded us what real faith looked like. For me, in Africa one century on, Sammy somehow opened up the possibility of not just listening to beautiful gospel music but of having some of that faith my-self. In the quaint but no-nonsense words of Baldwin, to do so was a simple if demanding proposition: "You need only to come face to face with your own personal helplessness without God and to acknowledge His grace and power."[11] Anyone, I reasoned, could do that, so why not me?

[11] Baldwin, *Samuel Morris*, p. 92.

4

Moghul Dawn

Pilate said to him, "What is truth?"

John 18:38

During the summer of 2014, while serving as an Anglican curate in Yorkshire, I was asked by a bishop to attend a meeting on his behalf in London, convened by some sort of advisory arm of the government. To this day, I have no idea who they were; the slick chair sounded mid-Atlantic, and the place we met was an upmarket office rental. In the audience were senior representatives of all the major religions in the country, about thirty of us in total. Over the course of the day, we were addressed by a series of senior civil servants, sociologists, and charity bosses. The message was broadly the same: we were in what they were calling "a post-secular age", where faith communities would have an opportunity to provide more key services, in partnership with local government, particularly in support of people trying to break out of cycles of poverty, addiction, and homelessness.

English may not have been the first language of everyone present, but most people knew where this was headed. As Britain ran out of money, anything to do with caring was being cut, and modest pots of money would be made available to faith groups who were already running such projects. Most of us had already seen this in practice: the pots were very modest and came with caveats about not "proselytiz-ing", which, since it was not a word I used very often, I had had to look up, only to realise that proselytizing was pretty much my job. If I could not tell people about Christ in a church hall, where could I tell them? In my experi-ence, drug addicts, the unemployed, and the homeless did not normally mind you praying for them.

Being gathered close to the heart of political power was certainly a nice change from being told we were bigots, but, as the day went on, I decided I preferred aggressive secu-larism to sweet-talking post-secularism. It also became clear that none of us in the room was going to have much of a speaking part in this relationship. Coffee came and went, the sun rose, and the trees in Saint James' Park looked love-lier by the hour. When one of them started talking about future trends, I had had enough and stuck my hand up. Did they realise that when it came to prophecy, some of those present might know a thing or two? That we might not have much in the way of statistics, but that when it came to des-tiny, we had our convictions. A couple of people in front of me turned and smiled, but the chair fobbed me off in the politico-academic way—thanking me for my point, refram-ing my point, and moving on as if I had not said anything.

I once worked with a Muslim in Yorkshire whom I used to go and visit. One day, as we were walking down his road, a man came from the other direction and stopped and talked with us. He spoke for a few minutes about East Africa, from which he had just returned. Before walking off, he said some-thing I had heard several times with committed Muslims, along the lines of: "May you one day come to know the truth." My colleague and I walked on for a while, and then I stopped:

"How come you are allowed to evangelise us, but if I

evangelise you, it's offensive? I should have told him I hope
he comes to know Christ as his Lord and Saviour."

"You should have done", he replied breezily. "We don't
mind if it comes from your heart."

Later, I asked a Muslim scholar what he thought about
post-secularism and the pressure to accept a "faith neutral"
society. In answering, he mentioned the sixteenth-century
Moghul emperor, Akbar, and his attempt to fuse all religions
into something he called *Din-i Ilahi*, "The Divine Faith".
What happened there, he said, was a warning to everyone.
I knew about Din-i Ilahi from a Christian account of the
debates Akbar had held in his capital before establishing the
hybrid. He had invited religious representatives from across
his empire, including Catholic Jesuits from Portuguese Goa,
where two had been chosen by their brethren to respond to
the invitation, Padre Rodolpho Acquaviva and Padre Antoni
de Monserrate.

Monserrate's journal surfaced in 1906, when a British
scholar uncovered the significance of the Latin manuscript
held in the archives of the Anglican Cathedral in Calcutta.
It had been there for years but was missing its cover and
front pages. How it had ended up on the antiquities market and then in Calcutta was likely to remain a mystery,
since plague and a silting harbour had long since reduced
Goa's possessions to a ghost town. Its tens of thousands of
words of invaluable evidence did not appear to have been
known to Jesuit historians, whose books had made no reference to it, suggesting the Calcutta document was the original manuscript.[1] Once shared with historians, its credibility

---

[1] C. H. Payne believes that a summary, also written by Monserrate, was
incorporated into a late-sixteenth-century account of Akbar written by Fr.
Barrista Peruschi and that a later history of the Indian missions written by Fr.
Pierre du Jarric had access to this Peruschi rendition of that summary, since he

was enhanced by how closely it corresponded to surviving records left by Abul Fazl, Akbar's prime minister. Most interest was on the light the document shed on the personality of Emperor Akbar ("The Great"), about whose reign much was known but whose character was little understood; on which subject Monserrate had written with insight and detail.

When Akbar's invitation to attend the debates arrived in Goa in 1579, the timbre of day-to-day life in the Portuguese colony was set by the religious and educational activity of the new Jesuit buildings. The Jesuits were a revivalist Catholic order not long set up in Europe by a Basque noble named Ignatius Loyola, whose famous story bears retelling. Injured during a siege as a young soldier, after such heroics that the French were said to have refused to take him prisoner, Ignatius went to recuperate at his brother's castle. Daydreaming of chivalry, whose grip on the Spanish imagination at that time would form the basis of Cervantes' masterpiece *Don Quixote*, he started reading Ludolph of Saxony's *Life of Christ*. Finding that the thrill of his chivalric fantasies left him flat, but the inspiration of the story of Christ kept burning long after he had finished, he decided in the uncomplicated way of soldiers to respond with action. As soon as he could walk again, he went to a monastery.

Over time, he would encounter a clerical culture of sloth and jealousy that appalled him, but it could never put him off. Quite the contrary. Like the poet Dante, who had de-

---

repeats Peruschi's spelling mistakes. Fr. Pierre du Jarric, S.J., *Akbar and the Jesuits*, trans. and ed. C. H. Payne (London: Routledge and Sons, 1926), p. 209 (1999 LPP facsimile used). According to the note written by Monserrate at the end of the document found in Calcutta, the fuller version of the story was written toward the end of his life, while in prison in Arabia.

picted more than one pope in hell, the sight of corruption
and compromise in the Church's ranks only sharpened Ignatius' resolve to help restore her to her purity, which he
began with himself. At the monastery, he developed a set
of spiritual exercises designed to provide a brutally honest
inventory of one's soul and a way to bind it closer to the
will of God. Having completed these exercises, he set out
on pilgrimage to Jerusalem. When he arrived there, the resident Christian curators of the holy sites, who were living
at the sufferance of the Ottoman Empire, were so horrified
at the reaction such a man might cause that they forced him
out. As Loyola walked back through Europe, news of his
integrity spread.

He went to the University of Paris to study theology,
to which he applied himself with the same rigour he had
once shown as a soldier, his asceticism impressing young noblemen from across Catholic Europe, some of whom left
great inheritances to join him. What they joined, eventually
with papal approval, was a movement based on three priorities: education, personal sanctity, and mission. In the four
decades since its inception, his "Society of Jesus" (colloqui-
ally, "Jesuits") had not only spread in influence around the
world but had managed to sustain the remarkable verve of
their founder. A case in point was the fate of the fourteen
missionaries with whom Fr. Rodolpho had sailed from Europe. One would go on to be poisoned in Japan, another decapitated in Java. One would be the first ever Christian into
Thailand, and two of them would enter China. These were
Christians looking to convert entire nations single-handedly
to Christ, with no thought of ever going home. In 1926,
C. H. Payne translated a collection of early Jesuit travel writings. Aside from the religious nature of their journeys, he
said, it was time to acknowledge what they achieved purely

as travellers: "[They] wrote so sparingly and withal so modestly of their adventures by sea and land that we are unaccustomed to think of them as travellers. Yet few men . . . have a better right to the designation."[2]

Given the intensity of early Jesuits, it was never likely that Akbar was going to get a pliant Christian representation at his debates from Goa, but this was perhaps especially true of the two who were chosen. Monserrate, forty-three, was from a noble Spanish family, and had offered himself as a novice to Loyola in person. An account of his early Jesuit career places him in Lisbon in 1567 during the time of a plague, tending the sick without concern for his own safety. He was sent to Goa seven years later, as one of forty Jesuits deployed to build and establish the new mission headquarters in India.

Despite the fact that Rodolpho Acquaviva, twenty-nine, had arrived in Goa after Fr. Monserrate, and was younger, he was to lead the embassy. This was presumably a gift of leadership discerned by his peers, and we know he had given up more than most to become a Jesuit. Italian-born, with German ancestry, his father was the Duke of Atri. When it had become clear that their son was set on a religious life (all-night prayer vigils, giving away clothes to beggars), his father arranged for him to join Rome's most illustrious seminary.[3] But Rodolpho wanted to be a Jesuit, an option forbidden not only because of his father's preference, but also on account of his perceived fragile physique. Undeterred, he absconded from his lavish seminary and presented himself at the door of the local Jesuit house. Aware of Rodolpho's

[2] Ibid., p. v.

[3] Account of Rodolpho's early life: Francis Goldie, S.J., *The First Christian Mission to the Great Mogul: Or, The Story of the Blessed Rudolph Acquaviva* (Dublin: M. H. Gill and Son, 1897).

family, and likewise unconvinced that he could put up with the rigours of missionary life, the superior sent him away. Eventually, they all relented, and since then Rodolpho had belied everyone's fears; for he himself was fearless. Given the wealth he had twice forsaken, there were few less likely to be mesmerised by the glitter of Akbar's court.

Their journey took them first by ship, up along the western coast of India to Surat, then upriver before disembarking and beginning a trek that would take them initially through a jungle and then up a long mountain pass. Akbar had provided them with a guard, which was put to good use on the pass, where they were ambushed by bandits. During the ensuing fight, one of their guards was killed. At the summit, the close air of the jungle was replaced by gales: "Fierce storms and violent whirlwinds are so frequent that not a house in the town would be able to retain its roof, had not God himself solved this difficult problem by supplying a natural abundance of marble slabs, which are used for roofing."[4]

In the plateau town of Gwalior, they observed a pilgrim site at the tomb of one Baba Capurius, a Muslim-born mystic who, said Monserrate, was convinced that perfect happiness "consists in the absence of all feeling and in insensibility towards the ills of the flesh and the troubles of the mind". He had chased this state of consciousness through a combination of vegetarianism and opiate tea, and a temple had grown up around the tomb, where his followers continued to congregate: "They eat only cooked pulse and any sweet food. Then they put their heads between their knees

[4] Father Monserrate, S.J., *The Commentary of Father Monserrate, S.J. on His Journey to the Court of Akbar*, ed. and trans. Banerjee and Hoyland (London: Oxford University Press, 1922), p. 21. Unless footnoted, all subsequent quotations are from this edition of Monserrate's account.

and sleep." Monserrate was not impressed: these acolytes
were revered for being idle, he said, adding that he doubted
whether they found much peace, since "in reality one is
more liable to be tortured by the incitements of the senses
when in a state of semi-insensibility."

When they reached Akbar's capital at Fatehpur Sikri, the
two of them found themselves "the cynosure of all eyes",
residents and visitors turning out to watch the black-robed
priests enter the two miles of ramparts, into a maze of alley-
ways, housing, markets, and the imperial palace. It was not
dissimilar to a European city, and Akbar had drawn talent
from as far as Italy to furnish it. What made it different was
Akbar, for no one was quite like this emperor, or the court
he kept, not even among his forefathers. Still only in his
thirties, so assured was his power that the phrase "as lucky
as Akbar" was used throughout the bazaars of Asia.[5]

When the two Jesuits were taken to meet him that evening, across carpeted halls, they were surprised to find the
emperor and his young sons dressed in Portuguese clothes.
Akbar's interest in European civilisation was not craven but
matched by a fascination in almost all aspects of human
life. According to Abul Fazl, Akbar had once ordered thirty
babies to be purchased from their mothers and kept in a
building in the palace gardens, to be fed and nursed by at-
tendants who were not allowed to speak to them, because
he was curious what language they would grow up speaking to each other: "If the fountain of speech bubbled over
in any one of them, he would regard this as divine speech,
and accept it as such."[6] The children were eventually returned to their mothers, but the bizarre cruelty of the ex-

[5] Jarric, *Akbar and the Jesuits*, p. 208.
[6] Ibid., pp. 245–46. In his edition of Jarric's history, Payne offers pertinent
translations of Abul Fazl's Farsi court records.

periment had barely registered in a court featuring human chess pieces and foot couriers with their spleens removed for greater speed.

Thirty-seven years old, Akbar had been emperor for twenty of those, born to a Moghul dynasty so entrenched within India that his only serious threats were from within his family. Such a war had begun his reign, the memory of which was a part of the aura that surrounded him. Monserrate noted "one could easily recognise, even at the first glance, that he is the King." He had broad, imposing shoulders, a wide forehead, and eyes "so bright and flashing that they seem like a sea shimmering in the sunlight". His moustache was "like that of a Turkish youth who has not yet attained to manhood", and there was a prominent mole on his upper lip. His nostrils flared wide "as though in derision". He was a sturdy, hearty, and robust man, honed by hunting and gymnastics. That night his attitude appeared "tranquil, serene, and open, full also of dignity".

Had Akbar simply been a charming despot, it would have been easier for Monserrate to criticise him in the days that followed, but his subjects seemed to like him, as did the two Jesuits. Although he could be ruthless with his nobles, he was said to be lenient with the people, commuting death sentences, tolerant of local customs, and open to petitions from the very poorest of his subjects: "It is hard to exaggerate how accessible he makes himself to all who wish audience of him." There was a temper ("when he is angry, of awful majesty") but also a restless melancholy one caught glimpses of from time to time. Abul Fazl, who had shown the missionaries their quarters and continued to host them, explained that at the age of nineteen, while fighting against his uncle in the Himalayas, Akbar had experienced a moment of peace so profound it had haunted him ever since.

Neither his whimsical experiments nor over one hundred wives and concubines had been able to satisfy that craving.

Kazakh by distant origin, this intriguing man's nomadic ancestors had drawn their language from Persia, their appearance from Asia, and their faith from Mecca, and it had proved an almighty combination. "Genghis Khan", "Kublai Khan", "Tamerlane", and "Babur" were names known throughout Europe, both for their ruthlessness (Tamerlane's army was reputed to have killed 100,000 people in a single day in its conquest of Delhi) and their elegance. Akbar's grandfather Babur had composed poetry and commissioned Hindu artists during his consolidating campaigns in the south of the sub-continent.

There had been weak links, notably Akbar's father, who had degenerated into opium addiction and watched his harem have sex with each other. There is a suggestion he also had epilepsy, though his death by falling from a palace window is generally thought to have been assassination, corroborated by the immediate stake to the throne by Akbar's uncle.[7] Akbar was a teenager when he rose so memorably to the occasion and also dismissed his tutors, remaining illiterate for the rest of his life. His shrewdness was not in dispute, and he had honed an instinct for watching and listening to peoples' mannerisms, as well as for reaching the gist of the reports that were made to him. All this would be evident in the religious debates that the two Jesuits were shortly to join.

In matters of religion, his spirit of exploration was well developed. Though Muslim-born, and with a fiercely pious mother, he often dressed like a Sikh, whose gurus had presented him with the accoutrements of that religion. He had several senior Hindu and Jain confidants, and from Persia

[7] Ibid., p. 215.

he had invited to his court priests of the pre-Islamic Zoro-
astrian faith, who spoke his mother tongue of Farsi. The
very furnishings of his palace spoke of divided loyalties: the
state rooms were decorated in the non-figurative patterns of
Sunni art, while his private quarters (where he had greeted
the Jesuits) were decorated with figurative work by Indian
artists.

With the Jesuits *in situ*, the debates resumed. Rodolpho
took the lead as representative of the Christian faith, speaking initially through a Farsi interpreter. The king sat on a
balcony, out of sight, but listening intently. The most frequent interjections, as Rodolpho began to lay out Catholic
doctrine, were from the mullahs. This was opposition he
and Monserrate were ready for and a form of apologetics
that clergy in southern Spain had become well versed in
during centuries of Islamic rule. The mullahs' main con-
tention was that Jesus was not divine; that he did not die
on a cross; and that what Christians call the Trinity (God
as Father, Son, and Holy Spirit) was akin to polytheism, the
pagan worship of different gods.

Rodolpho replied with reference to both Christian and
Islamic Scriptures, drawing for the latter on Saint Bernard of
Clairvaux's writings about the Qur'an. His grasp of Islamic
doctrine impressed his Muslim counterpart, Shah Abdulfasilius, who showed himself subsequently friendly, but it
stoked the rest of the mullahs to fury. Akbar sat over it all,
telling Rodolpho afterward that he was delighted at the way
he had begun. The mullahs, he warned, were his greatest
headache, and no one had ever countered them as well as
Rodolpho. Abul Fazl echoed this in his account:

> The religious debate [*Ibadat-Khana*] was brightened by the
> presence of Padre Radalf, who for intelligence and wis-
> dom was unrivalled among Christian doctors. Several carp-
> ing and bigoted men attacked him, and this afforded an

opportunity for a display of the calm judgment and justice
of the assembly! These men brought forward the old received assertions, and did not attempt to arrive at the truth
by reasoning. Their statements were torn to pieces, and
they were nearly put to shame; and then they began to attack the contradictions in the Gospel, but they could not
prove their assertions. With perfect calmness and earnest
conviction of the truth, the Padre replied to their arguments.[8]

After three such sessions, Akbar summoned the two Jesuits into his quarters and warned Rodolpho to be more
careful, for the mullahs were "unscrupulous villains". He
also asked Rodolpho to repeat, for his own satisfaction, how
it could be that one God could be three Persons, and how
God could be born as a child, since such things were "beyond his understanding". Rodolpho told Akbar that he must
pray to God in order to be allowed deeper understanding
of such mysteries and agreed to be more cautious with the
mullahs "not because we are afraid of them for ourselves,
but because we wish to obey you".

Indeed, fear would never be a problem with Rodolpho, so
convinced was he of heaven. Back in their own accommo-
dation, at prayer, Monserrate said he would sometimes tilt
his head, as if offering his neck to an executioner. Rodolpho
opened the next debate with the following statement: "It
is needful that he who desires thoroughly to learn the divine doctrines of Christianity should ponder especially two
matters—as (Christ) himself very frequently testified—in
order that the mind of such a one may be disposed to drink
in the divine light with the eyes of his soul, and to let as
it were the gentle rain of (God's) gifts soak into and thoroughly permeate his heart." First, he said, such a seeker
must try "with the greatest earnestness to avoid those sins

[8] Ibid., p. 222.

which divide the soul from God". Christian faith was not
a philosophy or a proposition, but a living truth that would
"not enter a soul that is full of evil wishes".

Wisdom, he continued, was not to be sought by achievement but was itself a gift from God. He quoted to them
from the prophet Zechariah: "Turn unto me and I will turn
unto you" and said this could never happen without heartfelt
repentance. On earth, Christ had "exhorted men to peni-
tence" throughout his ministry: "I believe that he wished to
teach the same lesson—the lesson of the necessity of fleeing
from sin—when, before raising from the dead the daughter
of the leader of the synagogue, he drove out the musicians
and the unruly crowd. For nothing is so successful as sin
in arousing that tumult in the soul which can prevent the
acceptance of Christ, who is the God of peace and calm;
nothing can so take away the sight of the eyes and prevent
a man beholding that light of faith which Christ himself
brings with him; nothing can so shut up a man's heart and
prevent its drinking in the heavenly showers with which
God floods it." All sin prevents holiness: "If you wish to
put on a clean garment, you must first take off the dirty
one." Rodolpho concluded by saying that if anyone, having
heard all this, still wished "to put on the new man, that
is, Christ himself", he must restrict himself to one wife,
repent of past sins, give generously to the poor, and pour
out prayers to God. Then he could freely visit the Jesuits at
their quarters, where, "without the spirit of controversy",
the priests would further explain the Gospel.

If this was meant to calm everyone down, miraculously
it almost worked. Rodolpho was so patently guileless that
both Abul Fazl and the Shah Abdulfasilius began visiting the
two priests. The news that they had turned down all gifts
of money from Akbar had meanwhile impressed the whole
capital, including Akbar, who exclaimed in court that he

"loved" these Christians and asked them to begin tutoring his eldest son, Prince Salim. Meanwhile, Rodolpho's Farsi, which he had begun learning in Goa, had reached a point where he could dismiss his interpreter.

The first concerted hostility came, not from the mullahs, but from the high-caste Brahmin Hindus in the capital. The Jesuits had been disgusted to observe the practise of *suti*, by which a widow was burned alive on her husband's funeral pyre and had challenged Akbar for allowing this to go on. He replied that "only God" could give the widows the fortitude to go through such a sacrifice, which Rodolpho disputed, insisting the women were often drugged and, "before they lose their resolution" were hurried to the pyre "with warnings, prayers and promises of eternal fame". If they hesitated, they were "driven on to the pyre: and if they try to leap off again, are held down with poles and hooks".

The emperor seemed to enjoy the novelty of being contradicted, said Monserrate, placing his hand on Rodolpho's shoulder and smiling, even as the latter rebuked him. Furthermore, he agreed to ban *suti*. This had incensed the Brahmins, priests, and beneficiaries of Hindu tradition, who stirred the people to hiss at the priests when they were in the streets. In fact, many started to show greater friendliness to the Jesuits, further inflaming the Brahmins. Muslim opposition was not far behind and centred on the king's mother, who had returned from the Haj to find her son toying with the idea of closing the harem. The harem was her seat of power, made up as it was of daughters from across the most powerful families in the empire. When she spoke in the harem, she had the ear of Muslim governors, Sikh and Jain noblemen, and Hindu *rajas*, whose daughters were under her care. In that sense, the harem was the glue that held the empire together.

There was also resentment toward the Jesuits for their association with the Portuguese. By dominating the Arabian Sea with their superior artillery, Portuguese ships had started to muscle a monopoly on Haj traffic from India, a lucrative but insulting move that the Queen Mother had unfortunately just experienced at firsthand. Compounded by the discovery that her grandson, and Moghul heir, Prince Salim, was being taught by the Jesuits, she made her outrage known through semiotics understood by everyone in the extended Moghul court. The effect was immediate, as Bengal and then Kabul came out in revolt.

If the rebels thought their speed would catch Akbar unawares, they underestimated his spy network, who had suspended the debates and gone into war-planning before rumours had reached the streets of the capital. The Jesuits did not see him for weeks, except on one memorable occasion. Salim was still attending lessons at their house, and, it being Christmas, they had built a crib with figures they had bought in the market. When they put this on display in the room they had turned into their chapel, it caused such public interest that Akbar came to visit with his generals and war council: "He examined everything, and began to talk about the birth of Christ." His comments caused a re-eruption of outrage among the mullahs who had accompanied him, to which Rodolpho responded by asking how they could, at one point, teach that Jesus was not killed before his Ascension and, at another, say that God promised to be gracious to Jesus at his birth, death, and Resurrection. This did not calm them down, but, apparently unperturbed, Akbar sent his other sons to see the crib that evening and asked that Rodolpho accompany the royal camp on his impending military campaign.

Rodolpho had taken ill, however, and it was agreed that

he would stay at the capital with Salim, while Monserrate
travelled with the camp, and act as tutor to Akbar's second eldest son, Pahari, who was to accompany his father.
On departure, under the same black banners that Tamerlane had once carried into battle, the army at first seemed
"remarkably small" to Monserrate. But once they were in
open country, forces began arriving from the provinces to
join them: "it increased so rapidly that it soon seemed to
hide the earth." Still others arrived, one flank now being
formed by armoured elephants, the other by mule cavalry,
light infantry, and foot lancers: "No beast, if surprised on
the way, could break through the ranks and escape. Even the
birds, wearied by trying to fly out of danger, and terrified
by the shouts of the soldiers, fell down exhausted to the
earth."

When the king rode down the lines, every man saluted as
he passed, there being no noise during the inspection except a
solitary drummer sounding his drum at short intervals, "perhaps at every tenth pace, with a slow and dignified rhythm".
Ahead of them were mounted scouts, clearing people and
beasts out of their path, as yet more contingents arrived.
Ahead of them were agents on the road to Kabul, promising
exemption from taxes for merchants who brought "grain,
pulse and all manner of provisions" to the army and sold
them at reasonable rates. At the back rode the harem on
female elephants, hidden from view within decorated *how-
dahs* and escorted by five hundred veterans "of very dignified and venerable appearance". There were two identical
royal camps, one always being set up a day's march ahead.
Still the army swelled, until elephants had to be estimated
in their thousands, cavalry in their tens of thousands, and
the infantry was "almost infinite". The elephants were not
only trained to obey the voice of their keepers, but to fol-

low senior elephants into battle, the latter with "a proud and insolent air, like a true general in the midst of his forces". The momentum of the entire force was such that, at one point, the vanguard burnt down an entire forest rather than stop anyone.

Monserrate tutored young Pahari *en route*, and Akbar was kept daily informed of all that he was learning. Hindu elders in the royal camp engaged Monserrate with an account of their own theology: "The Hindus throughout India worship Crustnu [Krishna] as a god. They say he was the son of Parabrama whom they call Para Maessuris, that is 'immortal God' and that he had two brothers, Messuris and Brahma, and a sister Sethis, who was born from the forehead of Paramaesseur." It reminded Monserrate of the mythology of the ancient Romans "who used to say that Saturn was the father of Jupiter, Neptune and Orcus, and that Minerva was born from his head." In one town, Monserrate visited a Hindu temple, dedicated to the monkey god Hanuman, where three hundred monkeys had been trained to take up arms and "dividing into two companies, fight like gladiators, ceasing again and laying down their arms at the sound of the same bell", the people "[imagining] this to be achieved by a divine miracle".

Delhi offered a more refined break: "Time fails me to describe the lovely parks and the many residential districts"; the avenues of the ancient city were filled with "a rich profusion of fruit and flowers". With his breviary and rosary beads, he was a lone Christian among a moving mass of now over a million people, but that did not seem to bother him. Meanwhile, the size of the army had become its victory, as the campaign turned into a triumphant procession. In one city, "the inhabitants, especially the women, filled the balconies and the roofs in their eagerness to see the King." The rebels turned and fled back toward Kabul, news of which sent joy through the royal camp, a number of whom had relatives among the rebel leaders.

Sensing it to be a good moment, Monserrate prepared in Farsi a brief summary of the events of Christ's Passion "and handed it to the King whilst he was in a state of delight". The emperor, "as though in a fit of absent-mindedness", ordered Abul Fazl to read it aloud. While he did, Akbar kept stopping him to quiz Monserrate on points that puzzled him: "Why did not the Lord Jesus, who was so anxious that the Jews should believe in him and be saved, accept the challenge of these same Jews, when he was on the cross: 'If thou art the Son of God, descend now and we will believe in you'?" Monserrate told him that faith came from the soul and not the eyes: "If Christ had come down from the cross, they would not have been made better, but would probably have put down the miracle to magic, as has frequently happened; for many miracles which could only be performed by God are attributed to the Prince of devils."

But if this is true, Akbar went on, why did Christ, appearing after his Resurrection, allow the doubting disciple Thomas to place his hands in his wounds? Monserrate answered: "Christ met Thomas' doubts, like a father pitying his son, of his own kindness and grace, showing him his hands and his side, lest Thomas should fall and be lost. Thomas himself made no conditions or demands." Christ's patience toward Thomas was "of advantage" to others, said Monserrate, but had he come down from the Cross, and never died, men could not have been redeemed by his sacrifice. Akbar nodded and repeated the answer to those around him. Why, he rejoined, did Christians say that God had no mortal body but that Christ sits "at the right hand of the

Father". Monserrate replied that this was no bodily, human sitting down: "we say that Christ sits at the right hand of his Father because, since Christ is God, he has the same glory, honour and power as his Father." Akbar declared himself pleased with these answers.

The embassy arrived from the rebels begging forgiveness, which Akbar received, observed Monserrate, with the melo-dramatic air of a bored parent. News then reached the camp that the Bengal revolt had also cracked. Monserrate did not speak to Akbar again after this moment but had reason to hope that the campaign had been positive for the mission. The emperor had already mentioned that he wished to have Salim baptised. Who could stop Akbar if he now also wished to make that step? For while the revolts might have been seen as a sign of divine displeasure at Akbar's openness to the Jesuits, the vanquishing of the same could surely now show that he was favoured?

In fact, Akbar had read the omens a lot farther than that. After they all returned to the capital, Akbar shut himself off from the two Jesuits. He had a high wooden platform erected in the main palace courtyard, and up to it he would climb each morning to "[watch] the dawn and [worship] the rising sun". Fazl recorded that "many thousands, men of all classes", flocked to be received into the new faith of Din-i Ilahi. At times this interest appeared to upset Akbar, who would say out loud: "Why should I claim to guide men?" But at others, he stepped more fully into the role with which he had now appointed himself. Receiving male initiates in his palace on Sundays, the latter would approach his throne on their knees, holding turbans in their hands, and bow their heads onto Akbar's feet: "His Majesty, the chosen one of God, then stretches out the hand of favour, raises up the suppliant, and replaces the turban on his head, meaning by these symbolical actions that he has raised up a man of pure intentions, who from seeming existence, has now entered into real life. His Majesty then gives the novice the *Shact*, upon which is engraved the 'Great Name', and His Majesty's symbolical motto, *Allahu Akbar*."[9]

It combined elements of Christianity (the use of Sundays); Islam (the terms "Great Name" and "Allahu Akbar"); Hinduism (the "Shact" badges referencing the threads conferred on Brahmins at maturity);[10] and Sikhism (his own turban had been ceremoniously presented to him by the Sikh Guru Amar Das). Sun worship bore echoes of Zoroastrianism, while the concept of a saint king bore the influence of his Jain confidants. Prince Salim was initiated into Din-i Ilahi together with his brothers and subsequently stopped coming for lessons. On witnessing the sun ceremony for themselves, the two Jesuits came to the decision that Rodolpho would stay in the capital so long as there was any hope, but that Monserrate would go back to Goa.

Akbar was displeased when he found out and initially forbade Monserrate to leave, but he eventually gave him permission to depart, together with a letter that he asked him to deliver in person to Philip II, King of Spain and Portugal. Akbar, said Rodolpho, was changing "into more numerous shapes even than Proteus". The letter urged Philip to resolve tensions on the Arabian Sea as a fellow spiritual man: "It is not concealed and veiled from the minds of intelligent persons who have received the light of divine aid and are illuminated by the rays of wisdom and knowledge, that

[9] Ibid., pp. 237–38.
[10] Ibid., p. 238.

in this terrestrial world, which is the mirror of the celestial, there is nothing that excels love." A man named Sayyid Muzaffer was sent to accompany Monserrate, and the two of them were almost killed, an assassination attempt they only avoided after being tipped off. If this was the hand of the Queen Mother and her faction, there would scarcely be more enthusiasm for peace in Goa, and the embassy proceeded no farther.

With regret, Rodolpho also now left the capital. He would later be asked to lead another mission, to the Hindus of Salcette country, south of Goa. There had been conversions there among people who had been working in the Portuguese colony, and Rodolpho was sent to administer sacraments to them and seek permission to build a permanent church. His party consisted of five priests, a group of Salcette converts, and a Portuguese merchant named Gonzalo Rodriguez. While they were waiting in one village for an audience with the chief, a convert rushed into the hut where they were and warned them that a massacre had been stirred up by the local Hindu priest. They hurried back toward the river: "Hardly had they gone a few steps, however, when they heard behind them a great clamour and war-cries. . . . [They] were armed with swords, clubs, lances, bows and arrows, and shouting: 'Kill these sorcerers, these disturbers of our land, these enemies of our gods, the destroyers of our temples and of our worship!'"

The merchant Gonzalo Rodriguez levelled his musket, but one of the Jesuits told him to lower his barrel and tried to appease the crowd in the local tongue. At this point, another group of about two hundred attackers rose from behind a small hill, while another ("still more numerous") appeared from the road by which they had planned to retreat:

"These last were led by two herculean young men, whose naked bodies, and dishevelled hair, were a signal of war to the death."[11]

All five priests stepped forward to shield the others, knelt on the ground, and made the sign of the Cross. When the assailants shouted: "Where's the great Father?" Rodolpho stood and walked toward them. One of them "flourished his scimitar" and gave Rodolpho a gash in his thigh, which made him sink to his knees. Unfastening the top of his cassock, he offered them his neck, crying out as he did: "Pardon them O Lord! Saint Francis Xavier, pray to God for me! Lord Jesus, receive my soul!" All six Europeans and thirteen of the converts were killed in the melee.

Monserrate meanwhile was sent to Ethiopia, on an embassy to the Coptic Church there. He sailed with a fellow Jesuit named Pedro Paes, both disguised as Armenian merchants, since their ship would have to go via the Gulf coast, at whose ports Christian missions were illegal. Their identity was betrayed, possibly by their captain, and the two of them were imprisoned in Dhofar. Brought before the Ottoman governor, they were first imprisoned in the Yemenese capital of Sanaa before being transferred to Mocha on the Red Sea, where they were put to work as galley slaves. When Fr. Monserrate's health broke, they were sent back to prison, where Monserrate had his belongings restored to him and wrote the document that was found in Calcutta years later. It ends with the line: "I finished copying and revising the manuscript at Sanaa in Arabia on the feast of Saint Damasus in the month of December, 1590 A.D." After six years, the Portuguese paid the Ottomans one thousand

[11] Francis Goldie, S.J., *The First Christian Mission to the Great Mogul, Or, the Story of Blessed Rudolf Acquaviva, and of His Four Companions in Martyrdom, of the Society of Jesus* (Dublin: M. H. Gill, 1897), p. 134.

gold ducats to release the two hostages, but Monserrate died soon afterward. Before he died, he wrote a letter to Akbar, a letter we know about because Akbar, in his inscrutable way, had asked for more Jesuits.

The new missionaries found life turbulent at the court, which had moved to Agra, after a fire at Fatehpur Sikri. They reported constant whispers of plots against the emperor, mostly centred around his heir, now married, the prince Salim. Salim had proclaimed himself a friend to the new mission and obtained permission from his father for them to baptise their Muslim and Hindi converts. He received the news of Padre Rodolpho's death with genuine feeling ("What a man! What a man!") and remained well disposed toward them. But as time went on, they had seen less and less of Salim, who spent an increasing amount of time out of the capital. There was a trickle of converts, despite enormous difficulties. One was attacked outside the mission by his family, the convert begging God to forgive them as they beat him. Afterward, "he assured the Fathers that never in his life had he experienced such comfort of mind as during this ordeal."[12]

Akbar's faith had not taken root, and very few, even within the court, still pretended to believe it. Very little was seen of Akbar, who had become reclusive, with the exception of an extraordinary episode that followed the arrival of a gift for the mission chapel, a copy of an ancient painting known as the "Madonna del Popolo", depicting Mary and the baby Jesus. When displayed to the converts under their care, the impact of the picture, the original of which stands above an altar in Rome, was so immense that word spread and crowds began forming outside the mission to view it:

[12] Jarric, *Akbar and the Jesuits*, p. 147.

"The picture affected them in a manner that was wholly miraculous; for it aroused in them not only wonder, but remorse for their sins, while at the same time it brought exceeding consolation to their hearts. In short, as they went away, the Fathers were amazed at the change that had come over them."[13] The crowds grew until "the daily attendance exceeded ten thousand persons", from the poorest to the rich: "Amongst the gentlemen and grandees who came was a great captain, accompanied by more than sixty men on horseback and many others on foot, who, as soon as he saw the picture, stood as one in a trance, so overcome was he with admiration."

Eventually, word came from the palace that Akbar wished to see the painting. The crowds groaned that they would never see it again. When it was uncovered before him, he descended from his throne, and, "partially baring his head, approached it and made a deep reverence". He let them take it away, but soon afterward his mother requested to see it. The Jesuits returned to the palace, where Akbar took it from them and carried it to his mother. It was later returned by one of the harem eunuchs and marked the last encounter between the Jesuits and Akbar.

The rise of Salim's popularity carried hope that the mission might be able to retain its foothold. But politics trumped affection, and when Akbar was poisoned, everyone (including the Jesuits) knew that Salim was behind it. Abul Fazl was no longer around to confirm the matter, having been recently executed by Akbar for lingering too long during negotiations with rebels in the Deccan. The Jesuit mission would not witness Salim's ascension as Emperor Jahanghir ("Conqueror of the World"). Their last act, before being

---

[13] Ibid., p. 162.

ordered by Salim's officials out of Agra, was to attend Akbar's funeral. Moghul tradition required that the sixty-three-
year-old body be carried by Salim, and Salim's son, through a
freshly breached gap in the city walls, out to a garden grave.

Some had wanted to give him an Islamic burial, but "did
not dare". Neither Salim nor his son wore mourning dress,
and those who did were back in normal clothes the next
morning. The man who had tried to embrace all religions
was mourned by none, not even his own. As the mission
departed, with their converts, books, and the Madonna del
Popolo, they were sure what it all meant. Akbar had drawn
close, but had "missed the greatest thing of all: the knowledge of the true God and His only Son Jesus-Christ, who
came to save mankind; so that, in spite of all his worldly
prosperity, he was unable to escape everlasting torment."[14]

The Moghul Empire lasted until the ascendency of the
British a century later and is remembered in tourist guidebooks largely for the Taj Mahal, the marble mausoleum
built by Salim's son Shah Jahan ("King of the World") for
his wife. By the time of its construction, the Portuguese
were a fading presence in India, as are now the British, but
the Church herself, self-led and self-evangelised, has never
grown faster on the sub-continent or throughout Asia than
she has since the end of European colonialism.[15] Indeed,
the most remarkable and inspiring Christians in the world
are often found in such places today.

[14] Ibid., p. 208.
[15] A classic Protestant account of this shift is K. P. Yohannan's *Revolution
in World Missions*, first published in 1986 by Gospel for Asia in Carrollton,
Texas.

5

To Praise Him

David danced before the LORD with all his might; and
David was belted with a linen ephod.

2 Samuel 6:14

"I get it, but why do we have to go every week?" asked my
son, aged thirteen. He had come to live with me two years
earlier, and, while this was still a less stubborn stance toward
churchgoing than I had taken at his age, it was still a question, and another difficult one to answer properly. Chesterton had once observed: "A child of seven is excited by being
told that Tommy opened a door and saw a dragon. But a
child of three is excited by being told that Tommy opened
a door."[1] To extend this line of thought, I would say that
a thirteen-year-old is often too busy being thirteen to pay
much attention to anything you are saying, but even if the
question contained little curiosity as to what I might actually think on the matter, I still saw it as a start. Having him
with me was such an unexpected blessing (and I was too
aware of my own history) to drag the matter out. When he
asked if he could join a soccer team that played on Sunday
mornings, I agreed, and soon his churchgoing was down to
once a month and involved shameless bribery, but I felt I
was in with a shout.

The answer to his question was "to honour God", but

[1] G. K. Chesterton, *Orthodoxy* (London: Hodder and Stoughton, 1999),
p. 71.

honouring God does not mean much if you do not know
who God is. My son was happy enough in the atmosphere
of heartfelt worship and preaching, but he was hardly what
the preachers called "born again"; football, computer games
and other teenagers remained his passion. Since I was not
going to force him to go to church every week, how could
I make him want to? I realised two things. First, this was
going to be a long game, perhaps taking the rest of my life.
Secondly, I had to trust the absolute goodness of what I was
offering. I would have to do what I could to provide witness
in my own life and being, on a sustained basis, to the fruits
of the Holy Spirit (love, joy, peace, etc.), but at some stage I
would also have to introduce him to the grand sweep of the
Bible, about which I knew he had no idea, since to present
God to someone without the Bible is to reduce theology to
a set of fridge magnets. But how to summarize two thousand pages of love and brutality to a thirteen-year-old? For
me, the Bible held everything together, giving a frame of
fathomless meaning to life, but did I know it well enough
to convey its coherence? Not yet was my hopeful answer.

A few years later, while working as an army chaplain,
I found myself in a famous seventeenth-century church in
Ethiopia called *Debre Berhan Selassie* (The light of the Trinity) with two British soldiers. As we stared up at the African-
looking angels painted on the ceiling, the senior of the two,
a warrant officer and veteran of war, asked me: "Is there
anything I can read to explain all this?" I knew he meant
Christianity. I stared back at the ceiling, resisting the urge
to suggest the Bible. Why did the angels look so peaceful?
Why did they not look scared, malevolent, or bored? The
apostle Peter once told early Christians: "always be prepared
to make a defense to any one who calls you to account for

the hope that is in you."[2] Other translations render that a "reason" or a "logical defence". The following is an attempt to lay out the vast logic of the Christian Bible with a sense of the coherence the Church has always found within its brutal and glorious pages. It will try to convey how believing the story, and believing you are part of the story, transforms the way you read it and the way it begins to read you. Any errors are my own, but eventually you need to answer these people.

Of all the moments in the Bible, my favourite growing up was where children are trying to reach Jesus and are being brushed away by the disciples. He says to them: "Let the children come to me, and do not hinder them; for to such belongs the kingdom of heaven."[3] In Yorkshire, I used to lead assemblies at a local school where the age of my twenty-minute audience ranged from four-year-olds at the front, twelve-year-olds at the back, and tired-looking teachers along the side. It was hard to know where to pitch my talks until I realised that almost none of them had a clue what I was talking about and that they stopped fidgeting whenever I spoke from the heart.

One day, I took a deep breath: "OK. What I'm trying to say is this. As a Christian, I believe that God created the trees and the clouds and the hills, and you and me, and that he came down to the world, not as a super-hero to zap all the baddies, but as a vulnerable baby. That he grew up and died in love for you and me." Afterward, a five-year-old ran up to me and said: "I love God!" "Me too", I replied, knowing that I should speak this simply more often. In an

[2] I Peter 3:15.
[3] Matthew 19:14.

age characterised by both lost theology and revelations of child abuse there is a danger we overcorrect the latter by idolising children. Children are not perfect. It is said that babies are unaware of any reality beyond their own needs and that the very existence of other people takes a while to dawn (a whole lifetime, in some cases). But, in amongst these flashes of selfish mania, children are also capable of seeing life very clearly. If "God is love", as the Bible puts it, then young children often understand what that means better than anyone.[4] It is a language in which they are still fluent: "Whoever receives one such child in my name receives me; but whoever causes one of these little ones who believe in me to sin, it would be better for him to have a great millstone fastened round his neck and to be drowned in the depth of the sea."[5]

Children have more trusting hearts than adults, and to abuse that is to abuse the language of heaven, since their unmatched ability to trust carries a spiritual genius. "Trust in the LORD with all your heart, and do not rely on your own insight", says Scripture, which is hard for many of us but second nature to someone learning the alphabet.[6] Consider the way young children listen to bedtime stories. You can tell them the same story repeatedly because they are as attached to your voice as to the plot. For them, a story is as much an assurance that all the parts of life hang together as it is about a frog or a princess. However cynical we become in later life, this need for stories does not disappear. A nineteenth-century British traveller, resident at a provincial Russian court, was told of an itinerant minstrel who had

[4] 1 John 4:8.
[5] Matthew 18:5–6.
[6] Proverbs 3:5.

been put to death for breaking in the middle of a story. Stories affect our minds in a unique way, touching our moods and aspirations, which is why advertisers use them. Films, books, song lyrics, the news, and even gossip assuage this adult craving for stories.

Then there are the fractal stories we dream in our sleep or the fantasies (paranoid and base) that play out in our daytime minds; they all run, as do memories, into the pool of our disposition. I once worked with prisoners who would queue for rosary beads after church to hang them on the corners of their beds to try to stop nightmares. Then there are the stories, the narratives of what is happening, presented to us by employers, families, media, and religion. It is no wonder people go mad. Our medieval ancestors may not have always liked what was going on, but they generally knew what was going on. "What is going on?" is the unique cry of a culture trapped in what Saint Augustine calls the "pell-mell" confusion of secularism. What we crave, from childhood on, is a story we can trust. Ultimately, we want the truth.

"What is truth?" asks the Roman governor Pontius Pilate when he meets Jesus in John's Gospel, not realising that the truth is standing in front of him. Jesus does not answer. I believe this meeting happened. I believe that there is a God and that Jesus of Nazareth is "his only begotten Son". I believe, without understanding how, that Christ was at His Father's side when time was created and that we humans are made in God's image. That is to say, we most resemble God and are the reason the rest of creation exists. That in some mind-boggling way the entire universe is waiting for us to get our act together. I hold the Bible to be a trustworthy account of how this profoundly mysterious story unfolds.

It tells me that the first two humans were a man and a

woman. Without having any more idea than a child how this could have happened, I read that God placed them in a garden, a garden he created and visited. That they had abundant food there and did not age. In every respect, they were in paradise, except that they were also free to make decisions, and the devil started to exploit that. I do not know why God allowed the devil to speak to them, but I know that we are still being tempted and tested now. The devil persuaded Adam and Eve to eat the one fruit God had forbidden them to eat, from the tree of the knowledge of good and evil, and thereby become equal to God. The fruit never really had that power in the first place, and it was wrong to try it. We may be made in God's image, but we are not God, and forgetting that has been the basis of all our bad decisions.

Our ancestors were banished from God's side and so began a long journey to get back here. We're still on that return, but we will eventually get there, because that was the promise made by God to Adam and Eve when he banished them. How it would happen is the rest of the Bible, told in visions, suffering, and history. After being evicted, they had to fend for themselves on less fertile and more dangerous ground. Something else had changed—they started to grow old. Slowly at first, for Adam is said to have lived to 930 years old, but then he did something that never happened in the Garden of Eden. He died.

Their first two sons fell out with one another, and Cain killed Abel. This was not only a bad start to the journey but suggested that it was going to be a hard and long road. They had other children, whom the Bible says encountered strange, ghostly beings roaming the earth, who started breeding with them. The Bible also says there were leviathan monsters lurking in the waters. All in all, it sounds horrible and must have been a torture for Adam and Eve, who remembered Eden, where even the beasts did not kill one another. Whatever they told their children of what had been lost, most of their descendants grew up as brutal as the world they were in, making decisions on impulse. God sent a flood to wipe them all out, save for one family, through whom the story continued.

Noah had survived by taking it seriously when he believed God had instructed his heart to build a wooden boat before the floods began. Onto that boat, Noah gathered animals, as well as his wife, three sons, and their wives. Afterward, they landed and began again. The earth had changed, but Noah's children grew dark once more. As they multiplied, their race grew confident and built a brick tower so they could reach God. Apart from being impossible, this showed that we had not changed, forcing God to have us back rather than sealing our hearts from temptation. God sent a spirit of confusion, making Noah's descendants start speaking in different languages. They could not understand each other, began to split into tribes, and roamed to cover the face of the world.

Near to where they had built the tower, a man named Abram believed he heard God tell him to leave his father's country and to travel into a region south of them. Abram and his wife had been unable to have children, but God promised that, were he to show faithfulness, he and his wife would give birth, not just to a family, but to a whole nation, the people who would eventually lead the world back to God. He set out with his wife and servants. Abram was not perfect, nor was his wife, but we are told they trusted God enough to please Him, and in mark of this pleasure, God renamed him *Abraham* ("father of a multitude")[7] and his

[7] Genesis 17:5.

wife *Sarah* ("princess of princesses").[8] Abraham remained
nomadic, but a miraculous child, whom they named Isaac,
was born to them when he and Sarah were approaching one
hundred years of age. Whatever Abraham told Isaac of his
heavenly destiny, it must have seemed strange, for his family
was so small compared to the tribes that lived about them.
These other tribes worshipped gods and idols and fought
each other for land, and had Isaac's family been any bigger,
they would have crushed it, but it was nothing, just a family
of herdsmen.

Isaac was followed by Jacob, who struggled with his destiny but kept returning to faith, who changed his name to
"Israel", which meant "wrestler with God".[9] The family
grew, as did the nations around them. One of the largest
was Egypt, whose influence cast a long shadow across the
whole region. As that nation spread its influence, so too did
tales of chariots, pharaohs, and palaces, making it harder
than ever before to believe that Jacob's family would lead all
nations, let alone back to God. When drought struck their
land, they were forced to go to Egypt in search of food, but
thanks to the gifts of Jacob's son Joseph, the Pharaoh there
looked kindly on them and offered them land on which to
settle.

The stay in Egypt proved better and worse than either Jacob or his twelve sons could have imagined. Over four centuries, they grew in size and strength, but this growth made
the Egyptians nervous and jealous. Finally, the pharaohs sent
their armies to enslave them, and they lost their freedom,
forced into backbreaking work overseen by violent keepers.
A nation had emerged, but it was now trapped in captivity.

[8] Genesis 17:15.
[9] Genesis 32:28.

The Israelites cried to God for help, and God heard them and started to prepare a man named Moses. Moses was an official in Pharaoh's government, but an Israelite by birth. One day, he saw a fellow countryman being beaten in the streets and, in a rage, killed the Egyptian beating him. Fleeing the city to avoid arrest, he sought refuge with desert herdsmen: "I have been a sojourner in a foreign land", he said.[10] He lived with the clan of a man named Reuel, and married Reuel's daughter, Zipporah. After forty years of this life, God spoke to Moses from the midst of a burning bush.

He told him he was sending him to Egypt to free the Israelites. Moses was beside himself with objections, not primarily about the power of the pharaohs or the Egyptian army, but because his own people would never listen to him. Trusting God is the great challenge of the Bible, but that does not mean God will not help us to answer it. He told Moses to throw down his staff, and it turned into a snake. Other miracles were performed that day in the desert until Moses believed him. When he complained that he did not have a strong enough voice to speak to a whole nation, the Lord told him that he would prepare Moses' brother, Aaron, to speak on his behalf.

As Moses approached Egypt, it was indeed his brother who was the first to come out to meet him, and the two of them went before Pharaoh. They asked that their people be granted permission to go into the desert for three days to hold a festival to God. Pharaoh laughed in derision, at which Moses threw down his staff, which turned into a snake. Pharaoh called in his court magicians to do likewise, which they did. Then God performed other miracles through Moses that the magicians could not follow. Plagues

---

[10] Exodus 2:22.

of locusts and hailstones were followed by gnats, blood in the Nile, and a sickness that ravaged the land. Eventually, Pharaoh screamed in despair and told Moses to take the people of Israel and get out of Egypt forever.

The Egyptian people had been so terrified by the plagues that they gave the Israelites jewellery and begged them to go quickly. Israel filed eastward out of Egypt, but they had not gone long when Pharaoh changed his mind and sent his army to call them back. The commanders caught up with them up against the shores of the Red Sea, with nowhere to run. Moses held up his staff, the sea parted, and the Israelites began to walk across on the seabed.[11] When they were across, Moses lowered his staff, and the waters closed in on the soldiers who were following after them. Led by Moses' sister Miriam, the people thanked God for their deliverance in song and dance.

If Moses thought such an astonishing miracle would be enough to secure the people's trust in God forever, he was wrong, for the Israelites were quick at forgetting and quick at complaining. Moses found himself leading a nation of worriers: What were they going to eat and drink while they crossed the desert? How were they going to survive among the nations they were headed toward? They had been slaves

[11] Rabbinic Greek (Septuagint), Latin, and subsequent English translations of Hebrew Scriptures name this "the Red Sea", although in the Hebrew the name is *Yam Suph*. *Yam* can mean "sea" or "water", and *Suph* is elsewhere used to describe the papyrus of Moses' basket and the seaweed in Jonah's whale. Red Sea, used on modern maps, may have been a name introduced by Greek geographers in reference to a type of red seaweed that grew there. The appearance of all these waters has changed since the construction of the Suez Canal, and similarity between the words "red" and "reed" is only in the English, but "sea of reeds" (as per *Yam Suph*) is thought by scholars to be a likely description of a northern extension of the Red Sea marked today on maps as the Gulf of Suez. This site would also make sense as the most direct (but still miraculous) route out of Egypt for Moses.

so long in Egypt that freedom was now a burden to them; they had been so harshly disciplined that self-discipline had been forgotten. God led Moses up a mountain in the desert and gave him rules for the people, basic laws by which to live well and worship God.

As for other nations, the message was: Follow these commandments and live righteously, and God would deal with those nations. But despite these laws and constant miracles, they kept losing heart and were scared to step out of the desert. In his last message to them before he died, Moses told them God was offering them two choices: "life and death, blessing and curse; therefore choose life."[12] It fell to his successor, Joshua, to muster their spirits. As they advanced, hostile nations turned on each other, cities fell into Israel's lap, and the people entered good land wide enough for all the tribes of Israel. They established towns, settled into the industry of life, and soon started to forget about God. Worship neglected, the laws gathered dust, and they started to resemble any other nation, which was not what God had chosen them for.

The nations around them were also growing, and some of them were reaching a size to rival Egypt. The Philistines, Babylonians, and the Assyrians all dwarfed Israel, and while they were wary of the God who so miraculously protected Israel, they waited for any sign of weakness. That weakness came, for God could not abide the decadence and disputes that Israel had fallen into and lifted His guard. Soon the attacks began and were not thwarted. Israel turned back to God in distress, and He kept them from being destroyed, but it was a hazardous and uncertain existence. The people longed for a strong king like the others to protect and lead

[12] Deuteronomy 30:19.

them, but God spoke through the prophet Samuel and told them that they did not need a king like other nations, for they had God Himself, if they would only obey Him. But they still wanted a king, so God told Samuel to appoint them one.

Saul looked like a king, but lacked faith, and looks without faith were not enough for a nation that needed miracles to survive. He grew vicious and paranoid, and the Philistines began to raid at will, capturing the Ark of the Covenant, the acacia box that contained the Ten Commandments and relics of what they had experienced in the desert. Losing that was like losing Israel's soul, but Israel had a way of coming back when it was on the edge of destruction. With sincere and repentant hearts, they prayed to God for help. Enter David, not yet old enough to join the army that was busy trying to hold off the Philistines, with whom his elder brothers were fighting. What God would do through David was certainly miraculous, and it was surely no accident that God used a youngster to achieve what he did. One day, David was sent to take food to his brothers on the front. Within the Philistine ranks on the other side of that front was a giant named Goliath, who would come out and taunt the Israelites and their God, challenging any man to fight him in one-to-one combat.

King Saul sat wretchedly in his tent. He had offered his daughter in marriage to anyone who could kill Goliath, and after David heard the giant ridicule the God of Israel, he walked out in front of both armies and challenged him. Goliath laughed and asked how he was going to do that, to which David replied: "You come to me with a sword and with a spear and with a javelin; but I come to you in the name of the LORD of hosts, the God of the armies of Israel, whom you have defied."[13] With that, he slung a stone from his sling into Goliath's temple, killing him instantly.

David's fame made an enemy of King Saul, who gave him his daughter but burned with jealousy as the people sang their songs about David's bravery. Among his many gifts, David played the harp, and when he played at court, his music soothed Saul's troubled soul. Part of the king loved David, and part of him loathed him so much he threw a spear at him during a royal banquet, aiming to kill him. David took off into the desert and was joined by a group of desperados. Together, they roamed the wilderness, as Saul and his men tried to hunt them down. They were often close to starving in the dry hills, and David composed songs during this period, psalms we still sing today, asking God why he was doing this to one who loved Him, and yet still praising Him. David grew into a man in the desert and was proclaimed king of Israel after Saul's death. Once crowned, he pushed the Philistines back, recaptured the Ark, and established a great capital at Jerusalem. This became a mighty city to which other nations came to trade, where sacrifices and festivals kept God at the centre of life. It was more than a city: this was Zion, the City of God, where heaven touched earth.

Had David been any more perfect, the story might have ended there, but David was not perfect, for what Saul and the Philistines had not been able to do to him, power and lust would. One day, he spotted a woman bathing naked from his royal rooftop and had her summoned to him. She was married, and her husband was away with the army, but he slept with her anyway, and when she became pregnant, David arranged to have her husband sent into the most

[13] 1 Samuel 17:45.

dangerous part of the fighting, where he was killed. His
sin having been uncovered by the prophet Nathan, David
begged God for mercy, which he was granted, but there were
still consequences to face, as Israel's first civil war erupted in
the final years of his reign, and his son, Absalom, was killed
in an attempted coup: "O my son Absalom, my son, my son
Absalom! Would I had died instead of you, O Absalom, my
son, my son!"[14]

He was succeeded by Solomon, who brought peace and
built a Temple for the Ark to live in permanently. Jerusalem
continued to prosper, and visitors came from as far as
Ethiopia to marvel at the city's splendour. But wealth and
power also led Solomon astray, and, for all his eloquence, he
grew decadent and cynical, leaving Israel fraught with dis-
cord. The nation split into two after his death, Judah in the
south (including Jerusalem) and Israel to the north, and now
these cumulative riches, which had once seemed so awe-
some, began to shine like prizes to the surrounding nations.
Very dark clouds appeared on the horizon, and no one saw
them clearer than the prophets, who became resented but
insistent voices as the inevitable drew closer, for Israel had
turned away from God, and God was turning away from it.

Empires took turns to plunder it in the centuries that followed. The elite of the nation were transported to the city of
Babylon, slaves again, and behind them rubble and stragglers,
the Temple in ruins, jackals haunting the pools of Jerusalem.
In exile, the words of the prophets were no longer hated
but treasured for their promises that God would not forget
Israel. One named Isaiah beheld a vision of something better
than a king, a miraculous Messiah: "a virgin shall conceive

---

[14] 2 Samuel 18:33.

and bear a son, and shall call his name Immanuel."[15] The name meant "God is with us", and he also saw a vision resembling Paradise: "The cow and the bear shall feed; their young shall lie down together; and the lion shall eat straw like the ox."[16] But generations passed, and no such Messiah came from God. Other empires rose, and the prophets fell silent, as Babylon's supremacy gave way to Persia, which in turn gave way to Roman occupation. The people returned to Jerusalem and rebuilt it, but it was no longer theirs, but an outpost of the Roman Empire, and not even an important one.

If it is hard for people today to believe that God was born as a human baby in Bethlehem, it was even harder for people in Bethlehem to believe it. For those who watched him grow up in Nazareth, his name was pronounced *Yeshua* (God saves). He left no writings, only the stories of what happened during the three years in which he taught and healed. These accounts, the Gospels ("Good News"), have been ridiculed from the beginning, and the paradoxes are overwhelming. He healed and yet was broken. He was God, and yet he wept. Before he was killed, Jesus asked his followers "Who do men say that I am?"[17] They told him that some thought he was one of the prophets brought back to life. "But who do you say that I am?" he asked. His disciple Simon Peter replied: "You are the Christ, the Son of the living God!" Jesus said to him: "Blessed are you, Simon Bar-Jona! For flesh and blood has not revealed this to you, but my Father who is in heaven."[18]

[15] Isaiah 7:14.
[16] Isaiah 11:7.
[17] Mark 8:27.
[18] Matthew 16:15–17.

When he had left them, his believers went through their Hebrew Scriptures in the light of what they now held to be true. That the Messiah had come, not as a political king, but as a saver of souls.[19] They confirmed details of his short life anticipated in those Scriptures (his birthplace; the colt on which he had entered Jerusalem; the number of days he had lain in the tomb, and disciples he had chosen; the "cleansing of the Temple"; the blessing of the Gentiles), and in his death they saw explained the mysterious and Messianic vision of a suffering man that Isaiah had seen seven centuries earlier: "He was wounded for our transgressions, he was bruised for our iniquities; upon him was the chastisement that made us whole, and with his stripes we are healed."[20]

It is said that on the Western front during World War I, where the use of heavy explosives meant that often the only structures left standing were the life-size crucifixes found at the entrance of Catholic villages, known as "Calvaries", British soldiers were drawn to these crosses. "It is a symbol they like", one officer wrote home, an appeal expanded upon by the wartime poet Edward Shillito in "Jesus of the Scars": "The other gods were strong; but Thou wast weak; / they rode, but Thou didst stumble to a throne; / But to our wounds only God's wounds can speak, / And not a god has wounds, but Thou alone." The French word for wound is *blessure*, from which English derives the word "bless".

---

[19] This is not to say he was apolitical. He drew crowds in one of the most volatile nations in the Roman Empire, was of royal descent within that nation, and was in the prime of his physical life. When Mark's Gospel describes him and the disciples approaching Jerusalem with the detail: "and Jesus was walking ahead of them", we are not to picture a man without political potency. That he chose not to act on that potency, however, paradoxically defined his power. As Napoleon observed on Saint Helena: "I know men, and Jesus Christ was no mere man."

[20] Isaiah 53:5.

Christians believe that Christ blessed us by bleeding for us, that he broke the curse of Adam by being "cursed on a tree". The formerly Christian world carries on largely negligent of this, and even those who go to church seem hardly to believe it. We do not want to trust God. We want to trust money, relationships or influence—things we can measure. It is invariably people who are without influence, or those suffering, who most realise the power of what Christ did and its eternal implications.

In the Second World War, a retreating German unit found itself surrounded by the Russian army. They maintained radio contact with their divisional headquarters, but there was nothing the latter could do to save them. One of the last messages the headquarters received from them was: "Send us Bibles! Send us Bibles!" Most German soldiers had grown up in the Hitler Youth and hardly knew what the Bible was, as later testified by a man who was in the headquarters at the time: "Why on earth did our boys call for Bibles to help them die? I don't know much what a Bible is like: Isn't it a Jewish book of some sort? Did they give them some Bibles? Yes, they dropped all the Bibles that could be found. There were not many around, you know. One fellow who escaped after capture told me that our soldiers would beg for just one page to hold in their hands."[21] People do not die clutching pages from *Great Expectations* or *The Brothers Karamazov*, *Das Kapital* or Freud's *Introduction to Psychoanalysis*. And yet each day people die listening to the words of the Bible. They get married to it, buried to it, and swear on it to tell the truth.

It is not an easy story. It is stern and beguiling and relentless in its message that we should trust God and abandon

---

[21] Mark Hayden, *German Military Chaplains in World War II* (Atglen, Penn.: Schiffer Military History), p. 39.

our delusions of self-sufficiency. It can seem pretty irrele-
vant until you know your lack of self-sufficiency, and then
it speaks to you clearer than a newspaper. I personally do
not always feel like reading about a God who wants me to
get over myself, but I do, because I do not want to rely
on calamity to strip away my nonsense, and it never feels
wrong. It feels right and good. When I think of angels praising God, I want to join them because I think it is the greatest
thing I can ever do.

All you need to do to know the joy of praising God is
to admit you are suffering without Him. He made you, He
loves you, He sent Christ to bring you home. What more
do you want? "That which was from the beginning, which
we have heard, which we have seen with our eyes, which
we have looked upon and touched with our hands".[22] The
four Gospels, the summit of the Christian Bible, have an
abiding power, not based on literary excellence, but because
they are telling the truth. O Lord, keep me from sin, for I
could never be apart from you again.

[22] 1 John 1:1.

POSTSCRIPT

How It Feels to Believe

Helen Berhane was a popular gospel singer and owner of a beauty parlour, where she was arrested by a Marxist regime trying to quash a revival erupting in Eritrean churches. A Pentecostal from a Catholic background, her crime had been telling people about Jesus in a public place. For two years, she was held in a shipping container on a desert military camp, knowing that she could be released by renouncing her faith. One night, she was attacked by a fellow prisoner who had gone mad. As the woman was dragged out, Helen tried to go back to sleep, but

> my scalp feels as though it is on fire, and I know that I will not sleep tonight. Sometimes I cannot believe that this is my life: these four metal walls, all of us corralled like cattle, the pain, the hunger, the fear. All because of my belief in a God who is risen, who charges me to share my faith with those who do not yet know him, a God who I am forbidden to worship. I think back to a question I have been asked many times over my months in prison: "Is your faith worth this, Helen?" And as I take a deep breath of the sour air, as my scalp stings, the mad woman rants outside, and the guards continue on their rounds, I whisper the answer: "Yes".[1]

[1] Helen Berhane and Emma Newrick, *Song of the Nightingale* (Milton Keynes, England: Authentic Media, 2009), p. xiii.

I met Helen Berhane in Denmark after her escape from the hospital to which she was eventually taken. She is one of the most impressive people I have met but also made me feel inadequate at the paucity of my own evangelism. Why on a daily basis did I not share the good news with more people?

In 1823, an English farm labourer named John Oxtoby attended a church meeting in northeast England at which was discussed the abandoning of a mission to the fishing port of Filey, where a culture of hard drinking and superstition had proved impervious to the Gospel. Oxtoby said he would go. On approaching the hill that overlooked the port, he fell to his knees and prayed for hours, sometimes crying out to God: "Do not shame me, Lord! Do not shame me!" Then he jumped to his feet, shouting: "Filey is taken!"[2] He marched down to the town, and within minutes men and women were sobbing and praying in the streets. The town was so transformed that people read about it in America. It should be that simple, but it rarely is.

Something was missing. One of the reasons Lord Byron gave for not believing in Christianity was division among Christians: "seventy-two villainous sects who are tearing each other to pieces for the love of the Lord and the hatred of each other." Whatever we make of him (bearing in mind that Byron knew the Bible back to front, wrestled with its claims all his life, and according to witnesses died repeating the words "Ah Christi!"),[3] he was surely right about this—a divided Church resembles an empty promise. People need

---

[2] Alan Botterill, *When Heaven Touched Filey* (York: Quacks Books, 2013), p. 22.

[3] Fiona MacCarthy, *Byron: Life and Legend* (London: John Murray, 2002), p. 518.

to hear the Gospel of love, but they need to see it, too. They no doubt saw it in Oxtoby's eyes, but Filey is a worldly town again today, and history shows how quickly revivals fade. The lost West requires not only individual people or places filled with the Holy Spirit, but a Church around which to rally. Helen Berhane told me she was shocked by the laxity of Western Protestants and that the Catholic churches in Eritrea had also experienced the revival there, and "very powerfully". Was a renewed Mother Church not what we were all waiting for?

In John's Gospel, Christ prays for his followers to be one "so that the world may believe".[4] For the believer, a united Church is inevitable, since Christ has prayed for it. Believing in Christ had to mean believing in "The Church", and I found it impossible to believe that Rodolpho and Sammy were not in the same Church. So, what did my Protestantism mean—what exactly was I "protesting"? Mary? The pope? Saints? Mass? Confession? Were these heretical, or fringe doctrines that could be outgrown for the sake of unity? If so, why did I miss them so much?

[4] John 17:21.

PART TWO

The Logical Catholic

Behold, I am the handmaid of the Lord; let it be to me according to your word.

Luke 1:38

Preface

According to her cellmate, a Communist named Else Gebel, Sophie Scholl had a dream the night before she was tried for distributing anti-Nazi leaflets.

> It was a fine, sunny day, and you were taking a child in a long, white robe to be christened. The road to the church climbed steeply up a mountainside, but you held the child firmly and securely. All at once a crevasse yawned ahead. You just had time to deposit the child safely on the other side. Then you plunged into the abyss. You interpreted the dream as follows: the child in the white robe is our ideal, which will surmount every obstacle. We are privileged to be its pioneers, but we must die for it beforehand.[1]

A Munich undergraduate, Sophie Scholl was guillotined the next day, together with her brother Hans and a man named Christian Probst. In the brief interlude between their return from the show trial and their execution, Sophie asked to pray with a prison chaplain. In a farewell letter, which she addressed to her fiancé, she also sent a greeting to Carl Muth, an elderly Catholic editor whose journal had been banned. Muth had introduced the Scholls to the writings of Saint Augustine and Catholic art, significantly "La Pietà", scenes depicting Mary's grief as she cradled her crucified son in her arms. Suffering, he had told them, could be noble and was not always to be avoided.

[1] Inge Jens, ed., *At the Heart of the White Rose: Letters and Diaries of Hans and Sophie Scholl* (Walden, N.Y.: Plough Publishing, 2017), p. 347.

For the siblings, their friendship with Muth had been part of a renewed interest in Christianity. Their mother was a devout Protestant, but their father had never been to church. The deeper the risks they took, the more Hans and Sophie had both felt drawn to faith. For Sophie, prayer had not come easily, as she had once confided to a friend: "I'm still so remote from God that I don't even sense his presence when I pray. Sometimes when I utter God's name, in fact, I feel like sinking into a void. It isn't a frightening or dizzy-making sensation, it's nothing at all—and that's far more terrible. But prayer is the only remedy for it, and however many little devils scurry around inside me, I shall cling to the rope God has thrown me in Jesus Christ, even if my numb hands can no longer feel it."[2]

She preferred Catholic liturgy ("it's a real service, not the lecture you get in a Protestant church"), and at times felt close to the Lord: "Sometimes I feel I can forge a path to God in an instant, purely by yearning to do so—by yielding up my soul entirely."[3] During the trial she had demonstrated her courage. When the infamous Nazi judge directed a torrent of vitriol at her, Sophie had calmly responded: "Somebody had to make a start." She and Hans had attempted to take on their heads responsibility for Christopher Probst's involvement (a young doctor, Probst was a father), but all three were sentenced to death. Back at the prison, Probst asked to see a priest in order to be received into the Catholic Church. Taken after that to share a final cigarette with the Scholls, a witness heard him say: "I didn't know that death could be so easy."[4]

[2] Ibid., p. 283.
[3] Ibid., p. 190.
[4] Annette Dumbach and Jud Newborn, *Sophie Scholl and the White Rose* (London: Oneworld, 2018), p. 161.

The defeat of an apparently unbreakable power sometimes turns on the action of an individual. At the battle of Isandlwana, a large Zulu army found itself pinned down by the fire of a well-armed but small British force. Finally, according to the Zulu account, a man got up and shouted: "Our grandfathers did not make us to be cowards!" He was instantly shot dead, at which the whole army rose to its feet and routed the British camp. The truth sometimes requires such a witness. Many Germans hated the Nazis, but it was easier to go along with the lies. Sophie had worked as a nursery teacher and knew handicapped children were being killed, while Hans had passed through Warsaw as an army medic on the Eastern front and seen the Jewish ghetto. Armed with the truth that lay behind the regime's propaganda, writers such as Saint Augustine led them to see the spiritual dimension to what they were doing. One of the leaflets they distributed read: "Every word that comes out of Hitler's mouth is a lie. When he says peace, he means war, and when he blasphemously uses the name of the Almighty, he means the power of evil, the fallen angel, Satan. . . . [W]hoever today still doubts the real existence of demonic powers has completely failed to understand the metaphysical background of this war."[5]

Shortly before the execution, Frau Magdalena Scholl was allowed to see her two children:

"Sophie, Sophie, you'll never come in that door again!"

"Oh mother, what are those few years anyway?"

"Sophie . . . remember Jesus."

"Yes, but you too."[6]

The distinction between saying such words and meaning

---

[5] Ibid., p. 196.
[6] Ibid., p. 160.

them is infinite. Just so, in the moments of renewal that have saved the Church from error, compromise, and hypocrisy, one cry has always resounded: *mean it*. It has never been a call to believe anything new but a call to believe what has always been believed, only with the agony of love.

6

The Motives of King Alfred

I am not writing history but biography, and the most out-standing exploits do not always have the property of re-vealing the goodness or badness of the agent; often, in fact, a casual action, the odd phrase, or a jest reveals character better than battles.[1]

Plutarch, *Life of Alexander*

The 1950s English writer L. P. Hartley began his novel *The Go-Between* with the words: "The past is a foreign country; they do things differently there." It is a crisp opening, but only a half-truth, for they also did exactly the same things in the past, and still do in foreign countries, which is part of their fascination. Everyone eats, sleeps, clothes themselves, and dies, albeit in different ways. Moreover, the past also has a past. One of the earliest preserved poems in Old English is called "The Ruin", found in a thousand-year-old book known to scholars as *Codex Exoniensis*. The poem describes a wanderer rummaging through the once-mighty Roman ruins of Bath. Adapted into modern English, its voice is as crisp as Hartley's:

Roofs have fallen, towers are ruinous,
the ring gate is destroyed, frost is on the mortar,

[1] Plutarch, *Greek Lives*, Oxford World's Classics (Oxford: Oxford University Press, 1998), p. 312.

the gaping protectors against storms are rent, have collapsed, undermined by age. . . . It fell to the earth, its future burst.[2]

We can go back even farther than that poet. Before the Romans ever arrived in Britain, British tribes were occupying hill forts, such as Danebury Hill Fort some forty miles from Bath. Archaeologists believe that Danebury Hill had been abandoned before the arrival of Romans in Britain in A.D. 43. In other words, Danebury Hill Fort was a ruin when the Romans laid the first stone of a city that would become the ruin our old poem wrote about. The past recedes but is always there, back to a mysterious and deeply contested horizon.

In my fifth year of service as a chaplain in the British army, I awoke one morning on a camp cot in my office. I had been drinking at a Christmas party the night before and decided not to drive home. Officially, it had not been a Christmas party, since the regiment's commanding officer had used his newly granted prerogative not to formally observe Christmas that year. It was to be an "end-of-year celebration". There was to be no carol service, no traditional Christmas lunch. He had let me know his views on religion while at the same time assuring me that he considered my pastoral role within the regiment to be invaluable. His warmth notwithstanding, I could not but see this as an ominous sign of things to come, a foreboding deepened by a Ministry of Defence announcement soon afterward regarding the launch of a "Defence Pagan Network". In the announcement, a general said he was "delighted" to see this

[2] R. E. Bjork, ed. and trans., *Old English Shorter Poems*, vol. 2: *Wisdom and Lyric*, Dunbarton Oaks Medieval Library (Cambridge, Mass.: Harvard University Press, 2014), p. 119 used with permission by the President of Fellows of Harvard College).

new "community" for witches and druids being launched within the British military. That night at the Officers' Mess, I drank more than I meant to and nearly got into a fight with some who had supported the Christmas ban. Now I woke with a headache and a cringe. Instead of driving home, I took the car to Hyde Abbey, north of Winchester, one of the places where Alfred the Great is thought to have been buried.

Hyde Abbey was so meticulously dismantled during Henry VIII's "Dissolution of the Monasteries" that few vestiges of it are left. A surviving 1538 document itemises the asset stripping that took place: "The stone, timber, slates, iron and glass, remaining within and upon the Church cloister, chapter house, dormitory, frater, the Convent Hall, with the lodgings adjoining to the Gatehouse, deemed by the King's Commissioners to be superfluous houses, to be razed and taken to the use of the King his majesty. And likewise all the lead."[3] A prison was later built on the site, and the inmates put to tilling the land immediately around the old church. One day, they hit upon a crypt, and a crowd gathered, including a Dr. John Milner, one of the first Catholic priests to be operating legally in England since the days of the Dissolution, who recorded that: "at almost every stroke of the mattock or spade some ancient sepulchre was violated."[4] A century later, Hyde became a Victorian suburb, a street of terraced houses running down the line of what had been the nave. Anything of value from the graves had by then been lost, but a mixture of bones was retained. In contemporary times,

[3] Christine Grover, *Hyde: From Dissolution to Victorian Suburb* (Winchester: Victorian Heritage Press, 2012), p. 14.

[4] David Horspool, *Alfred the Great* (Stroud: Amberley Books, 2014), p. 210.

these have been carbon dated to the ninth and tenth centuries, and it is possible that some of them are King Alfred's.

Monasteries were a part of King Alfred's reality and a part he liked. He founded two of them, his daughter became a nun, and three of his closest advisers were monks. He considered the discipline of prayer to be as noble as soldiering, once saying that a kingdom "must have praying men, fighting men, and working men". A piece of modern glass art has been installed at the end of the terraced street, depicting what the monastery may have looked like. Across the road blink the lights of an old leisure centre, and it is difficult to imagine.

It can be likewise hard to picture Alfred's character from reading biographies. Twenty-five years ago, the flagship academic publisher Oxford University Press published a major biography questioning Alfred's reputation as "Great", by a Professor Smyth, who described him as "a master of manipulating and projecting a desired image of himself to his own time and to a gullible posterity".[5] In a more generous entry for the *Dictionary of National Biography*, the medieval historian Patrick Wormald maintained Alfred was "among the most remarkable rulers in the annals of human government"[6] but also identified two problems in trying to get a real sense of the man. Firstly, there is more surviving documentary evidence about Alfred than about any other person living in the British Isles before or for two centuries after him, with the consequent danger that the volume of evidence may exaggerate Alfred's importance, especially given

[5] Alfred P. Smyth, *King Alfred the Great* (Oxford: Oxford University Press, 1995), p. 553.

[6] *Oxford Dictionary of National Biography* (online), https://doi.org/10.1093/ref:odnb/183.

much of it was generated by his own court. Secondly, said Wormald, the traditional summary of Alfred's reign (held as much in folklore as in history books) was so heroic that each successive generation tended to project its own image onto him. Thus, he had in turn been depicted as a great warrior, great Church reformer, great educator, great engineer, and always a great Englishman.

It was bleak to think our age was reinventing him as a great spin doctor, for if Alfred was not "Great", it is difficult to know who is. In their tendency to question all conventional "narratives", medieval historians have increasingly restricted themselves in recent years to extremely objective matters —coins, place name etymology, textual analysis, and very localised archaeology. Computer-mapping such data, they have picked holes in the old sweeping portraits of Alfred's reign without offering much to replace them. We learn a lot more about what Alfred was not than about what he was. To an extent, this must be healthy, for while we may have more evidence about this King Alfred than anyone else, it is hardly conclusive. There are so many gaps in what we know about him that a degree of creativity has been inevitable. As one antiquarian wrote of Alfred: "The Pieces we have being mangled . . . they seem rather the Rubbish of a Broken Statue than the whole Parts of a Perfect Image."[7] That said, to desist from any portrait of the man Churchill declared the greatest Englishman who ever lived is to turn what is healthy about revisionism into blanket self-hatred.

Professor Smyth's attack on Alfred's reputation centered on a long section in his book entitled *A Thousand Years of*

---

[7] Quoted in Beatrice Lees, *Alfred the Great* (New York: Putnam, 1915), p. 33.

Deceit, where his rejection of all previous biographies extended to the oldest, a life of the king written by a Welsh monk in Alfred's court named Asser. Smyth claimed that this was a forgery, written by a later monk for personal gain. On publication, Smyth's evidence for this was picked apart by fellow academics, and his book has not influenced subsequent study. Historians continue to accept Asser's biography as a frustrating, subjective, but contemporary description of the king.[8] Smyth's book was, however, evidence of a voice that had come to dominate British academia —uncomfortable about nationality, reductionist about religion, determined to contradict rather than develop traditional thought, and, in all this, seduced by the notion that human beings are only ever motivated by greed and that the Church should have no part in explaining her role in the history of these islands.

The critical demolition of Smyth's book was (hopefully) a high-water mark for such extreme revisionism as far as Alfred is concerned. Rather than offering us a sense of his subject, Smyth had been more intent with smashing all other portraits, in line with a contemporary ethos that considers the proposal of any coherent proposition about the past as akin to starting a dictatorship. Academic history can hardly survive such cynicism, and, in 2018, the Professor of Medieval History of Archaeology at Oxford, John Blair, felt the need to say something that his predecessors had been able to take for granted—that the past did happen: "I reject the relativistic position that all our perceptions of the past are our own subjective projections; events really happened

---

[8] An account of the critical fate of Professor Smyth's book is given in an appendix to Richard Abels, *Alfred the Great: War, Kingship and Culture in Anglo-Saxon England* (Harlow, England: Longman, 1998), pp. 323–24.

in Anglo-Saxon England, and, although most of them are irrevocably lost, we can recover some of them and make hypotheses that are either right or wrong."[9]

Inasmuch as biography continues under these bizarre conditions, the question most asked of Alfred is not so different from that asked of a tennis champion or goal scorer. "What were you thinking about?" or "How does it feel?" is always the most intriguing door to unlock, since so few of us can begin to imagine what being an Anglo-Saxon king meant. Offering fresh insights into the mind of a man who died twelve centuries ago may seem a tall order, but there is one key that never seems to get fully turned. All historians, including Smyth, agree that Alfred's faith was important, even where they mention it in passing, as if it was his hat size. Yet, Alfred believed in scriptures, creeds and sacraments that still command belief today, and a Church whose very authority rests on being apostolic and continuous. As the Bible Alfred knew so well states: "Jesus Christ is the same yesterday and today and for ever."[10] If one is bound in some ways to project oneself onto the past, then why not be conscious of this and open to its advantages?

To exploit common religious ground does not mean having to abandon discernment, for you can admire a person without idolizing him, just as I can share Alfred's faith without being identical to him. But time itself is less an issue, since liturgy takes us both back into the Paschal Mystery with an uncommon weight of presence, citing Scripture along the way that was ancient even at the time of Christ, with the understanding that we make the same mistakes,

---

[9] John Blair, *Building Anglo-Saxon England* (Princeton, N.J., and Oxford: Princeton University Press, 2018), p. 18.

[10] Hebrews 13:8.

seek the same assurances, and pray to the same God as remote ancestors. Indeed, we are bold enough to believe that
we worship a God who exists outside time, or we would
not call it worship. Alfred may have been an Anglo-Saxon
king, but he was also hoping to follow Jesus Christ to eternal
salvation, and it does not seem naïve to construct a portrait
from that perspective.

By the time I drove back from Hyde Abbey, the sun was
rising, and my head had eased, but a fire at the cancelling
of Christmas still sat in my stomach, and I decided to drive
back via Danebury Hill Fort. As confirmed at the Andover
Iron Age Museum, a university archaeology project working
at Danebury each summer for twenty years found evidence
of pagan human sacrifice there, not the only pre-Roman hill
fort where this has been found. In his *Commentaries on the
Gallic War*, Julius Caesar describes the druids he encountered
in Gaul. They were, he said, a privileged class, exempt from
military service and from taxes, and he specifically affirms
their connection to British druids: "It is believed that this
institution was discovered in Britain and transferred to Gaul;
and nowadays those who want to understand these matters in
more detail usually travel to Britain to learn about them."[11]
Writing five decades before Christ, he said the training of
these northern druids could take as long as two decades and
involved prodigious feats of memory. Once trained, they
settled disputes and performed public sacrifices, including
human ones:

> [T]hose who are afflicted with serious illnesses and those
> who are involved in battles and danger either offer human
> sacrifice or vow that they will do so, and employ the druids

[11] Julius Caesar, *The Gallic War*, trans. Hammond, Oxford World's Classics
(Oxford: Oxford University Press, 2008), p. 127.

to manage these sacrifices. For they believe that unless one human life is offered for another the power and presence of the immortal gods cannot be propitiated. They also hold state sacrifices of a similar kind. Some of them use huge images of the gods, and fill their limbs, which are woven from wicker, with living people.[12]

They considered it preferable, said Caesar, to use criminals, but if there was a lack of them, "they will even stoop to punishing the guiltless."[13]

The conversion of Caesar's successors to Christianity had affected both Gaul and Britain, as well as Ireland, where there was no direct experience of Roman occupation. It is thought that the first wave of conversions happened as much through the osmosis of trade and personal witness as through concerted evangelism, although there may have been missionary contact from the Coptic Church of North Africa, since the ornamentation on examples of early Irish Gospel-copying calligraphy is "extraordinarily similar" to Coptic textile design.[14] One way or another, the spread of Christianity prior to the Roman exit gave birth to what is known as the Celtic Church. By the time of Alfred's reign, over four centuries later, both sides of the Irish Sea had adopted the formularies of the Catholic Church, though Ireland was still capable of throwing up characters from another age. *The Anglo-Saxon Chronicles* record three monks being brought to Alfred's court from Cornwall in A.D. 871 after setting sail from Ireland in a boat of animal skin without oars and enough food for seven days. "Dubslane", "Macbeth", and "Maelinmum" told the Wessex king they had set

[12] Ibid., p. 128.
[13] Ibid.
[14] Christopher de Hamel, *Meetings with Remarkable Manuscripts* (London: Allen Lane, 2016), p. 118.

sail for the love of God, and "they did not care where."[15] A subsequent report had them reaching Jerusalem on their pilgrimage.

The late Roman Empire had never been a single-minded evangelical machine and had continued to spread many other influences than that of the Gospel. According to the Roman historian Tacitus, the indigenous British nobles had become particularly weakened during the period of occupation by a taste for pomp and decadence, "led into the demoralising vices of porticoes, baths and grand dinner parties. The naïve Britons described these things as 'civilisation', when in fact they were simply part of their enslavement."[16] The sixth-century British Christian Gildas described his own people as becoming "like timorous chickens" under Roman rule, while the Northumberland monk Bede lamented: "All the bonds of sincerity and justice were . . . broken."[17] It was not just in Britain where this effect was felt. The early-fifth-century Iberian Christian Orosius noted of Roman Spain and Portugal: "Men butcher their virtue as a sacrifice on the altar of luxury."[18]

The exception were the Germanic tribes, who had remained a thorn in the side of Roman dominance and relatively impervious to its decadence. It was German attacks on Rome itself that had prompted the evacuation of Britain in A.D. 410, leaving the timorous chickens in a poor state to defend themselves against the warbands that poured in from

---

[15] *The Anglo-Saxon Chronicles*, trans. and ed. Michael Swanton (London: Phoenix Press, 2000), p. 82.

[16] Quoted in Michael St. John Parker, *Romans in Wessex* (Salisbury: Wessex Books, 2008), p. 12.

[17] Bede, *Ecclesiastical History of the English People*, ed. Benedicta Ward and Rowan Williams (London: Bloomsbury, 2012), p. 56.

[18] Orosius, *Seven Books of History against the Pagans*, ed. A. T. Fear (Liverpool: Liverpool University Press), p. 202.

Ireland and Scotland and the more serious pagan invasions by
Angles, Saxons, and Jutes, the latter realising (as *The Anglo-
Saxon Chronicles* put it) "the worthlessness of the Britons
and the excellence of the land".[19] These Germanic tribes
were battle-hardened and had a reputation as such across the
Christian courts of Europe: "the Saxons, like almost all the
peoples living in Germany, are ferocious by nature. They
are much given to devil worship and they are hostile to our
religion."[20] Another called them "a race [which] causes terror".[21]

These were King Alfred's ancestors, whose elite had entered Britain in the vacuum left by the Roman withdrawal,
settling throughout what we now call England. Though
happy to fight each other if there was no one else to fight,
these "Anglo-Saxons" were in time converted by an influx
of Celtic and Catholic evangelists from Ireland and Italy respectively. According to Bede's account, the seventh-century
King Aethelberht, whose wife was Christian, was converted
by "the simple and innocent life" of the Roman Catholic
missionaries who arrived in his Kentish kingdom, "and their
delightful promise, which, by many miracles, they proved
to be most certain".[22] In Church history, miracles are often
associated with periods of conversion, and miracles occur
so often in accounts of this time in England that they are
difficult for modern historians to skim over: "In [the] Christian worldview, God was everywhere, able to intercede on
behalf of believers and to punish those who strayed from
the true path. This was a time when saints were not just

[19] *Anglo-Saxon Chronicles*, p. 13.
[20] Einhard and Notker the Stammerer, *Two Lives of Charlemagne*, trans.
Lewis Thorpe (London: Penguin, 1969), p. 61.
[21] Orosius, *Seven Books of History*, p. 379.
[22] Bede, *Ecclesiastical History*, p. 60.

stories but real living men and women, when miracles really seemed to happen."[23] The Catholic evangelists in Kent experienced so many miracles in the early days of their mission that Pope Gregory wrote to them warning them not to let all the miracles go to their head.

Within the records that survive, accounts of healings and visions are so entwined with details of more quotidian business that it is hard to separate them, as one might beautiful capital letters from illuminated Gospels. As in accounts of the supernatural in the Bible, there is no discernible change in tone, and many of those occurring to Anglo-Saxon Christians were on an equally homely scale. At a convent in Essex, a dying nun was reported to have called for a candle in her room to be extinguished:

> When she had often repeated this and yet no one did it, at last she said, "I know you think I speak this in a raving fit, but let me tell you it is not so; for I see this house filled with so much light that your candle there seems to me to be dark." And when still no one paid any attention to what she said, or gave any answer, she added, "Let that candle burn as long as you will; but take note it is not my light, for my light will come to me at the dawn of the day." Then she began to tell how a certain man of God who had died that same year had appeared to her, telling her that at the break of day she would depart to the heavenly light. The truth of this vision was confirmed when the virgin died as soon as the day appeared.[24]

It was a golden age for Church growth ("There had never been happier times since the English came into Britain",[25]

[23] Justin Pollard, *Alfred the Great: The Man Who Made England* (London: John Murray, 2005), p. 25.
[24] Bede, *Ecclesiastical History*, p. 122.
[25] Ibid., p. 118.

said Bede), looked back on with nostalgia in Alfred's day. The "minster" monasteries of that time were often oases of stone-built order in a land struggling to overcome the chaos caused by the Roman withdrawal. As well as the legal continuum the Romans had provided, albeit at a price, the infrastructure they left began to perish. The Anglo-Saxons were skilled house carpenters but lacked the ability or will to maintain the rotting river bridges, and "without them, the Roman road system was reduced to a series of discontinuous stretches."[26] The monasteries became sites, not just of liturgy, but hospitals, schools, breweries, markets, and coin mints; neutral places where treaties and agreements could be signed. The leading Anglo-Saxon families contributed clergy from their own number and furnished their churches with the best imported and manufactured craftsmanship that could be afforded. Land was given by nobles and kings in exchange for prayer, so that many minsters began to receive rental income. But this elevation came at a price, namely, worldliness, and began to attract unsavoury characters into the clergy, as interested in financial as in spiritual opportunities. In other cases, the nobility began to absorb minsters back into early towns, creating at best tension and at worst unholy alliances between spiritual and worldly power.

When the first Viking raids began at the end of the eighth century, they targeted the wealthy minsters on the east coast. The Northumberland monk Alcuin, who was at the court of Charlemagne in Gaul, wrote back to the monks on Holy Island, accusing them of having brought such punishment on themselves for degenerating into "drunkenness, vanity, lewdness, degeneracy and . . . lack of manliness".[27] There

---

[26] Blair, *Building Anglo-Saxon England*, p. 189.

[27] Thomas Williams, *Viking Britain: A History* (London: William Collins, 2017), p. 31.

was thus from the start of the Viking era a sense that God was punishing the Anglo-Saxons for allowing their Christian faith to be tarnished. King Aethelwulf of Wessex ("West Saxons") wrote to Charlemagne's successor, Louis the Pious, telling him of a dream one of his priests had reported, in which he had been shown a beautiful church. Inside, boys were reading, but when he approached to see what they were reading, he saw that every other line was written in blood. When he asked the figure showing him this in the dream, he was told: "The lines of blood you can see in those books are all the various sins of the Christian people, because they are so utterly unwilling to obey the orders and fulfil the holy precepts in those divine books."[28] Aethelwulf was Alfred's father and in Wessex was at arm's length from the initial Viking raids, but he interpreted the dream to mean that if he and his people did not rekindle their piety, a "great and crushing disaster will swiftly come upon them . . . pagan men will lay waste."[29] He was in part writing to inform Louis of his wish to pass through Gaul on his way to Rome, for he had decided to go on pilgrimage with his youngest son, Alfred, in order to initiate this spiritual reconciliation.

Early sources differ as to whether Alfred visited Rome once or twice as a child, but between the ages of four and seven he is believed to have spent at least a year there, and certainly with his father. The impact of this post-Imperial city of 30,000 or so people (London is unlikely to have held 1,000 at the time), with its magnificent churches, vestments, and processions, can hardly be imagined. In two separate incidents, kings of both Wessex and Mercia had given up

---

[28] Pollard, *Alfred the Great*, p. 40.
[29] Max Adams, *Aelfred's Britain* (London: Apollo, 2020), p. 54.

their thrones to move there. Alfred was brought before Pope Leo IV, who anointed the royal child, bestowing on him his papal blessing and patronage. To the impact on a young mind of such moments we need add the death in England before their departure for Rome of Alfred's mother, who was said to have cherished her youngest son as a favourite. She had been, said the monk Asser, "an exceedingly religious woman".

These were the foundations of a loyalty to the Church that would not just run through the trials of Alfred's adulthood, but be reawakened by them. As the youngest of four royal brothers (or five, depending on the source), for Alfred to have taken holy orders as a priest would have been so normal as to have been predictable, and Wormald suggests that there may have been conflict all Alfred's life between a secular and clerical calling: "If so, the conflict was never resolved. But it was arguably the key to his unique creativity."[30]

If ordination was the plan for Aethelwulf's youngest son, then the Vikings were to disrupt this and almost every other plan in Wessex. During Alfred's youth, the Viking raids began to move closer to Wessex, preceded by dreadful rumours. These raiders were principally looking for gold, silver, and slaves, but violence itself appeared to be a treasure to them. The Mediterranean Arabs, to whom they sold many of their slaves, hardly knew what to make of them, and one scribe, named Ahmed ibn Fadlan, left the most vivid description we have of a Viking funeral. First, he said, they dressed the deceased in trousers, tunic, and a brocade caftan with gold buttons. Placing the dressed body on cushions in one of their boats, they lifted the boat and carried it on

[30] *Oxford Dictionary of National Biography*, p. 5.

land into a large tent, placing alcohol, fruit, and basil next to the corpse, followed by bread, meat, and onions: "After that they brought in a dog, which they cut in two and threw into the boat. Then they placed his weapon beside him. Next, they took two horses and made them run until they were in lather, before hacking them to pieces."[31] Finally, a slave girl was brought in, killed, and laid beside the dead man. Then the whole affair was set on fire.

These vessels. with their characteristic high prows, square sails, and oars, could hold sixty men at a time and had shallow enough keels to probe deep into the river systems of Britain, using the tributaries like the lines of a London underground map, hauling boats overland on rollers when necessary. The Peterborough manuscript of *The Anglo-Saxon Chronicles* recounts 350 such vessels sat at the mouth of the Thames in 851.[32] They came to raid but, like the Anglo-Saxons before, developed an eye for conquest and settlement and were already "ploughing" in Northumberland, as the annals put it.

Considering the ferocity of the Vikings, it is possible to err with both caricatures of cartoonish savagery and romanticised ideas of paganism. For J. R. R. Tolkien, who, aside from writing *Lord of the Rings*, spent a career as an Oxford professor examining Scandinavian mythology, there was a danger of demanding too much precision of Viking doctrine, which he believed conveyed as much a mood as a rigid set of beliefs, and largely a mood of "doubt and darkness". He further argued that surviving oral sagas invoked a heroic age in Scandinavia *before* the Vikings, suggesting the latter was understood as a decay into violence and bar-

---

[31] Williams, *Viking Britain*, p. 159.
[32] *Anglo-Saxon Chronicles*, p. 65.

barism; "a triumph of Odin and the ravens, of bloodshed for its own sake, over the gods of corn and fruitfulness".[33]

Their armies carried banners with ravens on them into battle, and it was this military identity with merciless creatures that appealed to Adolf Hitler. His Fifth *Wiking* Panzar division was recruited from Denmark, Norway, and Sweden, and he saw in the Vikings an admirable and conscience-free war machine. Addressing a Hitler Youth rally in Nuremburg before the war, he demanded a similar mind-set: "Weakness must be stamped out. The world will shrink in terror from the youngsters who grow up in my fortresses. A violent, masterful, dauntless and cruel younger generation—that is my goal. There must be nothing weak and soft about them. Their eyes must glow once more with the freedom and splendor of the beast of prey."[34]

It was a culture that left only oral history, but also archaeological evidence of human sacrifice as well as a reputation that lasted long among the people they attacked. A thirteenth-century York account of Viking "blood-eagling" is the most infamous and possibly exaggerated torture they are associated with, in which a man's ribs would be pulled open and his lungs wrapped over them to resemble a bird.[35] Even rumour of their approach could cause carnage: a convent of nuns was said to have disfigured themselves with blades rather than be raped. To whatever extent fear may have fed the terror caused by the Vikings, for the biblical mind, all the signs were of a people deliberately invoking evil: "Ungodly men by their words and deeds summoned

[33] J.R.R. Tolkien, *Beowulf, A Translation and Commentary* (London: HarperCollins 2014), p. 330.

[34] Annette Dumbach and Jud Newborn, *Sophie Scholl and the White Rose* (London: Oneworld, 2018), p. 25.

[35] Horspool, *Alfred the Great*, p. 40.

death; considering him a friend, they pined away, and they made a covenant with him, because they are fit to belong to his party."[36]

Pagan reflexes had not been entirely torn out of the Anglo-Saxon soul. The strategy of the earliest missionaries had been, wherever possible, to turn their pagan temples into churches and erect crosses at sites previously used for pagan purposes, such as river fords and crossroads, as well as appropriating traditional calendar dates for new Christian festivals. In so doing, they had "swallow[ed] up the religious core of paganism", with the result that: "by the 730s, we can find no evidence for any surviving English paganism in the sense of a formal belief system."[37] But there were leakages to this system, which were emblematised in the semi-pagan artwork of Anglo-Saxon Christian tombstones and were being shown in the way supposedly converted Northumberland and Mercian nobles had by now switched loyalties to the Vikings.

Alfred was Christian, but what do we mean by that? It is important we do not transpose a modern picture of a man sitting in a church. For a start, there was not much sitting; in many ways, this was a less sedentary kind of Christianity. Kneeling, standing, and processions were the order of the day, and the majority of services were sung in plainchant, more demanding than easy choruses. Religion was as regular as household chores. People prayed about everything: crops, sickness, curses, while festival processions could see nobles and kings walking alongside children and beggars. The latter were not flawless public events carried out by flawless people, or else there would not be surviving exhortations for

---

[36] Wisdom 1:16.
[37] Blair, *Building Anglo-Saxon England*, p. 95.

people to practise them with fear and trembling, . . . "not mixed with vanities—as many are in the habit of doing—or levities, or vulgarities".[38]

For Alfred, who had experienced liturgy done to the highest standard in Rome, Mass would be daily, as were daytime and nightly prayers. As king, he saw the spreading of piety to be one of his heaviest responsibilities: "Kings who fail to obey their divine duty to promote learning can expect earthly punishments to befall their people."[39] Beneath the conviction shared with his father that the Viking onslaught was a result of the Anglo-Saxons' sinning against their faith was a medieval world view in which the punishment often suited the crime. In Dante's depiction of hell and purgatory, the punishment afforded a soul often reflects his sins while on earth: thus, gluttons wallow like pigs, the lustful are constantly unsettled by the slightest breeze, and so on. This kind of allegorical thinking was not restricted to artists or the afterlife, and to such minds the rape and plunder carried out by the Vikings was punishment for the lust and greed to which the Anglo-Saxons had themselves resorted, just as—and most clearly of all—the wrecking of beautiful monasteries was deserved by a people who had abandoned their piety.

The modern presumption that Alfred always acted out of self-interest needs to be held in the light of his belief in divine justice: "God had entrusted him with the spiritual as well as physical welfare of his people."[40] Spin would not be enough to fulfil that responsibility, and when it came

---

[38] Helen Gittos, *Liturgy, Architecture, and Sacred Places in Anglo-Saxon England* (Oxford: Oxford University Press, 2015), p. 134.

[39] From preface to Gregory's *Pastoral Care*, quoted in Abels, *Alfred the Great*, p. 220.

[40] Abels, *Alfred the Great*, p. 221.

to resisting backsliding, few had set a better example to the Anglo-Saxons than the Northumberland saint Cuthbert, whose stories Alfred knew. As a young man, Cuthbert once stood on the banks of the Tyne River watching monks, who had been caught in a storm, be driven out to sea on their rafts. A rescue attempt had been blown back and, as Cuthbert watched, a crowd beside him began jeering, "as though [monks] deserved such misfortune for spurning the life of the ordinary man and introducing new, unheard-of rules of conduct". Cuthbert said to them: "Do you realise what you are doing? Would it not be more human of you to pray for their safety rather than to gloat over their misfortune?" But they scoffed: "Nobody is going to pray for them. Let not God raise a finger to help them! They have done away with all the old ways of worship and now nobody knows what to do." Cuthbert knelt and prayed: "At once the wind changed right about and bore them safe and sound to land at a very convenient spot beside the monastery. Seeing this, the country people burnt inwardly with shame at their impiety. They gave due credit to Cuthbert's faith, and from then on never ceased to praise him. The man who told me the story, a worthy brother of this monastery, said he had often heard one of that very group, a simple peasant, incapable of lying, tell the tale before a large audience."[41]

When Alfred looked to rebuild the piety of his kingdom, he would have known that heavenly miracles were the surest way to do that. One of his favourite authors, whose writ-

[41] David Hugh Farmer, ed., *Age of Bede*, trans. J. F. Webb (London and New York: Penguin, 1988), p. 47. Many miracles of healing and guidance surrounded Cuthbert, even after his death. One of Alfred's early biographers, Simeon of Durham, was present when Cuthbert's body was transferred in 1104 and claimed to be one of the witnesses to its uncorrupted state. Cuthbert's body was said to be still intact when his tomb was broken open during the Reformation.

ing Alfred had translated from Latin into English so it could be read more widely, was Pope Gregory, who had considered the converting effect of miracles in a book called *Dialogues*. Gregory makes a point of mentioning the provenance and witnesses of each of the stories he discusses. Having given up a vast family inheritance and status to become a monk, he cannot easily be accused of using Christianity to regain what he had voluntarily forsaken. In the book, he put especial weight on the testimony of ordinary people, introducing one story thus: "a certain poor, old man was brought unto me (because I loved always to talk with such kind of men). . . ."[42] The Italian miracles he recounts range from prophetic visions, healings, and exorcism to domestic incidents such as the supernatural mending of a borrowed kitchen sieve. Responding to the accusation that he believed in old wives' tales when he accepted such things were possible, G. K. Chesterton once echoed Gregory in replying that in a life of knowing newspaper editors and professors, he found old wives to be more trustworthy, adding: "I have always been more inclined to believe the ruck of hard-working people than to believe that special and troublesome literary class to which I belong."[43]

One of the grounds on which Professor Smyth considers Asser's contemporary biography of Alfred to be a forgery is its inclusion of miraculous incidents in Alfred's reign. Since Smyth could not accept miracles as being anything other than "a tissue of folk tales and motifs, miracle stories, and sheer invention",[44] he was forced to ask how anyone

[42] Gregory the Great, *The Dialogues*, trans. Philip Lee Warner (London: Philip Lee Warner 1911), chap. 10.
[43] G. K. Chesterton, *Orthodoxy* (London: Hodder and Stoughton, 1999), p. 63.
[44] Abels, *Alfred the Great*, p. 322.

could be sure that Asser had ever met Alfred, or was named Asser, since he was clearly not telling the truth. Attempting middle ground, one historian suggests: "Asser did not strive for historical accuracy and objectivity. . . . [His] Life was meant to be an encomium, a celebration of Alfred's greatness for the edification of its multiple audiences."[45]

Such a genre of writing certainly existed. William of Malmesbury, author of the twelfth-century *Chronicles of the Kings of England*, was unashamedly romantic with his source material (he wrote a life of King Arthur) and freely admitted that he saw his primary task being to inspire readers to "frame their lives to the pursuit of good, or to aversion from evil", even at the cost of being strictly factual: "I hope truth will find no cause to blush, though perhaps a degree of doubt may sometimes arise."[46] As one Victorian observer of this genre noted: "Biography and history were . . . simple and direct methods of teaching character."[47] While Bede (who wrote the above account of Cuthbert on the Tyne), Pope Gregory, and Asser were certainly looking to edify, each was adamant that he was not writing that kind of book. In his preface to his life of Cuthbert, Bede wrote: "I have written nothing about the saint without first subjecting the facts to the most thorough scrutiny."[48] If such an author is to be dismissed, he should be dismissed for lack of integrity, as Smyth has the honesty to do of Asser.

The difficulty that modern historians have in going as far as Smyth is the fact that most written evidence about

[45] Ibid., p. 12.

[46] William of Malmesbury, *Chronicles of the Kings of England*, ed. J. A. Giles, (London, 1847), bk. 2, prologue.

[47] John Henry Newman, *Lives of the English Saints: Hermit Saints*, ed. Hurrell Froude (London: James Toovey, 1844), p. 80.

[48] Farmer, *Age of Bede*, p. 41.

the medieval world would vanish overnight if those including the supernatural were removed from bibliographies. The
medieval Church, put simply, is the source "not only of the
written evidence but also of the most substantial and impressive physical evidence".[49] As a result, modern historians cherry-pick and thus sideline the beliefs of the people
whose records they depend on, even when they are writing about the Church directly. In the preface to his book
The Church in Anglo-Saxon Society, Professor Blair writes: "Its
concerns are with the externals of Christian culture rather
than its spirituality; with churches as social and economic
centres rather than as sites of scholarship or the religious
life; with the topographical and tangible rather than the in-
tellectual and conceptual."[50] One of the reviews extracted
by the publisher advertises this approach as "*Comprehen-
sive*", which could easily imply—given the book's title—
more than the author is claiming. As practical as the early
"minster" monasteries were, and as interesting as this book
is about that aspect of their impact on Anglo-Saxon society, there was always a religious and spiritual dimension to
them, however ephemeral one thinks such matters are, or
they would not have been built and recognised as a part of
the Church.

The Vikings were certainly "tangible". Northumberland,
Mercia, Kent, and East Anglia had been the first to feel the
full weight of their furies, but landings on the Hampshire,
Dorset, and Devon coasts, and overland incursions from
Mercia and Kent, now brought the nightmare to Wessex.
In 871, the Wessex men fought no fewer than nine battles,
according to the *Chronicles*, with the Vikings sensing that

[49] Blair, *Building Anglo-Saxon England*, p. 113.

[50] John Blair, *The Church in Anglo-Saxon Society* (New York: Oxford University Press, 2005), p. 1.

this last unconquered kingdom of the Anglo-Saxon world was now on the verge of capitulating. Alfred's family led the resistance and at such great cost that on the death of his brother Aethelred, Alfred became king of Wessex, at the age of twenty-three. Asser tells us: "he did not think that he alone could ever withstand such great ferocity of the Vikings, unless strengthened by divine help, since he had already sustained great losses of many men while his brothers were still alive."[51] He paid *danegeld* that winter, giving the marauders gold to leave, and the Vikings returned north to bully their puppet kings in Mercia and Northumberland.

One option was to run, for Alfred had plenty of good favour in the courts of France and in Rome, and others in his position had run before him. Another was to invoke the old warlike spirit of his ancestors. Alfred is said to have charged "like a wild boar" into his first major battle, and now thoughts of a cloistered life had gone. This was a Saxon man for whom war and lust came quite easily. Of the latter he would later write: "The evil desire of . . . lust disturbs the mind of wellnigh every man that lives. Even as the bee must die when she stings in her anger, so must every soul perish after unlawful lust, except a man return to virtue."[52] Asser tells us that as a young man Alfred had found it so difficult to restrain his concupiscent impulses that he was known to lie on the floor of a church praying for help. One day, says Asser, he prayed for a physical affliction, not visible to others, that would keep his mind off such pleasures and promptly developed haemorrhoids so excruciating that he

---

[51] John Asser, *Alfred the Great: Asser's Life of King Alfred and Other Contemporary Sources*, ed. Simon Keynes and Michael Lapidge (Harmondsworth, Middlesex, England, and New York: Penguin, 2004), p. 81.

[52] Quoted in Abels, *Alfred the Great*, p. 101.

begged God for another condition. Intestinal pains haunted him for the rest of his life. He could hunt and fight and fathered five children but was always, said Asser, either recovering from such an attack or anticipating the next one. Smyth dismisses the whole thing as a deliberately Messianic invention by the "pseudo-Asser", while paleo-medical history has suggested it may have been akin to Crohn's disease and the "haemorrhoids" the perianal abscesses and ulceration that can precede that condition.

Ancient legend, that most versatile of historians, has Alfred going hunting in Cornwall during this lull in fighting. The first account of this episode was written a century and a half after the event and may be entirely made up, but it contains what would become a persistent theme; namely, that Alfred needed to learn humility before God would give him victory. It was said that he went to visit his half-brother, Athelstan, who had removed himself from royal life when Alfred was a boy and become a monk and later a Roman missionary to the Celtic Church in Cornwall, and who was canonised after his death as "Saint Neot". An elder brother named Athelstan is mentioned by both Asser and the Anglo-Saxon Chronicles and depicted fighting against the Vikings in Kent, but his fate is not mentioned by either thereafter. Inasmuch as they pursue it, modern historians tend to follow the line taken by Smyth that "by 855 Athelstan is clearly dead."[53]

Legend has a better story, and the Victorian cleric Hurrell Froude points out that of the one Anglo-Saxon and four early Latin lives of Saint Neot, all state positively that the saint was the eldest son of King Aethelwulf and was brought up a soldier. "Again, all the old historians agree

[53] Smyth, *King Alfred the Great*, p. 184.

that [Aethelwulf] had but five sons. Athelstan by an early marriage; Alfred and his three brothers by a late."[54] While it does not prove the story, it is worth reminding ourselves that, if Athelstan was still alive, aside from at least one sister who had married away, he constituted all that was left of Alfred's family. In his meeting with Alfred in Cornwall, Athelstan is said to have admonished his younger brother for being "proud, self-willed, overbearing" and told him that his people were "discontented" with him and that he should accept his present humiliation as a divine chastisement.[55]

If the story captures (to use Tolkien's phrase) the mood in Alfred's kingdom at the time, so do the legends told about him in the period following the return of the Vikings to Wessex. When the Vikings reappeared in 878, a surprise attack on the royal hall at Chippenham saw Alfred nearly captured. Many of his nobles fled overseas out of "poverty and fear", says Asser, and "very nearly all the inhabitants of that region submitted to [the Vikings'] authority."[56] Alfred and a small group of family, servants, monks, and loyal nobles escaped to the Somerset Levels, where they "journeyed in difficulties . . . through the woods and fen [swamp] fastnesses" before building fortifications on a marsh island at Athelney, which remains neatly hidden even to this day.

The most famous story goes that Alfred took shelter one day in a peasant cottage. The farmer's wife asked him to watch something baking in the hearth but returned to find Alfred deep in thought and the cakes burning. Not knowing who he was, she scolded him: "You hesitate to turn the

[54] Newman, *Lives of the English Saints*, 2:82.
[55] Ibid., p. 110.
[56] Asser, Keynes, and Lapidge, *Alfred the Great*, p. 83.

loaves which you see to be burning, yet you're quite happy to eat them when they come warm from the oven!"[57] For G. K. Chesterton, this was the moment, legendary or not, when Alfred grew up and lost his arrogance. In Chesterton's ballad version of the story, the woman rescues the cakes and slaps him. Alfred's knuckles whiten, "And torture stood and the evil things / That are in the childish hearts of kings / An instant in his eyes." Then he laughs at himself, and in that laugh he loses his pride and finds the will to prevail: "This blow that I return not / Ten times will I return / On kings and earls of all degree / And armies wide as empires be." British soldiers used to chant the ballad in the trenches of World War I: "Up on the old white road, brothers, / Up on the Roman walls! / For this is the night of the drawing of swords, / And the tainted tower of the heathen hordes / Leans to our hammers, fires and cords, / Leans a little and falls."[58]

Writing of a more ancient ballad, *Beowulf*, Tolkien tells us that the Old English for a hero was *wrecca*, originally from the Germanic *rocke*, meaning a person of renown, but which had developed a second meaning in Anglo-Saxon Britain before Alfred was born, closer to our word "wretch", conjuring the idea of an exile, a man driven from the land of his home: "the position of a *wrecca* was unhappy. Only a man of commanding character and great courage could long survive in a state of outlawry."[59] Whatever exactly happened to Alfred in the wilderness around Athelney, the fact appears to be that he went into hiding a lost cause and returned an inspiration. We all need such history, and we need to be able to sing it:

[57] Ibid., p. 198.

[58] G. K. Chesterton, *The Ballad of the White Horse* (New York: John Lane, 1911), pp. 62–63.

[59] Tolkien, *Beowulf*, p. 260.

"Alfred underwent, according to legend, a deeply religious or mystical experience which changed the whole course of his life."[60] If we are to rely on physical evidence alone for what happened on Athelney, we will never say much, for swampland is not kind to physical evidence. What we have are folk stories and the admission, even among secular historians, that *something must have happened*.

Imagination is unavoidable when bringing the past back to life, whether singing a deliberately melodramatic song, or "reconstructing a ninth-century royal mead hall from the dark stains of post holes in the ground".[61] One does not need to be resistant to the truth, or abandon shrewdness, to say that legends and sagas can sometimes inform us of deeper truths than post holes and help clothe the latter with life, since "facts refuse to remain bare and isolated in our memory."[62] Another legend about Alfred, this one from the eleventh century, has a beggar appearing to him on Athelney while his men are out looking for food. The king gives him something to eat and sees him on his way. That night, both Alfred and his wife Ealhswith are met by Saint Cuthbert in their dreams, who reveals that it was he who appeared as a beggar and that, in return for Alfred's kindness in the midst of his distress, God would give Alfred victory over the Danes. While today's historians are quick to point out that heavenly figures disguised as beggars are a common "hagiographic trope", found in many medieval saint stories, it may also be that this is how God works sometimes, or that the trope itself is more penetrative than we allow. "History has a way of resembling myth",

[60] Douglas Stuckey, *Alfred the Great* (Newton Toney, England: Wessex Books, 2000), p. 26.

[61] Abels, *Alfred the Great*, p. 46.

[62] Newman, *Lives of the English Saints*, p. 75.

said Tolkien, "partly because both are ultimately of the same stuff."[63]

Asser tells us that Alfred chose the feast of Pentecost on which to ride out to meet his fate, the sort of detail that Professor Smyth again dismisses as deliberately Messianic. But Catholics are encouraged from childhood to make the Church calendar personal (following Christ into the desert during Lent; rejoicing with the angels at Christmas, etc.), so riding out to defend Christian culture on the Church's birthday can as well constitute humble obedience as delusions of grandeur or posthumous image-building. Either way, messages were sent out from Athelney through present-day Somerset, Hampshire, and Wiltshire, calling men to rally at a place called Egbert's Stone. The Viking leader, named Gudrun, left Chippenham and went out to fight. One historian has Alfred's force at about 5,000 men. Others estimate it as low as 2,000. It is all guesswork, and the Viking force the same. The veterans on Alfred's side would have been battle-hardened from the last spate of fighting, the elite among them with chain mail ("supple-linked shirts", as the Old English puts it), spears taller than themselves, and round shields; many would have been peasant farmers and self-armed. Asser said they received Alfred at Egbert's Stone with joy, "as if one restored to life". Froude, never afraid of imagination, pictures what Alfred may have said to them: "Our homes are desolate, our fields wasted, our holy places are destroyed, our priests are fled, and the hands of these heathen hounds run red with the blood of our dearest kinsmen. We have suffered, we have been forgiven. The day of retribution is come."[64]

[63] Tolkien, *Beowulf*, p. 338.
[64] Newman, *Lives of the English Saints*, p. 128.

The Vikings camped at an old hill fort, implies Asser, and came out to meet them at a place called Edington. As far as we know of such battles, men of both sides would line up shoulder to shoulder, lock their shields together to form a shield-wall, and advance against the enemy, shield-wall pushing against shield-wall until a breach was made, and then all hell would break loose. Even without sustaining a wound, so physically exhausting could these close-quarter fights be that neither side could endure more than a few hours of sustained combat. But if one side turned and fled, the pursuit of fleeing foes could go on until nightfall, while sieges of enemy encampments or fortified towns could go on for months.

Alfred submitted himself to the fortunes of war, as Asser phrases it, and prevailed, "hacking them down; he seized everything which he found outside the stronghold—men (whom he killed immediately), horses and cattle—and boldly made camp in front of the gates of the Viking stronghold with all his army."[65] When the Viking leader Gudrun, nephew of the King of Denmark, agreed to surrender, Alfred rode him and thirty of his men down to Athelney and had them baptised at the church on Aller. It is Asser who adds that in standing in as Gudrun's godfather, Alfred named him "Athelstan", which is confirmed by evidence of Gudrun later using that name on coins. It was of course the name of Alfred's half-brother, the purported Saint Neot. In the decades that followed, the emergence of an Anglo-Scandinavian Church down the eastern areas where Vikings had settled suggests they were starting to weary of their demons and that such conversions were not wholly strategic. Certainly, everyone emerged from the church in Aller

[65] Asser, Keynes, and Lapidge, *Alfred the Great*, pp. 84–85.

with something. Alfred was now a *de facto* national figure, to whom messengers from Mercia, Wales, Kent, Northumberland, and the distant Picts would arrive regarding the ongoing fight against other Viking armies.

Having defeated this Viking horde, Alfred had to shore up his exhausted kingdom against further attack and restore its beleaguered spirit. In the years that followed, he had several books translated into English that he considered would be beneficial for his nobles and clergy to start reading. One of them was *Seven Books of History against the Pagans* by the monk Orosius, a fifth-century *cri de coeur* that included a line regarding the dangers of complacency: "if only the feeble fickleness of the human mind could in times of prosperity keep to what it decided on in adversity."[66] Many of the authors Alfred chose to translate are still read today, such as Pope Gregory, Boethius, and Saint Augustine, but Orosius has become an obscure writer, though a salient one for those of us who would wish to have a Christian understanding of history. He set out to write a history of the world as one who "took the view that previous historians, because they were pagans, had necessarily missed the underlying message to be found in history . . . the unfolding of God's plan on earth".[67] Or, as Orosius himself put it: "to give an account of the true forces of history, not a mere picture of the past". This premise has not enamoured him to recent historians. In 1955, Eric Hobsbawn wrote of Orosius: "No historian today cares a rap what [he] wrote."[68]

His book was written while he was staying as an exile with Saint Augustine in Hippo, as Iberia fell to Germanic hordes. Indeed, it was the collapse of the Roman Empire

[66] Orosius, *Seven Books of History*, p. 104.
[67] Ibid., p. 8.
[68] Ibid., p. 25.

across Europe that drove Orosius' need to write, since the Christian faith had never existed without the Roman Empire, and he wanted to assure fellow Christian scholars that the Church was more lasting than worldly empires and that the fundamental human journey from the Garden of Eden, through Israel and the Cross, back to God's presence remained on course. Although Britain did not feature greatly in the book, it did feature, thus drawing Alfred's Wessex into this grand Christian understanding of history.

Knowing that standards of learning and devotion had been dropping for a long time in Wessex, including among the clergy, he invited scholars from Wales, Mercia, and the Continent to help rejuvenate his Church. The common "book language" of Latin allowed this influx of talent to Wessex, just as it had in the past seen Anglo-Saxon scholars travel to courts on the Continent. One who arrived was a French monk named Grimbald, accompanied by a note from his archbishop: "I do not allow him to be torn from me without immense grief. . . . [But] I know that one God is being served in all places and there is one catholic and apostolic Church, whether it is at Rome or across the sea."[69] With such scholars assembled, among them the Welsh biographer Asser, the king developed what became a voracious appetite for wisdom. His Latin was patchy but began to improve: "By day or night, whenever he had any opportunity, he used to tell them to read aloud from books in his presence."[70] One day, he found he could translate Latin into English himself, a miracle to those present, if rationalised thus by a modern scholar: "He was hearing religious texts constantly. Small wonder if their vocabulary, their mode of expression and

[69] Asser, Keynes, and Lapidge, *Alfred the Great*, p. 185.
[70] Ibid., p. 93.

argument, and their themes and images became part of his
habitus."[71] From the translations he contributed to, which
survive, and the comments he inserted before books were
sent out to his bishops, it is clear that Alfred thought deeply
about life, duty, and God. In his torrid life, he had experienced parental love, grief, faith, fury, glory, treachery, oblivion, and exhilaration, and the wisdom of Christian scholars, and the Bible itself, reflected the pitch of that carousel:
"Whoso will have eternal bliss, must fly from the dangerous
beauty of this world, and build the house of his mind on
the firm rock of humility, for Christ dwelleth in the valley
of humility, and in the memory of wisdom."[72]

Alfred still echoed his father's belief that God had sent
the Vikings to wake them up: "We were Christians in name
alone."[73] He could see that to stay awake in easier times required education and spiritual accountability: "The mind
itself lies to itself about itself."[74] But there were also legal
ways to stop them drifting back to how they were before the
Vikings. They had grown selfish: "everyone was more concerned with his own particular wellbeing in worldly matters than with the common good."[75] No one in the future
could "expect to live on [his] own terms in a realm that
is common to all".[76] In the Law Code that now emerged
from his court, Alfred and his advisers fused the Bible and

[71] Nicole Guenther Discenza, *The King's English: Strategies of Translation in the Old English Boethius* (Albany: State University of New York, 2005), p. 34.

[72] Quoted in Lees, *Alfred the Great*, p. 291.

[73] Asser, Keynes, and Lapidge, *Alfred the Great*, p. 127.

[74] Gregory the Great, *Pastoral Care, in Nicene and Post-Nicene Fathers of the Christian Church*, vol. 12, ed. Philip Schaff, trans. James Barmby (New York: Christian Literature Company, 1895), chap. 9.

[75] Asser, Keynes, and Lapidge, *Alfred the Great*, p. 109.

[76] Boethius, *The Consolation of Philosophy*, trans. H.R. James (London, 1897), bk. 1, chap. 2.

Anglo-Saxon traditions, introducing fines to stop honour killings, compulsory holidays for the poor, and the protection of women from rape. The significance of this might be overstated, for one in ten of the population was still a bonded slave, but Alfred at least had a desire for equality of all before the law, and that included himself and the nobles: "Position does not give dignity."

He also attacked the situation culturally, forcing clergy to study harder for ordination, threatening to strip titles from any noble who refused to learn how to read. Above all, it was a spiritual overhaul, a return to God, and the figure of Christ loomed over every book he had translated: "While daily snatching the souls of captives from the hand of the old enemy, He took blows on the face from insulting men; . . . while washing us with the water of salvation, He hid not His face from the spittings of the faithless; . . . while delivering us by His advocacy from eternal punishments, He bore scourges in silence."[77] He was piloting a ship, said Asser, "even though all his sailors were virtually exhausted".[78]

There was luxury but little ease in the royal court from which these initiatives were generated, a court that moved constantly around the shires, inspecting ordered fortifications against the Vikings, drawing taxes, judging suits. The court stayed in a series of royal halls dotted around the kingdom, "marvellously constructed of stone and wood", says Asser.[79] These halls were more edifices than palaces, decked ahead of the court's arrival with rich furnishings and tapestries, the latter as much against the cold as for colour. It is thought such a royal "mead hall" or "vill"/villa might typ-

---

[77] Gregory the Great, *Pastoral Care*, chap. 12 (translated in *Nicene and Post-Nicene Fathers of the Christian Church*, vol. 12).

[78] Asser, Keynes, and Lapidge, *Alfred the Great*, p. 101.

[79] Ibid., p. 101.

ically have consisted of a central area around 20–25m [65–82 feet] long, with a pair of annexes at either end, which likely included the royal chambers. With "high roofs, low walls, and raking external supports", they are thought to have had the appearance of large wooden tents.[80] Because they were wood, little trace of such halls can be found, and they may even have been torn down and rebuilt on a regular basis. Professor Blair suggests that "outside" and "inside" carried far less distinction than it does for us now and that tents themselves were still very much a part of royal life.

Either way, it was far from the luxuries known in royal France, where Charlemagne's court had largely taken over Roman towns and imperial prestige. In Britain, the Roman ruins were just that and only latterly would become eyed for reconstruction and habitation. Asser tells us that when Alfred got sick of candles constantly blowing out in the drafts, he decided to design his own lantern out of horn. This was a far cry from Charlemagne's court at Aachen, let alone Rome. Midden dumps from the period suggest wooden and horn eating utensils were still as common as pottery. Archaeologists have found remains of one house with glazed windows, tiled roof, and a water mill, but such glimpses of the future occurred to the east, closer to the influence of the Continent, where such things were commonplace. The almost complete invisibility to archaeologists of ninth-century housing in Wessex suggests that the majority of people (including their kings) continued to live in single-floor wooden houses built with Anglo-Saxon or Scandinavian carpentry traditions. A still-standing eleventh-century wooden church in Greensted, Essex, is not unlike the simple timber design associated with Scandinavia today.

[80] Blair, *Building Anglo-Saxon England*, p. 123.

As the court moved about, so moved falconers and dog-keepers, craftsmen, visitors, and a royal elite guard made up of nobles' sons. Asser tells us that Alfred was interested in everything, from the dogs to jewellery, and would judge disputes brought to him with the focus of an astute investigator. He describes him as once cross-examining a petitioner while washing his hands in his room. To mitigate against further Viking attacks, he had ordered the construction of a series of "burgh" fortifications and the organisation of the army into three levies, to be strictly rotated so that crops would not be left. He drove these plans, said Asser, by "gently instructing, cajoling, urging, commanding and (in the end, when his patience was exhausted) by sharply chastising those who were disobedient".[81]

It was a discipline he expected of himself. Asser says he had clock candles made in order to divide his day into three parts: eight hours of reading and prayer, eight hours for refreshment of the body, and eight hours for the business of the realm. Whether it was the building of burghs, signing of treaties, or the construction of boat-ships to rival the Vikings, the disproportionate amount of documentary and archaeological evidence from Alfred's reign indicates an immense activity, described by one writer as "the most extraordinary piece of statecraft by any ruler at any time in these islands".[82] In modern language, Alfred was probably capable of being a control freak, competitive, and determined to do everything well, whether it was hunting or being a good king or Christian. But that is not a crime, and if he projected an image of himself that was inspiring, then that, too, was a part of statecraft and not always to be collapsed

---

[81] Asser, Keynes, and Lapidge, *Alfred the Great*, p. 101.
[82] Pollard, *Alfred the Great*, p. 198.

into pride. In the translation of Boethius, he had read, if not personally written the words: "all your actions are done before the eyes of a Judge who sees all things", and for Alfred, that transparency before God extended even to one's thought life.[83]

When the Vikings did attack, toward the end of his life, another fraught season of violence began. The defence network creaked but worked, the new boats were cumbersome but helped, and perhaps, above all, the confidence of a people who had soundly beaten them once held out. No Dane was now going to ruin Alfred's legacy. A century after his death, a Winchester Saxon noble described Alfred as: "the immovable pillar of the West Saxons, a man full of justice, keen in arms, learned in speech, imbued above all with the divine writings".[84] Four centuries before Alfred's life, Saint Augustine wrote that "the tide of trouble will test, purify, and improve the good, but beat, crush, and wash away the wicked."[85] Alfred's suffering had improved him.

To receive Mass every day is no small thing for a Catholic, particularly one with as "imbued" a faith as King Alfred. His was a visceral faith for whom anxiety and temptation kept prowling "like a hungry lion", for whom Mass was a shield and taste of heaven. In his translation of Saint Augustine's *Soliloquies* lay a challenge: "It is not to be supposed . . . that all men have like wisdom in Heaven. For everyone has it in the measure which he here merited. As he who toils better here and better yearns after wisdom and righteousness, so has he more of it there, and likewise more

[83] Boethius, *Consolation of Philosophy*, epilogue.

[84] Quoted in Lees, *Alfred the Great*, p. 434.

[85] Saint Augustine, *City of God*, trans. Walsh, Zema et al. (New York: Image Books, 1958), p. 46.

honour, and more glory."[86] Once he had committed himself afresh to the Church, he was always going to do so
with the same zeal he applied to everything else in his life,
echoing Saint Cuthbert: "Then let us storm Heaven with
prayers."[87]

If it all seems too good to be true, occasionally it was. Alfred's headaches and compromises usually revolved around
land: nobles wanted it for their loyalty; monasteries wanted
it back after it was recovered from the Vikings. At times he
boxed clever and received at least one scolding from Rome.
But he also established a monastery at Athelney and a convent at Shaftesbury, and in A.D. 883, according to the *Chronicles*, he received a fragment of the True Cross as a gift from
Pope Marinus. Alfred belonged to a Church that could handle both his pride and his repentance. The books he read
were not read in a vacuum, but out of need. In his preface
to the translation of Gregory's *Dialogues*, he wrote: "there
is the most urgent necessity occasionally to calm our minds
amidst these earthly anxieties and direct them to divine and
spiritual law."[88]

The messy socio-economic realities that modern history
and archaeology have revealed about Alfred's reign reveal
more about his day-to-day life than do the smooth fantasies of hero-worship, for these were the rivalries, threats,
and problems he had to cope with and try to stay above.
In one of the most well-balanced biographies of the king,
published in 1915, Beatrice Lees said that whatever was
good about him would still reveal itself as good under
the scrutiny of a new and unsentimental school of history: "Though modern scientific research often shatters old

---

[86] Quoted in Abels, *Alfred the Great*, p. 221.
[87] Farmer, *The Age of Bede*, p. 57.
[88] Asser, Keynes, and Lapidge, *Alfred the Great*, p. 123.

beliefs, their fall may reveal unexpected truths and hidden beauties."[89]

At the end of his translation of Boethius' *Consolation of Philosophy*, Alfred added a prayer of his own composition. If one wishes to understand the mind of a Christian, listen closely to their prayers:

> Lord God Almighty, maker and ruler of all creatures, I beseech You on behalf of Your mighty mercy, and through the sign of the Holy Cross, and through St Mary's maidenhood, and through St Michael's obedience, and through the love and merits of all Your saints, that You guide me better than I have done towards You; and direct me according to Your will and my soul's need better than I myself am able; and strengthen my mind to Your will and to my soul's need, and confirm me against the devil's temptations; and keep far from me foul lust and all iniquity; and protect me from my enemies visible and invisible; and teach me to perform Your will, that I may inwardly love You before all things with pure thought and clean body, for You are my Creator and my Redeemer, my sustenance, my consolation, my trust and my hope. Praise and Glory be to You now and forever, world without end. Amen.[90]

Alfred had translated many of the psalms into English, a project cut short by his death. Each was prefaced by a few words of commentary, in which he repeatedly mentioned the biblical king Hezekiah, which is unexpected since Hezekiah is not mentioned in any of the psalms. But one can understand that king's significance to Alfred, for both men had come to the throne at the age of twenty-five and reigned for equivalent periods (Hezekiah, twenty-nine years; Alfred, twenty-six). Hezekiah had fought a pagan army (the

---

[89] Lees, *Alfred the Great*, p. 337.
[90] Asser, Keynes, and Lapidge, *Alfred the Great*, p. 137.

Assyrians) that all other nations had yielded to and at one point was trapped "like a bird in a cage" and paid his enemies off. When he kept on fighting, despite being under siege in Jerusalem, the Assyrian general issued a proclamation that the city would be slaughtered unless the king surrendered. The Bible says that Hezekiah went to the Temple with the prophet Isaiah, put the proclamation on the altar, and prayed. A miraculous victory followed.

There were other biblical characters he must have identified with. David, author of many of the psalms; a youngest son and one-time fugitive, propelled to power after an act of heroism, who struggled with arrogance and lust. Simon Maccabeus, who led his people's resistance against a pagan occupier and who rallied his followers with the words: "You yourselves know what great things I and my brothers and the house of my father have done for the laws and the sanctuary; you know also the wars and the difficulties which we have seen. By reason of this all my brothers have perished for the sake of Israel, and I alone am left."[91] Alfred, whom even the Vikings are said to have called "The Mighty", knew more of the intensity of life than any his biographers. He did so as "the emerging Roman conception of Christianity, rationality, humility and renunciation" wrestled in his soul with "tenacious old Anglo-Saxon emotions".[92]

Whether he grew up thinking he was going to be a priest or not, as a youngest son he cannot have imagined being king for so long. "I did not unduly desire this earthly rule."[93] Faced with the turmoil that put him on that throne, he went deeper into the faith he had known since his child-

[91] I Maccabees 13:3–4.
[92] Katherine Proppe, "King Alfred's 'Consolation of Philosophy'", *Neuphilologische Mitteilungen*, vol. 74, no. 4 (1973): 646.
[93] Asser, Keynes, and Lapidge, *Alfred the Great*, p. 132.

hood anointing in Rome. Whatever happened on Athelney, something good was saved. One of the psalms Alfred translated runs as follows: "He reached from on high, he took me, he drew me out of many waters. He delivered me from my strong enemy, and from those who hated me; for they were too mighty for me. They came upon me in the day of my calamity; but the LORD was my stay. He brought me forth into a broad place; he delivered me, because he delighted in me."[94]

Aside from the texts, we have post holes, coins, rubbish dumps, and the knowledge that "England" would be launched on its improbable journey, the most extensive empire since Rome, in which it might be thought to have gained the whole world and lost its soul. But that was hardly Alfred's fault, who fought gallantly and thought piously. As Chesterton reminded his generation: "How can we say that the Church wishes to bring us back to the Dark Ages? The Church was the only thing that ever brought us out of them."[95] Faithful people experience their faith more as the ability to tolerate mystery rather than to solve it, but there are also moments when concrete battles are mysteriously yet definitively won. I can only offer an analogy as to how this might affect someone: a drowning man, however strong he is, cannot pull himself out of the middle of an ocean without something to hold onto. When a Christian prays and senses a hand outstretched, he clasps it and does not care if the rest of the world calls it an illusion. If Alfred's faith was at all like mine, or mine like his, then his heart bore a mixture of gratitude and terror.

[94] Psalm 18[17]:16–19.
[95] Chesterton, *Orthodoxy*, p. 220.

7

Artwork

I hope to come to you soon, but I am writing these instructions to you so that, if I am delayed, you may know how one ought to behave in the household of God, which is the Church of the living God, the pillar and bulwark of the truth. Great indeed, we confess, is the mystery of our religion: He was manifested in the flesh, vindicated in the Spirit, seen by angels, preached among the nations, believed on in the world, taken up in glory.

1 Timothy 3:14–16

What a strange country this is.

Polish television series Dekalog *(1989), episode 8*

On the night of 19 October 1984, an unmarked Polish police car, a Fiat 125, pulled alongside a Volkswagen Golf and ordered it to stop. Both cars pulled over on what was a remote, forest stretch of highway, and for two minutes nothing happened. It was dark and quiet on the road. Then three men got out of the Fiat and walked toward the other car, the only one in police uniform ordering the driver out. The Golf's driver was an ex-paratrooper, and now working as a bodyguard, but was pinioned as soon as he stood up, handcuffed, and pushed into the front seat of the Fiat, his mouth gagged. They then turned their attention to the passenger.

Father Jerzy Popiełuszko was a Catholic priest and an outspoken opponent of the Soviet regime. He was pulled out on to the ground, beaten, and then put into the boot of the Fiat. Leaving the Golf behind them, they sped off, only slowing when the highway went through a town. There the bodyguard, a man named Waldemar Chrostowski, managed to open his door and fall out in front of another car, which stopped in front of him. The Fiat sped off, but, within a couple of days, the thirty-seven-year-old priest's face was in the newspapers, the government denying they knew anything about the disappearance. Following Chrostowski's testimony, the three policemen were arrested, and Popiełuszko's body was found in Włocławek dam, a hundred miles from where he had been abducted. Charged with acting without orders, Captain Piotrowski confessed to having tortured the priest, before tying bags of rocks to him and throwing him into the water. He was not sure whether the priest was already dead when they threw him in the water.

Poland had become no stranger to death, but this stuck in the throat. Although he was chaplain to a banned protest movement, everyone knew Fr. Popiełuszko was a good man who had preached nonviolence. His coffin was carried out of the morgue by fellow priests, but to get it through the crowds that had formed outside, a group of workers took the casket from them and placed it in the back of the waiting government hearse. On the drive to Warsaw, said a priest who was travelling with the body: "hundreds of taxis and automobiles followed. [It was] a concert of horns. The procession moved slowly westward, so that the setting sun illumined the way. I will never forget that red sun. At the village of Żółtki, the limit of the Archdiocese of Białystok, the convoy stopped. Everyone got out of the cars to recite the Angelus with the inhabitants of the village who were waiting for us, kneeling on the roadway. Emotions were high. Even our driver was weeping."[1]

When they reached the priest's old church of Saint Stanisłaus, in Warsaw, it was a foul night, but around ten thousand people were outside, with candles, and a group of men from the steelworks lifted the coffin into the church. There was not room for everyone inside, but, as the singing began, it spread outside. Within, the anger was so palpable that, during the Lord's Prayer, one of the priests stopped the Mass and had everyone repeat the line: "as we forgive those who trespass against us". He later recalled: "That was when I noticed Jerzy's mother, kneeling in the first rows. Clutching in her hand [her son's] cross and the rosary, she turned around toward the people and said, 'I forgive.' Even today I have difficulty holding back the tears when I recall that moment."[2] This was the liturgy for receiving the body into the church; the funeral itself would happen the next day in the park opposite.

Three years later, not far from the dam where Jerzy's body had been found, a piece of choral music was premiered at the Bydgoszcz Music Festival. The composer, Henryk Górecki, was already internationally known and was considered one of the best of his generation in a country where music and poetry were treated as forms of national therapy. Like Jerzy Popiełuszko, he had spent the last seven years being intimidated, having his phone tapped, his passport taken away, and his music forbidden public performance. The piece premiered at the festival had been written years before, but banned because of Górecki's alignment with

---

[1] Bernard Brien, *Blessed Jerzy Popiełuszko: Truth Versus Totalitarianism* (San Francisco: Ignatius Press, 2018), p. 94.

[2] Ibid., p. 94.

opponents of the regime, and included the arrested rural protesters to whom the work was dedicated. The murder of Fr. Popiełuszko, so close to where it was now performed, added to the poignancy of the premiere. The Latin title of the piece, *Miserere* ("Have Mercy"), was a familiar Catholic theme, drawing on the psalm in which King David begged God for forgiveness. Górecki's thirty-minute exploration of that theme is mesmerising and graceful, begging God for both forgiveness and help.

The thaw in censorship that allowed it to be performed was part of an ongoing strategy by the Communist government to raise Poland's image abroad and increase foreign investment. Another beneficiary of this relaxation had been a French film called *Shoah*, one of the most talked-about releases in recent European cinema. A nine-hours-long documentary about the Holocaust, it was a series of interviews with witnesses, perpetrators, and survivors, many of whom were still young enough to have clear memories of what had happened. Anti-semitic remarks made by some Polish interviewees in the film had provided some of the most disturbing moments, to the extent that the Polish government had initially asked the French state to stop the film being released at all. Among other things, the film contradicted the account of the Holocaust as taught under the Communist curriculum in Poland, which had exaggerated the number of Polish people systematically killed alongside Jewish people in the camps, teaching that four million people had been killed at the gas chambers of Auschwitz-Birkenau, as opposed to the actual figure of 1.2–1.5 million people, almost all of them Jewish. Many Poles had died in the Nazi camps that operated in their occupied country, but mostly from hunger, sickness, or other lethal means during spells of forced labour. This skewing of facts had helped portray

the Russian Army (200,000 of whom were still in Poland)
as liberators rather than occupiers of the Polish nation.

In a sequence of brutally candid interviews with Polish
peasants, people who had, in the words of one writer, "seen,
heard and even smelled the Holocaust to a degree unimag-
inable in Western Europe", opened up about how they felt
about it.[3] Several of those in the film cheerfully described
moving into abandoned Jewish houses, taking over rural Jewish businesses ("they were dishonest"), or recalled how they
used to leer at the "pretty Jewesses" who lived among them.
One man, who lived near the railway line, chuckles as he
remembers as a boy running alongside the incoming trains,
pulling his finger across his throat at those on board. A Jewish survivor recalls being on such a train, arriving in Poland
after days without water from Czechoslovakia. Whenever
the train slowed enough for them to catch people's attention, he says: "99 percent of them laughed."[4]

Complaints from among those involved in the filming
done in Poland that the director, Claude Lanzmann, had
picked the very worst bits in the edit could not disguise what
had been said and was now watched throughout the world.
Górecki had grown up twenty miles away from Auschwitz-
Birkenau and had gone there aged twelve with his school,
months after the end of the war: "I had the feeling the huts
were still warm. The piles of hair, glasses, teeth, suitcases,
false limbs, the size of it! The human ashes had been used
to fertilise the cabbages growing between the huts. But the
paths themselves—and this image has never left me. The
paths were made from human bones. Thrown on the path

[3] Anne Applebaum, *Iron Curtain: The Crushing of Europe* (London: Penguin Books, 2013), p. 150.
[4] Claude Lanzmann, director, *Shoah* (Les Films Aleph and Why Not Productions, 2010), DVD released by Eureka Entertainment, Ltd.

like shingle. We boys; how to walk on this? This is not sand, not earth. We were walking on human beings!"[5]

The poet Czesław Miłosz, in trying to explain the role that artists are expected to play in Polish life, wrote of poetry what was true for music and increasingly true for film in Poland: "In Central and Eastern Europe, the word 'poet' has a somewhat different meaning from that which it has in the West. There a poet does not merely arrange words in beautiful order. Tradition demands that he be a 'bard', that his songs linger on many lips, that he speak in his poems of subjects of interest to all citizens. Every period of history has understood the poet's obligations differently."[6] Górecki had grown up under Nazi and Soviet occupation and thirty minutes from what many considered the most evil place in history. Processing his responsibility as an artist in the sense Miłosz described would take up most of his life.

Poland's history was uniquely tumultuous. In the seventeenth century, the Polish Commonwealth (which included present-day Lithuania as well as parts of Belorussia and Ukraine) was the largest state in Europe, capable of sacking Moscow, its cities as impressive as any, its politics abnormally democratic. Around 25,000 families would elect a king and enjoyed freedom of speech to the extent of there being something that one historian has called "a legalised form of civil war", called confederation, which meant an armed force could be formed "by any individual or group of individuals. It could be formed by the King, or against him."[7] Voting in Poland's Parliament was a tumultuous af-

---

[5] Tony Palmer, director, *The Symphony of Sorrowful Songs* (Górecki/Upshaw/Zinman/London Sinfonietta), Voiceprint Records, 2007.

[6] Czesław Miłosz, *The Captive Mind* (London: Penguin, 2001), p. 175.

[7] Norman Davies, *God's Playground: A History of Poland*, vol. 1 (London: Oxford University Press, 2013), p. 295.

fair, since each law had to be passed with complete consen-
sus, and a single vote could cause debates to begin again.
Not all the families represented were still rich, and "street
nobles" or "nobles in clogs", who wore wooden swords
when they could not afford real ones, had as much a vote
as a representative from the Wiśniowiecki family, who by
this point owned 230,000 serfs and a private army.[8] Karl
Marx had commented that "the history of the world knows
of no other example of similar noble conduct by the nobility", and, although the majority of Poles were rural and remained in near poverty, there were signs of the enfranchise-
ment at large, especially in the cities, where public libraries
and free education were available.[9] Free speech extended to
religion, accommodating Catholics, Orthodox, Protestants,
and Jews. Outside the cities, most were Catholic, except in
the Orthodox eastern reaches of the Commonwealth, but
Protestantism had been taken up enthusiastically among the
elite, who embraced it as a form of emancipation. This included a number of nobles, though very few of their people:
"Even in the case where their master went over to Calvin-
ism, the peasants clung to their old faith with surly tenacity,
walking miles to the nearest Catholic church."[10]

Royal charters in 1264 and 1551 had afforded levels of
protection to Jewish settlers unavailable elsewhere in Europe. Poland was not necessarily the most exciting prospect
for early migrants, but, as the sixteenth-century rabbi Is-
seles Remuth put it: "It is better to live off dry bread,
but in peace, in Poland."[11] By 1648, as many as 450,000
Jewish people were living within the borders of the Polish

[8] Ibid., p. 355.
[9] Adam Zamoyski, *Poland: A History* (London: HarperPress, 2009), p. 71.
[10] Ibid., p. 70.
[11] Davies, *God's Playground*, p. 176.

Commonwealth, and, at the time of the demise of that Commonwealth a century later, a staggering four-fifths of all Jewish people in the world lived there.[12] The collapse of the Polish Commonwealth was a disaster for everyone, caused by the rapid growth of states around Poland and alliances between those states. Between 1792 and 1795, Russia, Prussia, and the Austrian Hapsburg Empire, having already removed the Ukraine and Silesia from the Commonwealth, went for Poland itself, agreeing between them "to excise the name of Poland from all future documents, to remove any reference to it in diplomatic business, and to strive by every means for its oblivion."[13]

In the Prussian partition, the Polish language was banned in railway stations, courts, government offices, and post offices. On the Russian side, Polish and Jewish underground units fought side-by-side, but to no avail, and thousands of potential resistance leaders were deported to Siberian prison camps. The poet Zygmunt Krasiński described the Tsarist regime there as "a huge, merciless machine". This machine turned a blind eye to the violence of Ukrainian nationalists, who had resented Polish and Jewish migration into their territories during the Commonwealth and who in one wave butchered 20,000 villagers under the slogan; "Pole-Jew-Dog: all one faith."[14]

Conditions in the Austrian partition were far less severe, mainly because the Austrians were fellow Catholics, and here Polish artists were able to express some kind of grief and outrage at what was happening. The version of recent history that emerged from their pens was of an enlightened commonwealth that had been too democratic for the despots

[12] Zamoyski, *Poland*, p. 304.

[13] Ibid., p. 216.

[14] Davies, *God's Playground*, p. 392.

and barbarians who surrounded them to bear. Adam Mick-
iewicz went so far in one play as to proclaim Poland "Christ
of the Nations", prompting one historian to point out that
Poland now had two Chosen People and no land. On the
Jewish side, there were Jewish Polish nationalists, including poets, as well as committed Zionists. There were hate
figures, particularly the *arandators* to whom absentee Polish landowners had leased lease rent-dues, but there were
also respected doctors and professors in the city; there were
Jewish atheists as well as a myriad of Rabbinic traditions; in
some places there was tension, while in others the priests
and rabbis would walk side-by-side at funerals. The poet
Cyprian Norwid, who would die penniless in exile in Paris,
was particularly wary of associating identity with excessive
nationalism: "No nation fashioned or saved me; / I recall
eternity's span; / David's key unlocked my lips, / Rome
called me man."[15]

Life went on, and urbanisation and industrialisation occurred in the partitions as elsewhere in Europe. By the
1890s, the Jewish population had risen to three million people within old Commonwealth boundaries.[16] An estimated
800,000 of these were moving over the border anti-Semitic
pogroms in the Russian partition, most of them headed for
emigration either to America via the Baltic ports or to Warsaw, where by 1897 a third of the population was Jewish. After the defeat of both Germany and Austria in 1918, and the
overthrow of the tsar by Communists in Russia, Poland suddenly, and almost accidently, found itself back on the map
at the Paris Peace Conference that followed World War I.
When the future Pope Paul VI spent a year there as nuncio

[15] Cyprian Kamil Norwid, *Selected Poems*, trans. Czerniawski (London:
Anvil Press, 2004), p. 41.
[16] Zamoyski, *Poland*, p. 285.

soon afterward, he found less a spirit of euphoria than heightened defensiveness. The Bolshevik army had been repulsed at the "Miracle of the Vistula" in 1920 (an apparition of the Virgin Mary was said to have appeared over the frontline) while the repression of German-speaking settlers in Silesia was a less noble episode in the new republic's life. Meanwhile, systematic Soviet anti-Semitism was driving further waves of people across the border: by the eve of World War II, Jewish donors in America were helping an estimated one million Jewish refugees surviving in Poland. And then the Nazis invaded.

When Górecki was five, the national trauma began in earnest, as 1.5 million German soldiers invaded Poland from the west, followed two weeks later by the Russian army from the east. For a few weeks, the Poles fought both, but there was no miracle this time. In the west, the Nazis declared martial law under which people could be shot without reason, and in Kraków the entire faculty of the university was arrested. Thousands of potential leaders, including poets, were tracked down and executed. In the east, "Stalin was outpacing Hitler in his desire to reduce the Poles to the condition of a slave nation."[17] All religious instruction was stopped, crucifixes were removed from classrooms, and monasteries closed. Twenty-one thousand Polish officers were killed in one day, and, in Gniezno, the oldest cathedral in Poland was destroyed by tanks. An estimated 1.5 million potential leaders were moved to work camps in Siberia between 1939 and 1942.

In 1942, the systematic killing of Jewish people in the Nazi-occupied territories began. Czesław Miłosz was fighting with the Polish underground when the uprising began

[17] Davies, *God's Playground*, 2:344.

in the Jewish ghetto in Warsaw. In one poem, he described
a merry-go-round situated next to the Jewish quarter that
continued to run throughout the uprising and the Holocaust
that followed:

> The bright melody drowned
> the salvos from the ghetto wall
> and couples were flying
> high in the cloudless sky.
>
> At times wind from the burning
> would drift dark kites along
> and riders on the carousel
> caught petals in midair.
> That same hot wind
> blew open the skirts of the girls
> and the crowds were laughing
> on that beautiful Warsaw Sunday.[18]

He later described the poem as "dishonest", as it cast him
as an innocent observer: "What is poetry which does not
save?"[19] Poland, he said, was "sullied, blood-stained, dese-
crated" by the Holocaust.

In the demonic bloodlust incited by World War II, Ukrainian nationalists slaughtered some 50,000 Polish-speaking
women, children, and old men, after which an armed unit
of the Polish resistance went over the border to rape and kill
in revenge. When the Nazi advance finally ground to a halt
in Russia, the Polish Resistance, including some of the country's finest young minds, staged an uprising in German-held
Warsaw, only to be crushed by the retreating Nazi army,

[18] From "Campo dei Fiori", in Czesław Miłosz, The Collected Poems (1931–
1987) (London: Penguin Books, 1988), pp. 33–34.
[19] From "Dedication" in Miłosz, Collected Poems, p. 78.

who killed 200,000 partisans and so thoroughly flattened the capital that postwar planners at one point considered leaving the entire city as a monument to war. It was in any case too late to save Warsaw's Jewish population, who had by then been systematically murdered, at a rate of 10,000 to 20,000 a day, at the Treblinka death camp. By the end of the war, around six million Polish citizens had been killed, just over half of them Jewish.

Henryk Górecki had lost an aunt in Auschwitz and a grandfather and uncle in two other camps. As a young composer, his first efforts were angry, manic, and discordant. One used a poem he had written, which translates: "they all delved / into the empty matter of blood / the lifelessness of a scream [scream]-ing / and / the searcher / searches for the function of the voice / AT BEING GOD / ARRANGING."[21] But if the shadow of World War II was not enough, Górecki now had to process Soviet occupation, which was not inducive to artistic integrity. Stalin was convinced that "propaganda and communist education could alter the human character permanently" and had ordered his agents to infiltrate every layer of Polish society.[22] Miłosz recalled attending Communist writers' congresses at this time where (as they realized what was expected of them) the faces of writers turned from anger, to fear, to amazement, to distrust, "and finally to thoughtfulness". He went into exile, but those who stayed and agreed to write Soviet propaganda got better apartments, the use of holiday villas, and overseas travel. In a state where by 1954 the secret police had files on about six million people, even half-heartedness was difficult; how hard you laughed at a joke could end up in a file.

The art form accepted by the Soviets was known as "So-

[21] Adrian Thomas, Górecki (Oxford: Oxford University Press, 1997), p. 28.
[22] Applebaum, Iron Curtain, p. 163.

cialist Realism", which for architects meant patching "folk art onto massive Soviet-style structures".[23] For musicians, acceptable genres included "Soviet style cantatas, operas, ballets and pieces for children", and music for parades.[24] Writers were to tell stories in which someone loyal to Communism overcomes resistance from those wanting to keep the old ways, while a 1950 national art competition called for entries on the themes such as: "the technology and organization of cattle slaughter"; and "bull and swine breeds in Limanowa, Nowy Targ and Miechów".[25] The Ministry of Culture controlled both commissions and the means of publication, building, or broadcast.

The only other possible source of commission was the Catholic Church, which, like the rest of Poland, was reeling after World War II. Many priests had been in prison or in Siberia, and their bishops were rebuilding dioceses that had been decimated in the war; few were looking for trouble. Both Lenin and Stalin's policy toward the Church before the war had been one of total annihilation (including a "Five Year Atheistic Plan" in the 1930s) but the Nazi invasion of Russia in 1941 had forced Stalin to mend bridges with the Orthodox Church in order to sustain morale. Thereafter, his policy had shifted to infiltrating and controlling the churches. In Soviet Poland, this job fell to Julia Brystiger, a Jewish Communist who had spent the war in Russia and who ran a department entirely dedicated to neutralising the Church, a mission she described to Party colleagues as "one of the most difficult tasks in front of us".[26] Her tactics included setting up organisations with the same name as

[23] Ibid., p. 371.

[24] Lisa Jakelski, "Górecki's Scontri and Avant-Garde Music in Cold War Poland", Journal of Musicology 26, no. 2 (Spring 2009): 209.

[25] Applebaum, Iron Curtain, p. 359.

[26] Ibid., p. 275.

Catholic community groups and the rewarding of "progressive priests" with the same kinds of privileges being offered to compliant artists.

The head of the Catholic Church in Poland, Cardinal Wyszyński, faced an almost impossible task. On one hand, there was a 1937 papal encyclical regarding Communism, *Divini Redemptoris*, which stated: "Communism is intrinsically wrong" and that any cooperation with it was impossible.[27] On the other, he was spiritual leader of a country whose capital had been flattened and whose society needed rebuilding. He had read Marx, was sympathetic to some Communist aims, and believed that the massive rebuilding projects offered an opportunity to overhaul a system still based on inherited nobility that left so many Poles disenfranchised. To that end, he had proposed to the government the setting up of a "Joint Commission", where Church and Party officials could meet to discuss the rebuilding on which they could cooperate. This offer was accepted but quickly manipulated by Brystiger's propaganda department, and when Wyszyński objected, he was arrested and imprisoned in an abandoned monastery for two years.

There he had an epiphany that would directly affect Górecki. Having read Marx (more, he realised, than his captors), he knew its strength lay in the poverty it called intolerable. As Miłosz had put it, "it isn't difficult to criticise Capitalism."[28] Poland had been as bad an example of inequality as anywhere, and Wyszyński had been willing to cooperate with anyone who addressed it. But Communism did the opposite, and by the 1950s Poland was proof of this, where it had become "state capitalism", favouring the

[27] Pius XI, encyclical letter *Divini Redemptoris* (19 March 1937), 58.
[28] Miłosz, *Collected Poems*, p. 17.

few, enforced by tanks and secret police. Furthermore, as
the 1937 papal encyclical had prophesied, the atheism inherent in Communism meant that for the first time in history, "we are witnessing a struggle, cold-blooded in purpose
and mapped out to the least detail, between man and 'all that
is called God'."[29]

But Wyszyński also realised in prison the extent to which
he needed to be spiritually renewed. Page after page of his
prison diaries are filled with him wrestling with his spiritual
poverty: "My Jesus is still tiny. But I want him to grow";
"It is much easier to be a prisoner of the Church defending its rights than a prisoner of Christ defending His rights
to my soul"; "More and more I fear freedom rather than
prison"; "Prayers of praise bring greater joy and strength
than prayers of petition"; "Do not ever tell me I am worth-
less. Do not tell it to anyone who is still capable of love";
"The strength of the Church depends on public profession";
"I must recognise that the most delicate point in the struggle of faith and disbelief turns within me and on me."[30]

On his release, Wyszyński went to the small southern
city Częstochowa and to the monastery of Jasna Góra. The
Polish Church may have had her oldest cathedral destroyed
by the Soviets, but nothing symbolised her more than the
icon Jasna Góra guarded, a painting of Mary and the baby

[29] Pius XI, *Divini Redemptoris*, no. 22. In his book *Why Marx Was Right*,
Terry Eagleton argues that Soviet Communism was an aberration and that
there remains room for cooperation between Christianity and Marxism.
However, elsewhere in the same book, he also mentions that Marx's "main
model for popular self-government" was the Paris Commune of 1871. During that Commune (although Eagleton does not mention it), sixty-two Catholic priests were executed in one day, on Rue Haxo, and the Church banned
from public life.

[30] Quotes from: Stefan Cardinal Wyszyński, *A Freedom Within*, trans. Krzy-
wocki-Herburt and Ziemba (Sutton: Aid to the Church in Need, 1986).

Jesus known as "The Black Madonna". So old that tradition attributed it to the hand of Saint Luke, and the wood it was drawn on to a table made by Jesus, it had been at this monastery for six centuries and was seen as more than just a painting, but a "transmitter of supernatural power".[31] Two slashes on the Madonna's right cheek, made during an attempt to steal it in 1430, looked like tears and only added to the picture's aura. Many miracles were associated with this painting and, consequently, the monastery that held it, most famously in 1655, when fewer than 200 Polish troops and monks held off a siege by 9,000 Swedes. An academic book published in 2010 about the icon's cultural significance quoted one Pole as saying: "If there was not the image of Our Lady of Częstochowa in Poland, then the country would simply not be on the map."[32]

Wyszyński had a copy of the icon painted by the artist Leonard Torwit and sent to Rome to be blessed. It was then sent on a "peregrination", to visit every single parish in Poland, beginning that year of 1957 and to end on the Marian Feast of the Immaculate Conception on 12 October 1980. Wyszyński planned to use the first nine years of the tour as a "novena", building up to the anniversary of 1966, which would mark 1,000 years of Poland accepting the Catholic faith.[33] Whatever the thinking was behind all this, by 1966 crowds around Poland had grown so large that

---

[31] Anna Niedźwiedź, *The Image and the Figure: Our Lady of Częstochowa in Polish Culture and Popular Religion* (Kraków: Jagiellonian University Press, 2010), p. 16.

[32] Ibid., p. 45.

[33] Novenas are traditionally a period of nine days devoted to prayer, matching the nine days when Mary and the disciples waited in prayer between the Ascension and the Pentecost. A novena is sometimes extended to nine weeks or nine months. The intent behind Wyszyński's nine-year novena was nothing short of the restoration of the land to God.

towns were coming to a stand-still as the car arrived with
the painting, flowers decorating every window the car would
pass by. Eventually, in September of that year, the painting
was "arrested" while on its way to Górecki's home city of
Katowice.

Two days later, in Katowice, the peregrination continued
with an empty frame and the crowds grew larger, the singing
louder. The Party was in knots. When one official banned
the decoration of apartment windows past which an empty
frame would be driven, people spent all night decorating
the parish church instead and then went to sing hymns outside the Party offices.[34] Cardinal Wyszyński wanted artists to
help break the Party's grip, reinvigorating what were known
as "Catholic Intellectuals Clubs", of which Górecki set up a
branch in Katowice. Like other artists, he was finding himself drawn more and more to liturgy: "Faced with the injustice, falsehood and drabness of socialist reality, people of
all classes sought solace, truth and beauty in the Catholic
faith."[35]

For Górecki, music was in some ways proving an easier art form with which to dodge the Soviet censors than
others, dealing as it did with the less censorable elements
of tempo and rhythm. *Collisions*, the first composition to
bring Górecki notice among his peers, was good enough, in
its angry, frenzied way, to dominate attention at the Warsaw Autumn International Festival of Contemporary Music, a gathering of musicians, audiences, and critics from
across the Eastern Bloc. It was not without its critics. The
Soviet musicologist Leonid Entelis berated the piece for

---

[34] Maryjane Osa, "Ecclesiastical Reorganization and Political Culture:
Geopolitical and Institutional Effects on Religion in Poland", *Polish Soci-
ological Review*, no. III (1995): 204.

[35] Zamoyski, *Poland*, p. 358.

undermining "the essence of music",[36] while an East German critic complained that it expressed "only fear, terror, and airlessness". Of course this was also what he intended, and what he felt, and even some of the official reviewers conceded its boldness: "He strongly feels the feverish, accelerated rhythm of the age, the pulsing of a great anxiety."[37] He would be helped to secure his job at the Katowice music school by one prominent critic admiring its "spontaneity, daring, passion and a sense of experimentation".[38]

As the 1960s went on, Górecki extended this experimentation into incorporating strands of folk music and fragments of hymns or liturgy, drawing on time spent in the Tatra mountains for the former, where folk music flourished. Even so, there was still a darkness to Górecki's music. *Three Dances* sounds like the deconstruction of a dance by a man who cannot dance, while his choral pieces were so slow and austere as to sound almost like parody. Promotion to rector of the music school brought him into regular contact with Party bureaucrats, whom he considered "yapping little dogs", but he liked his students, now had a young family, and, when the World Ice Hockey Championships were hosted in Katowice, duly wrote bugle-calls for the Party organisers.

Katowice was an easy place to be dark, dominated as it was by giant industrial plants and mines. People would fall ill from growing vegetables, and in winter the snow fell black. By the 1970s, urban Poland had become a charmless place of "alcoholism, bad drains, long queues, peeling

---

[36] Jakelski, "Górecki's Scontri", p. 224.
[37] Ibid., p. 213.
[38] Ibid., p. 234.

plaster, overcrowded homes and buses, polluted air".[39] By
then, the regime was increasingly being run by people who
had joined the Communist Party out of ambition, rather
than idealism, managers with undisguised contempt for the
people they were meant to represent, obsessed with the
"nomenklatura" lists that revealed Party appointments. In
time, that generation would give way to a brazenly self-
interested mafia within the Party. Membership was volun-
tary, and never more than 6.5 percent of the population
belonged, though all had to live under its spiralling dysfunctionality. The threat of Soviet invasion remained its guar-
antor, and when Polish students tried to emulate protesting
students in Czechoslovakia in 1968, no one came out to
join them. Later, when workers marched in protest at price
rises at the end of 1970, the students stayed in, and the front
ranks were gunned down.

During the 1970s, Górecki got to know the archbishop
of Kraków, Karol Cardinal Wojtyła, who held artists in particular esteem. Speaking a dozen languages, he was a poet
himself, who had written as a student for the theatre, remembered prewar Poland, had played goalkeeper for a Jewish football team, helped the resistance, and, like Górecki,
had been scarred by the loss of a beloved mother as a child.
He knew what suffering, anger, and guilt were, but would
later hold a Mass for artists in which he urged those present:
"You must all strive to express the depth of human life and
the heart of reality . . . the one who believes, who hopes,
in the Christian sense, enters into a new world . . . authentic artists share sincerely in all that is truly human, including the tragedy of man, but they know how to uncover from

---

[39] Davies, *God's Playground*, 2:451.

that tragedy the hope that is given to us. This world needs beauty in order not to fall into despair."[40]

However much of this message the archbishop shared with Górecki during their conversations in the 1970s, at some stage during that period it began to occur to the composer that he might contribute to beauty, rather than merely reflect brokenness. It was during this period, in 1976, that Górecki completed his masterpiece, *Symphony of Sorrowful Songs*, a lamentation so deep, and yet so beautiful, that it seemed by a different composer altogether. The piece consisted of three movements, in each of which Górecki incorporated Polish texts to be sung by a soprano. The first text was from a fifteenth-century manuscript held in a monastery library, in which Mary was pictured talking to Jesus from the foot of the Cross:

> My son, my chosen and beloved,
> Share your wounds with your mother,
> And because, dear son, I have always carried you in my
> heart
> And always served you faithfully,
> Speak to your mother, to make her happy,
> Although you are already leaving me, my cherished hope.[41]

The second movement used graffiti found scratched on the wall of a Nazi dungeon in the Tatra mountains:

> No, Mama, do not weep.
> Most chaste Queen of Heaven

[40] John Paul II, Homily at the Mass for Artists (20 May 1985) (author's translation).

[41] Lamentation of the Holy Cross Monastery from the "Łysa Góra Songs" suite, fifteenth century. From the liner notes to Henryk Górecki, *Symphony No. 3*, Elektra Nonesuch, 1992 (translated by Krystyna Carter for Boosey and Hawkes).

Support me always.
"Zdrowaś Mario" [Hail Mary].[42]

Górecki liked the prisoner's lack of self-pity, or anger: "It was nothing tragic, or melodramatic. Not 'I am innocent' or 'Kill them', simply 'Mama don't cry.'" The third text was in Silesian dialect, from a folk song Górecki had always liked the words to, in which a mother mourned the death of her soldier son: "It is not sorrow, despair or resignation, or the wringing of hands: it is just the great grief and lamenting of a mother. . . ." "I don't think a 'professional' poet would create such a powerful entity."[43]

Where has he gone,
My dearest son?
Perhaps during the uprising,
The cruel enemy killed him

Ah, you bad people
In the name of God, the most Holy,
Tell me, why did you kill
My son?

Never again
Will I have his support
Even if I cry
My old eyes out

[42] Prayer inscribed on wall 3 of cell number 3 in the basement of "the palace", the Gestapo's headquarters in Zakapone. Beneath is the signature of Helena Wanda Błażusiakówna and the words "18 years old, imprisoned since 26 September 1944." From the liner notes to Henryk Górecki, *Symphony No. 3*, Elektra Nonesuch, 1992 (translated by Krystyna Carter for Boosey and Hawkes).
[43] Thomas, *Górecki*, p. 81.

Were my bitter tears
To create another River Oder
They would not restore to life
My son.

He lies in his grave
and I know not where
Though I keep asking people
Everywhere

Perhaps the poor child
Lies in a rough ditch
and instead he could have been
lying in his warm bed.

Oh, sing for him
God's little song-birds
Since his mother
Cannot find him

And you, God's little flowers
May you blossom all around
So that my son
May sleep happily.[44]

In all three, Górecki had seen the powerful difference between lament and despair. Lament did not lessen the pain
felt but poured it out to heaven. In the book Lamentations
in the Bible, where the prophet Jeremiah laments the destruction of Jerusalem, his anguish ("Is it nothing to you,
all you who pass by? Look and see if there is any sorrow like
my sorrow?")[45] is met internally by an unbreakable faith:

[44] Opole folksong, trans. Carter, Boosey, and Hawkes Music Publishers
Ltd., 1992 (in sleeve notes to Henryk Górecki's Symphony No. 3).
[45] Lamentations 1:12.

"But this I call to mind, and therefore I have hope: The steadfast love of the LORD never ceases, his mercies never come to an end; they are new every morning; great is your faithfulness."[46]

Primo Levi, the Italian Jewish survivor of Auschwitz, was not a man of faith and was affected for the rest of his life by what even Jewish prisoners did to each other in the concentration camp, but he also wrote of two things that sustained him. One was the kindness shown to him by an Italian worker, Lorenzo, who brought him a piece of bread and extra rations every day for six months: "Thanks to Lorenzo, I managed not to forget that I myself was a man." The other was the need to express what had happened: "The need to tell our story to 'the rest', to make 'the rest' participate in it, had taken on for us, before our liberation and after, the character of an immediate and violent impulse, to the point of competing with our other elementary needs."[47]

Górecki never experienced the unique horror Levi did and therefore reacted angrily to the suggestion that *Symphony of Sorrowful Songs* was about the Holocaust. His obligation as a Polish artist was to express what he had experienced, which was growing up in the shadow of that evil and living in a country that one historian calls *God's Playground*. It was a love song, he told an interviewer. To another, he said: "I wanted to express a great sorrow. I have no other words to say what I mean."[48]

Górecki's audience up to that point had been the kind of experimental avant-garde who would congregate each summer in Darmstadt, West Germany, and for them the slow

[46] Lamentations 3:21–23.
[47] Primo Levi, *If This Is a Man/The Truce* (1960; London: Little Brown, 2019), p. 10.
[48] Palmer, *Symphony of Sorrowful Songs*, 2007.

paces of *Symphony of Sorrowful Songs* sounded too normal, while being too slow for more traditional classical music promoters. It was performed once in German, and a recording was made in Poland, and then it slipped into obscurity. One person who realised the work's significance was Cardinal Wojtyła, and, in 1978, he commissioned Górecki to write a major piece for the Kraków diocese, to commemorate the 900th anniversary of the martyrdom of Saint Stanisław. Weeks after giving Górecki the commission, the death of two popes in quick succession saw Wojtyła being elected as the first non-Italian pope in four centuries, and the first ever Polish pope, to be known as John Paul II.[49]

Once the Polish government recovered from the shock of its most persistent critic being set on the world stage, it did not take long for the secret police to be questioning Górecki about his friendship with the pontiff and his commission. His phone was tapped, and his job at Katowice music school threatened. Although a soft-spoken figure, whose health had never been great, Górecki had a fiercely uncompromising

[49] The American evangelist Billy Graham was on a visit to Poland during the conclave that elected the new pope and happened to be preaching at Kraków Cathedral on the day of the announcement. He and Wojtyła had not yet met, but Graham had warm links with Catholics in the United States, who had helped arrange the tour, commenting in 1966 that he found himself "closer to Catholics than radical Protestants", adding: "I think the Roman Catholic Church is going through a second Reformation". After hearing the new pope preach during his 1980 tour of Canada, Graham would comment: 'I'll tell you, that was just about as straight an evangelical address as I've ever heard.' After John Paul II's death, the American evangelist described him as "unquestionably the most influential voice for morality and peace during the last 100 years". Of their meeting in 1990, he recalled: "Suddenly the pope's arm shot out and he grabbed the lapels of my coat. He pulled me forward within inches of his own face. He fixed his eyes on me and said, 'Listen Graham, we are brothers!'"

side, as his early music had shown. One friend recalls having watched him storm out of performances of his music
twice, waving his fists and screaming "This is a scandalous
outrage!"[50] He proved in no mood to cower, and his job at
the music school was duly terminated, photographs of him
were removed from its walls, and students were forbidden
to mention his name.

The writer Anne Applebaum describes travelling around
the former Soviet bloc and entering a hotel room in the
Baltic port of Svetlogorsk. The room summed up what
society had become under this system. "The sink had no
drainpipe, so water leaked straight onto the floor. The toilet
flushed not with a handle, but with a bit of twisted wire.
The shower head was set so low that any normal adult would
have to kneel to wet his head. An inoperable ventilator, un-
connected to any source of electricity, hung from the wall."
It was no better in the bedroom, where half the tiles were
muddy blue and the other half hospital green, and neither
reached the ceiling, below which were several inches of un-
adorned cement. There were no pillows, no sheets, and a
cockroach:

> Someone had ordered the construction of this hotel. Some-
> one else had built it. Someone had placed the mismatch-
> ing tiles on the wall, someone had installed the ill-fitting
> sink. Someone had chosen the colors of the paint, some-
> one had failed to make the beds. Many decisions had been
> made but no one had been responsible for the hotel room.
> No one was forced by the need for money or the need to
> keep a job or even by pride of ownership to make the ho-
> tel room pleasant. It was just a place, created to fill the plan

[50] Jane Perlez, "Henryk Górecki", *New York Times*, 27 February 1994.

of a distant bureaucrat who would never see it and would never care.[51]

For those living amid such dysfunctionality, late 1970s Poland offered some grim humour ("They pretend to pay us, and we pretend to work" was one joke) but not enough. There was Church, but there was also vodka, promiscuity, and suicide. Farmers were selling goods out of vehicles rather than government shops, and without the black-market, malnutrition would have been unavoidable. On a national scale, heavy industrial goods were still being produced but were exported to Moscow under imposed deals, which meant less and less as the ruble depreciated. What budget there was went on increased security for, as the situation grew worse, the government grew more paranoid about its grip on power. Anger was everywhere, but even angry people could be intimidated if they were desperate enough, and the number of paid informers did not decrease, adding to the collective sense of "physical and moral inertia".[52]

It was into this national quagmire that John Paul II was granted permission to make his first visit as pope to Poland in the summer of 1979. Behind closed doors, the regime had insisted on his promising that he would not make any political statements, which he had agreed to, but Party officials were still fully aware of the threat his visit posed. No public advertising was to be allowed for the open-air Masses he would celebrate, and the television coverage was forbidden from showing the crowds. A memo was sent from the Politburo in Moscow to Polish schools:

[51] Anne Applebaum, *Between East and West: Across the Borderlands of Europe* (London: Penguin Books, 2015), p. 31.

[52] Lech Wałęsa and Pierluca Azzaro, *Sur les Ailes de la Liberté* (Paris: Parole et Silence, 2012), p. 21 (author's translation).

> The Pope is our enemy. . . . Due to his uncommon skills
> and great sense of humour he is dangerous, because he
> charms everyone, especially journalists. . . . He goes for
> cheap gestures in his relations with the crowd . . . puts
> on a highlander's hat, shakes hands, kisses children. . . . It
> is modelled on American presidential campaigns. . . . Be-
> cause of the activation of the Church in Poland our ac-
> tivities designed to atheize the youth not only cannot di-
> minish but must intensely develop. . . . In this respect all
> means are allowed and we cannot afford any sentiments.[53]

Górecki's commissioned work was scheduled to be premiered on the last night of the pope's tour, in Kraków. Because of the composer's rogue status, none of the country's
conductors or leading baritone singers had been prepared
to be involved in the project, so Górecki was conducting
the rehearsals himself and training an unknown baritone for
what was the main choral part.

On arrival at the Warsaw airport, the pope had kept to his
word, as he was officially greeted by ministers in front of the
world's press, whom he thanked for allowing him to come,
announcing: "I come here today as a pilgrim. I welcome
all from the depths of my soul and embrace, in my heart,
every person living in Poland today." His first day was spent
with Church members and civil authorities in the capital,
and people lining the streets to see him looked uncertain as
to how to behave, said one foreign journalist. Indeed, the
Western press corps were already dampening expectations
regarding what the trip would achieve. An editorial in that
morning's *New York Times* had said: "the pope's visit does

[53] Gracjan Kraszewski, "Catalyst for Revolution: John Paul II's 1979 Pilgrimage to Poland and Its Effects on Solidarity and the Fall of Communism",
Polish Review 57, no. 4 (2012): 30.

not at all threaten the political order in Poland."[54] The correspondent of the evening Paris paper, *France-Soir*, initially filed his article that first day with the title "Le Pape a Fait un Bide" (The pope flops) until a colleague persuaded him to change the title and wait to see what happened later that day.

What happened later that day would, with two decades of hindsight, be described by the *Wall Street Journal* as "one of the greatest spiritual moments of the 20th century".[55] The lack of advertising had done little to diminish the size of the crowds who turned up for the open-air Mass on Victory Square. Crowds around the country would grow bigger as the week went on, but it was the quarter of a million people who turned out in Warsaw (the very lowest estimate) who witnessed the culmination of Cardinal Wyszyński's resolve in prison to take on Communist atheism. The pope spoke of those who had first brought the faith to Poland, who had brought them Christ, who was "the key to understanding that great and fundamental reality that is man". The concrete buildings that surrounded the square, part of Warsaw's postwar reconstruction, bounced every word from the loudspeakers back at the crowd:

> Man cannot be fully understood without Christ. Or rather, man is incapable of understanding himself fully without Christ. He cannot understand who he is, nor what his true dignity is, nor what his vocation is, nor what his final end is. He cannot understand any of this without Christ. Therefore Christ cannot be kept out of the history of man in any part of the globe, at any longitude or latitude of ge-

[54] Bernard Lecomte, *Les Secrets du Vatican* (Paris: Tempus, 2006), p. 233 (author's translation).

[55] Peggy Noonan, "We Want God!", *Wall Street Journal*, 7 April 2005.

ography. The exclusion of Christ from the history of man
is an act against man.

The crowd kept bursting into song: *My chcemy Boga* ("We
want God").

The pope said he was going to kneel before the Tomb of
the Unknown Soldier in Victory Square, holding in prayer
as he did "every seed that falls into the earth and dies and
bears fruit", whether the blood of a soldier

> or the sacrifice of martyrdom in concentration camps or
> in prisons. It may be the seed of hard daily toil, with the
> sweat of one's brow, in the fields, the workshop, the mine,
> the foundries and the factories. It may be the seed of the
> love of parents who do not refuse to give life to a new hu-
> man being and undertake the whole of the task of bring-
> ing him up. It may be the seed of creative work in the uni-
> versities, the higher institutes, the libraries and the places
> where the national culture is built. It may be the seed of
> prayer, of service to the sick, the suffering, the abandoned
> —"all of that of which Poland is made".

He told the crowd he would lay all this in the hands of
Mary, at the foot of the Cross, in the Upper Room of the
Pentecost. He would lift all Poland's history, "including the
people that have lived with us and among us, such as those
who died in their hundreds of thousands within the walls of
the Warsaw ghetto . . . I cry—I who am a Son of the land
of Poland and who am also Pope John Paul II—I cry from
all the depths of this Millennium, I cry on the vigil of the
Pentecost: Let your Spirit descend. Let your Spirit descend.
And renew the face of the Earth, the face of this land."[56]

---

[56] John Paul II, Homily in Victory Square, Warsaw, Poland (2 June 1979).

By now, the late afternoon sun was making everything
in the square radiant. Lech Wałęsa, one of the leaders of
the workers' protest movement, said that as the pope was
driven away, even secret servicemen in the crowd were making the sign of the cross as he passed. In the days that
followed, an estimated one-quarter of Poland's population
went to see "our pope", sleeping under hedges and in road-
side churches to get there. Thirty million also watched on
television. No Polish figure in history, no king, had ever
experienced such an outpouring, and there was no need to
be inflammatory toward the regime; he dwarfed them. "[It]
was as if the great lie of our enemy was unmasked", said
Wałęsa: "as if the pope had said to us 'Take courage, do
not be afraid! With the Holy Spirit anything is possible!' "[57]
He visited Auschwitz, which he called a "Golgotha of the
modern world", and instructed Poles to pray not only for
freedom, but for holiness: "From every victorious test the
moral order is built up. From every failed test moral disorder
grows."[58]

On his last night in Poland, the pope attended the premiere of Górecki's work, the title of which the composer
had taken from a psalm: *Beatus Vir* ("Blessed is the man").
He had spent longer agonising over the texts than the music,
in the end drawing them all from the psalms. They begin
with some of the most needy and desperate lines ("Hear my
prayer, O Lord, give ear to my supplications!"; "I stretch
forth my hands unto thee; my soul thirstest after thee, as
a thirsty land"; "Make thy face to shine upon thy servant:
save me for thy mercies' sake" [Psalms 143 and 31, KJV]).
These are sung by the lone voice of the baritone, the choir

[57] Wałęsa and Azzaro, *Sur les Ailes*, p. 24.
[58] John Paul II, Homily in Kraków (10 June 1979).

and orchestra echoing his prayers and, after a manic start, gently filling in his pauses. He seems unaware of them at first, so locked is he in his despair, but the musicians and the rest of the choir get bolder, until they all join forces, like a superb, heavenly army, proclaiming the words: *Deus meus es tu!* ("You are my God!")

It is an extraordinary moment, and one can only imagine how it sounded that night, after such a papal tour. The crescendo occurs halfway through what is a thirty-five-minute piece of music, and the voices and instruments thereafter subside into sublime praises ("O taste and see that the Lord is good: blessed is the man that trusteth in him" [Psalm 34:8, KJV]) repeated again and again. Teresa Malecka, a friend of both the pope and Górecki, said both men burst into tears when they saw each other afterward: "Górecki's devotion, simple way of life and sense of justice moved the Holy Father."[59]

A year later, strikes started at the shipyard in Gdańsk. As other workforces, from bus drivers to big industrial plants, came out in support, the 17,000 strong sit-in at the shipyard became the centre of a 200,000-strong strike across the city. When other cities began to follow suit, the security forces cut the phone lines out of Gdańsk, but the leaders there began using dispatch riders to communicate with the other strikes, as momentum grew, and farmers began bringing the strikers food. On the gates of the shipyard at Gdańsk, which a huge crowd prevented the security forces from approaching, were displayed two pictures, one of the Black Madonna of Jasna Góra and the other of Pope John Paul II. Crucially, students and intellectuals immediately came on board and were smuggled through the gates, bringing the movement

---

[59] Perlez, "Henryk Górecki".

credibility in the eyes of the overseas press, who were covering developments, and a media-aware savviness: soon T-shirts and flags bearing the name of the protest movement were being seen everywhere: *Solidarność* (Solidarity).

The strikers brought integrity, and, at Huta Warszawa steelworks in Warsaw, they asked for a priest to come and say Mass for them. Several declined, and in the end Father Jerzy Popiełuszko was sent: "I will never forget that day or that Mass that I said. I was terribly nervous; I had never been in a situation like that. What sort of atmosphere would I find? How would they receive me? Where would I celebrate the Mass? Who would read the readings, who would sing? . . . At the doors of the steelworks, I had my first major shock. A dense crowd was waiting for me. . . . They applauded me, and I thought for a moment that a celebrity was walking behind me." He found an altar had been constructed, and a steel cross erected by the entrance:

> The lectors were there, too. You had to listen to them, those hoarse voices accustomed to swear words, solemnly reading the sacred texts. Then from thousands of mouths came a cry like thunder: "Thanks be to God." I noticed also that they knew how to sing, and better than in the churches. Before beginning, they went to confession. I was sitting on a chair, with my back leaning against a heap of scrap iron, and these rough men in blue work clothes [knelt down to make confession] on the dirty, oil-stained floor.[60]

The bishop of Gdańsk was a "progressive priest" and refused to help, but the priest who did go was astounded at the revivalist atmosphere: "Although vodka was brought to them, they poured it away and stayed sober. Some confessed every day, others had ripped up their Party cards and were

[60] Brien, *Blessed Jerzy Popiełuszko*, pp. 41–42.

confessing for the first time in thirty years."[61] The movement's leader, Lech Wałęsa, was an electrician and former
army corporal with only three years of formal education, but
there were Wałęsa ancestors who had frittered away land in
French casinos. He understood the working man, because
that was all he had ever been, but there was something of a
"street noble" about him, and a shrewd one at that.

The government wavered between sending in tanks, breaking up the strikes through subterfuge, or sitting down to
talks. In the end, they did all three. To get people back to
work, they sat down, live on television, with Wałęsa and the
strike committee. An agreement was signed, Wałęsa signing
with a souvenir pen bearing John Paul II's face, which allowed Solidarity to become a legal union. For a moment, it
appeared as if the whole fate of the Soviet Empire might be
hovering over an electrician's flat in Gdańsk. But controlling
the government in Warsaw were Soviet bosses in Moscow
who knew better how to play this type of chess. During the
years of the Russian Partition, Tsarist agents had developed a
pattern for dealing with Polish uprisings. They would make
immediate concessions, followed by a slow season of harsh
repression. Within eighteen months of the Gdańsk Agreement, tanks were on the streets of Poland, Solidarity was
banned, Wałęsa in prison, and the pope was recovering in
Rome from an assassination attempt.

In the Rome hospital where he was taken, doctors donated their own blood to keep John Paul II alive. The perpe-
trator was a professional Turkish assassin, named Ali Ağca,
and the world's suspicions immediately fell on Moscow.[62]
As a storm of denials and theories began, the pope asked for

[61] Roger Boyes, *The Naked President: A Political Life of Lech Wałęsa* (London:
Secker and Warburg, 1994), p. 65.

[62] Ali Ağca's mental health did not do anything to help resolve the debate as
to who had hired him, and it is more than possible he never knew his ultimate

a file to be brought to him. Here we enter a subplot difficult for the Protestant mind to follow, in which two further
works of religious art and Marian devotion are somehow
involved in the downfall of Soviet Communism.

The documents that the pope asked to see related to a vision of Christ's Mother reported by three Portuguese children near Fatima in 1917. John Paul II had been shot on 13
May 1981, the anniversary of the first appearance and, as
such, the Church's feast day marking the apparitions, which
had eventually been given the official status of "private revelation".[63] It was the three "messages" said to have been
given to the children on the second appearance, as reported
to a bishop by the eldest child, Lucia Santos, that he wanted
to see.

Lucia reported being shown a vision of hell ("Plunged
in this fire were demons and souls in human form") followed by a message about the ending of the ongoing world
war and a warning that "if people do not cease offending
God", a worse war would break out. The third message,
and subsequently the most controversial, was a vision in

---

paymaster, since he always claimed to have been hired by a gangster in Sofia.
The pope visited Ali Ağca in prison in 1983: "We spoke at length. Ali Agca,
as everyone knows, was a professional assassin. This means that the attack
was not his own initiative, it was someone else's idea, someone else had commissioned him to carry it out. In the course of our conversation it became
clear that Ali Agca was still wondering how the attempted assassination could
possibly have failed. He had planned it meticulously, attending to every tiny
detail. . . . The interesting thing was that his perplexity had led him to the
religious question. He wanted to know about the secret of Fatima. . . . This
was his principal concern; more than anything else, he wanted to know this."
Pope John Paul II, *Memory and Identity* (London: Weidenfeld and Nicolson,
2005), p. 185.

[63] For a summary of papal teaching on the non-binding status of "private
revelations" such as at Fatima, see Fr. Benedict J. Groeschel, C.F.R., *A Still
Small Voice: A Practical Guide on Reported Revelations* (San Francisco: Ignatius
Press, 1993).

which they had seen a bishop "dressed in white, we had the
impression it was the Holy Father, other bishops, priests,
men and women religious going up a steep mountain at the
top of which was a big cross. [Before] reaching there, the
Holy Father passed through a big city half in ruins, and half
trembling with halting step, afflicted with pain and sorrow,
he prayed for the souls of the corpses he met on the way."
Having reached the top of the hill, and knelt at the foot of
the cross, he was shot by a group of soldiers: "who fired
bullets and arrows at him". To prevent this, our Lady told
the three children that "Russia" (which they presumed was
a girl's name) would have to be "consecrated to the Immaculate Heart of Mary". The vision had ended with our Lady
telling them to pray what became known as "the Fatima
prayer" used today by Catholics reciting the rosary: "O my
Jesus, forgive us our sins, save us from the fires of hell. Lead
all souls to heaven, especially those who have most need of
Thy mercy."

A growing number of people from as far away as Lisbon
began to gather for the encounters, which Mary had told the
children would take place on the thirteenth of each month
for five months, and reported witnessing strange sounds and
lights as Mary spoke to the children. By the time of the
last encounter, there were 70,000 people present, including representatives from two sceptical Lisbon newspapers
(*O Dia* and *O Seculo*) and a professor of natural sciences.
Portugal was experiencing a period of fierce anticlericalism
at the time, in which the ringing of church bells had been
banned, much church property seized, and around 2,000
priests, monks, and nuns murdered. It started raining as the
children made their way out to the spot and knelt in readi-
ness. What happened then was seen not only by people miles
away, but was reported by the newspapers that had come
to pour scorn on the phenomenon: ". . . the sun trembled

and made sudden incredible movements outside all cosmic laws—the sun 'danced' according to the typical expression of the people."[64] The professor, Dr. Joseph Almeida Garrett of Coimbra University, similarly reported that the sun "seemed to loosen itself from the firmament".

When struggling to appreciate the extra-scriptural importance given to Mary prior to his conversion to Catholicism, Saint John Henry Newman's conversion came while studying the way in which the early Church had overcome the Arian heresy. That heresy, still extant, denies the full divinity of Christ and, by the turn of the fourth century, had convinced many bishops. At the Council of Ephesus in 431, it was overthrown by a clear doctrine of the Incarnation and the proclamation of Mary as *Theotokos* ("God Bearer"). Lifting Mary up, realised Newman, was to exalt the One she bore and pointed to. Once he saw this, he looked at Marian devotion with new eyes.

A 1974 papal exhortation to bishops on Marian devotion by Pope Paul VI conceded that "certain forms of popular piety"[65] had become excessive but reaffirmed the veneration of Mary as a duty and a joy of Christians. He traced a traditional line in Scripture, between the "woman" in Genesis whose offspring God promised would "crush the head of the serpent", to the woman in Revelation: "a great sign appeared in heaven, a woman clothed with the sun, with the moon under her feet, and on her head a crown of twelve stars."[66] It is a thread traditional theology sees running through the "Daughter of Zion" and "Wisdom" in the Old Testament and, most movingly, in John's Gospel,

---

[64] David Baldwin, *Fatima: A Pilgrim's Companion* (London: Catholic Truth Society, 2017), p. 29.

[65] Paul VI, apostolic exhortation *Marialis Cultus* (2 February 1974).

[66] Revelation 12:1.

where at both his first miracle and from the Cross, Christ refers to his own mother simply as "woman". She is the "model of the virtues", Paul VI said, the living "Mother of the Church" in heaven, where she exists "in harmonious subordination" to Christ.[67]

Convinced of the significance of having been shot on the feast day commemorating the apparitions at Fatima, John Paul II had the bullet from his abdomen sent to Fatima to be fixed on the crown of stars gracing the statue of our Lady that had been made based on the children's description. Later, he would have a copy of the same statue placed in a purpose-built new church in a forest near the Poland-USSR border, facing Russia. With instructions for all Catholic bishops around the world to follow suit, he then held a service, consecrating the entire world to "the Immaculate Heart of Mary" on 25 March 1984. A papal nuncio was sent to see Sister Lucia at her convent and asked her:

"Is Russia now consecrated?"

"Yes, now it is."

"Now we wait for the miracle."

"God will keep his word."[68]

Weeks later, Lech Wałęsa came of age when 400,000 people turned out for Jerzy Popiełuszko's funeral in Warsaw, and he

[67] Mary is thus seen as foremost among the "cloud of witnesses" mentioned in Hebrews, as well as those who have endured "the great trial" mentioned in Revelation, who are alert before the throne of God rather than awaiting the general resurrection. Luther wished to remove both Hebrews and Revelation from the Reformed Bible. For Newman's wrestling with the key issues, *An Essay on the Development of Christian Doctrine* and *Apologia Pro Vita Sua* are more readable than their titles suggest, while Scott Hahn's *The Lamb's Supper* and Leona Choy's *My Journey to the Land of More* are part of a growing library of Evangelical-to-Catholic literature.

[68] Timothy Tindal-Robertson, *Fatima, Russia and Pope John Paul II* (Devon: Augustine, 1992), p. 25.

addressed the crowd: "We bid you adieu, Servant of God, while promising not to bow to violence. . . . [W]e will respond to falsehood with truth and to evil with good. . . . Rest in peace. Solidarność lives, because you gave your life for it."[69] Ten million people had now joined the technically illegal movement. At the trial of Fr. Popiełuszko's killers, it was learned that the priest's last words were: "The worst you can do is kill me."[70]

Weeks after that, in Moscow, a man named Mikhail Gorbachev was appointed chair of the Foreign Affairs Committee, and Poland began to be more isolated in its problems, as Russia dealt with its own. The pope had been back there in 1983, a desperate concession by the Party to trade on the feel-good factor that had left everyone smiling in 1979. It came at a price, for John Paul II was in his prime and delivered what a foreign journalist described as "a masterpiece of prudence and boldness". One and a half million people attended his Mass at the old airfield in Gdańsk, while about a million made the pilgrimage to the Jasna Góra monastery, where the pope made his devotions before the icon of the Black Madonna. When the crowd saw him appear on the monastery ramparts, they erupted into song for so long that eventually he waved his arms to stop them:

"I would like to ask if a man who comes to Poland from Rome has the right to speak?"

"Please go ahead!" "Come closer!", came the shouts. To the bewilderment of his bodyguard, he walked to the edge of the ramparts.

"Any other requests?" he joked to a crowd that might have filled ten of the largest football stadia in the world.

---

[69] Brien, *Blessed Jerzy Popiełuszko*, p. 96.
[70] Boyes, *Naked President*, p. 151.

"Stay here for ever!"; "Stay here for ever!"[71]

A mesmerising piece of *a capella* music for massed choir, written by Górecki to mark John Paul II's third pilgrimage to Poland in 1987, premiered at the Salzburg Festival. *Totus Tuus* ("Totally Yours") is a fifteen-minutes-long expression of Poland's devotion to "Our Lady", its title from the motto Archbishop Wojtyła had taken on becoming pope, drawn from the writings of Louis de Montfort, whose prayers to Mary had been a source of comfort to him as a young seminarian during Nazi occupation: "I understood that I could not exclude the Lord's Mother from my life without neglecting the will of God-Trinity, who willed to begin and fulfill the great mysteries of the history of salvation with the responsible and faithful collaboration of the humble handmaid of Nazareth."[72]

In Moscow, Gorbachev was now general secretary and had announced that Soviet Communism needed overhauling; when this proved impossible, he announced its demise. In 1991, he sat down with President Yeltsin, inside the Kremlin, live on American television, and they told the world: "This experiment has been a tragedy for our people" (Yeltsin); "The model has failed" (Gorbachev). An attempted coup by hardliners a few weeks earlier had seen Yeltsin barricaded in the Russian Parliament building with no way of communicating to the world that he was still alive and resolute. By chance, a Belgian-based Catholic media company had recently sought permission to start broadcasting to Russian Catholics, and its radio transmitter was in a Moscow warehouse awaiting customs clearance. It was smuggled by a van into the Parliament buildings under fruit

[71] Ibid., p. 132.
[72] "Pope Reveals Mary's Role in His Life", *ZENIT News Agency*, 15 October 2000.

and vegetables and allowed Yeltsin to broadcast until the coup was broken.[73] In thanks, he agreed to let the production company broadcast a joint pilgrimage of Catholic and Orthodox Russians to Fatima live on television. The greatest icon of the Russian Orthodox Church ("The Mother of God of Kazan") had been stolen from Saint Petersburg during the Bolshevik Revolution in 1917 and later surfaced on the international art market. Its buyer had donated it to the shrine that had been built at Fatima, and it would eventually be given back to the Russian Church, but was in Fatima for the joint pilgrimage, which was broadcast live throughout the Soviet Union, including Poland.

The producer recalls an incident that occurred during a live link that was set up with an audience at the Novosti television centre in Moscow: "the presenter went over live to Moscow, and invited any person who would like to do so to ask a question. It was then that a young girl immediately asked . . . [what] turned out to be the central question of the whole broadcast. The question was of union, and of unity between Christians. 'Why was there division between Christians?' She was very insistent about it, it was very moving. . . . She said: 'You have devotion to the Blessed Virgin and we do too; you love her, and so do we; so why are we so separated? Why are there so many disputes?' "[74]

The following year, a new recording of Górecki's *Symphony of Sorrowful Songs* was made in London and ended up outselling anything by any other living composer. The New York producer of the record, Robert Hurwitz, later said he had had to reissue the composer's first royalty cheque because he would not bank it. "It may just have been such a

[73] Tindal-Robertson, *Fatima*, p. 92.
[74] Ibid., p. 131.

shock."[75] Lech Wałęsa became president of Poland, a role he would prove to be far less enamoured of than that of being an underground leader, "fidgety, yawning and breaking pencils" in government meetings. Negotiations between Poland and a newly unified Germany were almost derailed after Wałęsa declared that if Germany ever became aggressive again, it would be "blown off the map of Europe". On an aeroplane, he was overheard saying: "I have been warned so many times not to trust Jews!"[76] Being Wałęsa, he got the chance to apologise, in person, on Israeli soil, "on behalf of every Pole who had ever harmed a Jew".[77] His trip included a visit to Yad Vashem—The World Holocaust Remembrance Centre, with its "Righteous of the Nations", listing the names of over 27,000 non-Jews who risked their lives to save Jews during the Holocaust. Some 6,863 of those names are Polish, including that of Karol Wojtyła.

After his death in 2010, Górecki's effects included the score to a final symphony, parts of it already orchestrated, the rest eventually completed by his son, Mikołaj Górecki. Called *Tansman Episodes*, its title bore a tribute to the Polish Jewish composer Alexandre Tansman, who died in Paris in 1986. Toward the end of his life, Tansman had explored the Jewish and Polish music with which he had grown up and had followed events in Poland, naming a lovely guitar piece "Homage à Lech Wałęsa". In the symphony, Górecki explored his own youth, weaving strains of folk and classical music with a harsher presence of avant-garde distortion. Which would prevail? In the symphony's last movement, we enter what could be a jaunty soundtrack to one of the

[75] William Robin, "How a Somber Symphony Sold More Than a Million Records", *New York Times*, June 9, 2017.

[76] Boyes, *Naked President*, p. 245.

[77] Zamoyski, *Poland*, p. 401.

silent Yiddish films being made in 1920s Warsaw, with plots about brides, ghosts, and farmers. Then we are somewhere in the mountains, with the carpet rolled back, and for about ten seconds Górecki is almost dancing. The twilight journey stumbles on between nostalgia and self-mockery until collapsing in exhausted silence, which drumming leads us out of, into a flourish as clamorous and distinct as a bugle call, one sounding neither victory nor defeat, but resilience against the common enemy of mankind.

8

The Sacrifice of a Protestant

The heroic man is simple, and in his heroic act becomes the simpler.[1]

Dietrich Von Hildebrand

One summer's evening, in 1867, an English couple named the Freeses decided to take a walk to see the gardens of a new acquaintance. The invitation to do so had been accompanied by a key to the gardens in question, part of the residence of the officer commanding the Royal Engineers in Gravesend, a post currently held by Lt. Colonel Charles Gordon. With its lawns, mulberry trees, and view of ships turning on the lower reaches of the Thames, it was a glorious spot, especially in summer. A bachelor, Gordon had brushed off their thanks, assuring them he was "not particularly interested in flowers". On this, their first use of the key, it quickly became apparent that others had also been given keys. A number of elderly people were walking on the paths, while fruit and vegetables were being gathered by some of the poorest people in the town. The gardens were, in fact, quite busy that evening. There was, said one of the Freese children later, "an indefinable air of mystery and love" about Charlie Gordon.[2]

---

[1] Dietrich von Hildebrand, *Transformation in Christ: On the Christian Attitude* (San Francisco: Ignatius Press, 2001), p. 104.

[2] John Pollock, *Gordon of Khartoum: An Extraordinary Soldier* (Fearn: Christian Focus Publications, 2005), p. 155.

Four years earlier, on the south coast of China, a Scottish doctor named Halliday Macartney had gone looking for Gordon, at the urgent request of his imperial Chinese employer, for whom Gordon was also supposed to be working. He tracked him down to a house in Quinsan, present-day Hangzhou, where he found Gordon sitting on the side of a bed sobbing. The room was so dark that Macartney could hardly make anything out at first, but then Gordon pulled a human head from under his bed, and said to him: "Do you see that? Do you see that? . . . It is the head of the Lar Wang, foully murdered!"[3]

Gordon would once enthusiastically share the workings of a theory he had developed with the British superintendent of the Botanical Gardens in Mauritius. The theory involved river maps, Hebrew, and sketches of fruit, and demonstrated Gordon's reason for believing that the Seychelles were the original location of the Garden of Eden. He was nearly fifty, and by then many in London thought Gordon was mad. The Victorian public, however, loved him for his eccentricity, his disdain for fortune, and his repeated courage in battle. He was, wrote a journalist in *Vanity Fair*, "a fine, noble, knightly gentleman, such as is found but once in many generations".[4] A nation drifting away from religion also appreciated Gordon for his old-fashioned piety, and even the most cynical strategists in government still valued him for one thing: there was no one in the empire better at sorting out what were euphemistically called "native problems". Time and again, and in different parts of the world, Gordon had been able to quell revolts, and that sometimes single-handedly. Even tax-burdened, militarily harassed colonial subjects appeared

---

[3] Lord Elton, *General Gordon* (London: Collins, 1954), p. 81.
[4] Ibid., p. 286.

convinced that Gordon (as mad as he might be) would keep his word.

At Cambridge in 1977, the medieval historian Kathleen Hughes gave a lecture entitled "The Early Celtic Idea of History and the Modern Historian". In it, she acknowledged the difficulty of writing about people who themselves see history differently. She was addressing the frustration sometimes felt by her colleagues that so many medieval documents were preoccupied with genealogy, legends, and miracles, rather than hard facts. Less frustration, she promised, opened the way to a better relationship with the past: "Our rational analysis of evidence, even our imaginative apprehensions, are different. But from a sympathetic and sensitive questioning of what they were attempting, history emerges."[5] To write about Charlie Gordon is to write about a person almost as different to our own age as were the ancient Celts to whom he was incidentally related.

In 1880, aged forty-seven, Gordon had been appointed private secretary to the new viceroy of India, Lord Ripon. As one biographer puts it, "it would be hard to imagine a post less suited to Gordon's peculiar qualities and character, requiring as it did extreme tact, a calm temper, and a subservient nature."[6] Gordon accepted the job because he admired Lord Ripon, who had spent years in the political wilderness since forsaking Freemasonry and the Church of England to become Roman Catholic.[7] Gordon was not

[5] Kathleen Hughes, *The Early Celtic Idea of History and the Modern Historian: An Inaugural Lecture* (Cambridge: Cambridge University Press, 1977), p. 24.

[6] Anthony Nutting, *Gordon: Martyr and Misfit* (Bungay: Reprint Society, 1967), p. 169.

[7] Not unlike Akbar's Din-i Ilahi, modern "Freemasonry" began in London in 1717 as an attempt to synthesize all major religions and philosophies into an "enlightened" and "rational" brotherhood. Managing to be quasi-sacramental and clandestine, while at the same time "progressive", Masonry

Catholic but admired anyone who acted out of principle. Ripon had been appointed as a reformer, someone who would start the process of devolving power to Indians, and Gordon was seen as a militarily savvy proponent of that agenda.

At a formal dinner held in London before the viceroy's party sailed, Gordon insisted on eating all his courses from one plate ("We'll have to rough it in India, you know?") and spent most of the passage out talking with Fr. Kerr, Ripon's Jesuit chaplain. Once in Bombay, he was disgusted at the poverty: "The way people live here is absurd. . . . It is only the upper ten thousand in England who benefit by it."[8] The character of the European residents there was also worse than he had imagined: "they seem so utterly effeminate and not to have an idea beyond the rupee."[9] This was sad proof for Gordon that the chivalric Christian mission of England was dying. He had seen the decline elsewhere in the empire ("I feel sure it is nearly over. . . . It is money, money, money with us")[10] but never so blatantly as in Bombay. The reformist press in Bombay had hoped he would

has been forbidden by successive popes, but became fashionable within the Church of England (there is a Masonic window in Durham Cathedral) as well as other Protestant denominations. Although ostensibly encouraging diverse religious faiths, the persistent implication within Masonic doctrine is that Freemasonry holds a truth beyond any religion. The movement's political influence probably peaked during the successive American presidencies of Roosevelt and Truman, both senior Freemasons. Between 1949 and 1955, eight out of nine judges in the Supreme Court were Freemasons, during which time the role of the Church in state-funded American education was abruptly curtailed (John Salza, *Masonry Unmasked* [Huntington: Our Sunday Visitor, 2006]).

[8] Nutting, *Gordon*, p. 170.

[9] Charles Gordon, *Letters of General C. G. Gordon to His Sister, M. A. Gordon* (London: Macmillan and Company, 1902), p. 159.

[10] Ibid., p. 140.

pick a fight with such greed, but, rather than fire him up, it sickened him and made him want to leave. Having been there a week, the viceroy was sent a gift of poems by an Indian noble, and Gordon was asked to acknowledge the gift and say that Lord Ripon would read it with much pleasure: "He left the room repeating to himself 'Will read it with much pleasure—I know he will never look at it. I *cannot* write such a reply.'"[11]

On resigning, he insisted on paying the cost of his passage and apologised profusely to Ripon, one of whose staff drily observed: "Gordon is not an ordinary man."[12] Despite, and perhaps because of, such scruples, he was still in demand, and before he left Bombay a telegram arrived from the head of the British Legation in Peking, asking that he sail on to Shanghai urgently. The British Empire was both at the zenith of its powers and stretched to the limit of its human resources, and Gordon's reputation for resolving thorny native problems was nowhere higher than in China.

Gordon had first gone to China in 1860, aged twenty-seven, volunteering for active service while serving as adjutant at the Royal Engineers' depot in Kent. His progress within the army until that point had been successful and already out of the ordinary. As a subaltern, he had fought in the Crimean War, at the siege of Sebastopol, and afterward been seconded to the body responsible for mapping the borders of Bessarabia, Armenia, and the Caucasus. This had taken him into nomadic and unpopulated regions ("We have passed sixty miles without meeting a single village") and kept him away from England for four years. Neither the dangers of war nor the discomforts of his delayed return did

[11] Pollock, *Gordon of Khartoum*, p. 257.
[12] Ibid., p. 255.

he seem to mind in the least, for Gordon was not someone who missed society. He also admitted to his family that he had found his first taste of war "indescribably exciting".[13]

Whether to marry or not probably troubled him more than getting killed. His letters from this time record the charms of the women he encountered at diplomatic parties, on board ships, and in mountainous villages; "There are some very pretty ladies in Kutais [Georgia], who dance their national dances capitally"; "a very stylish person. . . . I like her very much"; a "very lively young lady". Offsetting those charms was the belief that when a man entered the army, "we sold our lives at so much a day." Money was also an issue when it came to the possibility of marrying, for Gordon came from an honourable but threadbare military family on his father's side, while the commercial interests his mother had inherited had been lost by his uncles. He would be expected to marry into money, since an army commission was prestigious but barely paid, and this would involve a circle of dinner parties and balls that Gordon loathed with a passion. The cadet school he had attended, he once informed his sister Augusta (when she upbraided him for poor punctuation), had taught him neither grammar nor dancing, and he was happy enough with that. Throw in a religious zeal that saw any form of self-denial as a personal challenge, and at another time Gordon might have joined the desert monks he once visited at Mar Saba in the Kidron valley. Mrs. Freese, who encountered him in his mid-thirties, described him as "a mystery you wanted to solve". His favourite book, apart from the Bible, was *The Imitation of Christ*, an uncompromising medieval

---

[13] Charles Gordon, *General Gordon's Letters from the Crimea, the Danube and Armenia*, ed. Demetrius Boulger (London: Chapman and Hall, 1884), p. 92.

roadmap to personal holiness. He was also a chain-smoker and drinker and a *Punch*-reader, and all these contrary influences fidgeted around a small frame with blue eyes that one fellow officer described as looking as if "they had lived for 1,000 years".

That was after his first tour in China, where his eyes had seen a lot. Joining the staff there under General Staveley, he had taken part in the advance on Peking, designed to enforce treaty terms on the Chinese Empire. In retaliation for the earlier execution of a British ambassador, Gordon was ordered to burn down the Imperial Summer Palace, not dissimilar to being told to demolish the Egyptian pyramids. Destroying things was part of his job as an engineer (in the Crimea, he had spent weeks mining Russian docks), but it was his intuitive understanding of siege tactics that impressed General Staveley, not to mention his remarkable initiative. During a lull in Peking, Gordon had taken it upon himself to ride up to the Great Wall of China and assess its current military significance.

When the Chinese court, having agreed on terms, asked for help in fighting a rebellion that had erupted in the south of the empire, Gordon was selected. This was the Taiping Rebellion, and Gordon was sent to assist the Imperial military commander, Li Hung Chang, who was trying to extinguish what was so perilously close to a civil war that the European merchants in Shanghai had funded a 3,000 strong army of Chinese irregulars, under white mercenary officers and armed with modern munitions and riverboats, to defend the port. Optimistically called "The Ever-Victorious Army", it had proved an immediate liability, as thousands of ex-criminals roamed the countryside around Shanghai under the charge of an unhinged American who would later join the Taiping rebels. Gordon's job was to replace him, make the force battle-worthy, and join Li Hung Chang in his work of eliminating the rebel strongholds.

The men he took over were so mutinous that he had a soldier shot dead on parade to restore order, while his personal courage, kindness, and rigid consistency won not just the Ever-Victorious Army over but the Chinese through whose lands they travelled. His own pay went on medicines, and a Frenchman travelling in China years later wrote: "It requires but few days journeying through the countries which were his battle-fields to find in all mouths words of reverence and honour for the brave English officer."[14] To the point of being accused of having a death-wish, he would not only direct sieges, but lead them, often at the head of the charge, armed with a cane and a revolver. Had this merely been daredevil arrogance, Li Hung Chang would not have been so impressed: "He is superior in manner and bearing to any of the foreigners I have come into contact with and does not show outwardly that conceit which makes most of them repugnant in my sight."[15] For a year and a half, the two men took on and broke the rebellion fort by fort, doing so with stealth, resolve, and a tactical use of gunboats masterminded by Gordon.

Although he was still only a captain, promoted to acting major for the secondment (without extra pay), when he was temporarily wounded, the news reverberated through Shanghai and was announced in London by the British prime minister, Lord Palmerston. But Gordon was soon back at it ("planning by night and executing by day, planning by day and executing by night! He is a glorious fellow", said Chang). His contingent were now being paid directly by

[14] Pollock, *Gordon of Khartoum*, p. 135.
[15] Elton, *General Gordon*, p. 58.

Peking, and he fought constantly for better pay for his troops (chiefly to stop them looting), while having his own pay reduced from £3,200 to £1,200 per annum, determined to show the Chinese that "we are not all actuated by greed."[16] The emperor's court in Peking was delighted with him, but joined a growing list of people bemused by Charlie Gordon: "We do not know what to do with him", they told the British minister in Peking: "He will not receive money from us."

So widespread had been the havoc, including resultant starvation, that estimates today put the total number of deaths caused by the Taiping Rebellion at between twenty and seventy million people. Many of these were never buried. Certainly, no one outside China could appreciate the scale of what Gordon had witnessed, and he once grew so furious back home when asked by his family to talk about his war stories in China that he destroyed all his diaries relating to that period. From letters and the accounts of others, we have such scenes as him once trapping a rebel column against a high riverbank and killing around 1,200 of them in an hour-long barrage. But this was war, and even the enemy were said to respect him, partly because Gordon would always insist on giving them generous terms when they surrendered. After the war, a Taiping leader said that the rebel commanders had considered Gordon so extraordinary that they would sometimes prevent their own European marksmen from taking shots at him.[17] When Chang reneged on a cease-fire with the rebels in order to allow his men to plunder the city of Soochow, Gordon snapped. The following, which appeared in *The Times* on 29 January, 1884, claimed

[16] Ibid., p. 72.
[17] Charles Beatty, *His Country Was the World: A Study of Gordon of Khartoum* (London: Chatto and Windus, 1954), pp. 107–8.

to relay a witness account by one of his European officers: "The *Carthage* has just come in from Shanghai. It appears that the rebel chiefs refused to surrender on the Governor's word that no unnecessary blood would be shed, whereupon Gordon got the Governor's promise to himself, and gave his word, on which they capitulated. The Governor got in, had his troops concealed about, and, when Gordon was outside, commanded a wholesale massacre—men, women and children. Gordon heard of it, gathered a few men together, among the rest a Count or Prince Wittgenstein, and broke into the place; and the scenes there witnessed were so revolting that the Prince says they all fired and loaded and fired again on every Mandarin they met. Gordon is said to have shot 25 *buttons* (Mandarins) himself."[18]

In the immediate aftermath of Soochow, Gordon disappeared from the front with the decapitated head of the rebel commander and remained at his rooms at Quinsan, refusing about 500kg [1,102 lbs.] of silver borne to him there at the order of Peking as well as the appeal of Dr. Macartney to reappear. Eventually, he did return to help Chang finish the campaign and was duly awarded Imperial China's highest accolade, the "Yellow Jacket". Gordon accepted this honour but declined an invitation to go to the capital for a ceremony, arranging instead for a riverboat to return him immediately to the coast under cover of night. Chang tipped off his troops, who lined the bank for a mile and a half with lanterns to wave him off.

Chang and Gordon had corresponded in the intervening years, the former rising to such prominence in China that the British minister in Peking had heard rumours that

[18] Quoted in ibid., p. 88. In the Mandarin system, buttoned bonnets were used to signify rank.

the French and Germans were encouraging him to stage a coup d'état. At the same time, China was threatening to go to war with Russia over a border dispute, a war it was thought China would probably lose, even if it might provide the British with welcome relief from Russia's ambitions regarding India. These were the headaches being faced by Sir Thomas Wade in Peking, who wanted Gordon to speak to Chang to find out what was going on. Onto such a stage of tense double-dealing thus entered a man who had just resigned from a post over the insincerity of a thank you letter.

On arrival, Gordon ignored Wade's invitation to stay with him and went to see Chang immediately. Instead, he told Chang to stop listening to Europeans, including the British, whom he said were only after their own interests. He then went to see the emperor's inner council. Through an interpreter, he told them bluntly that they would not win a war against Russia, because Peking was too close to the coast and Russia had a navy. If they were prepared to burn Peking and move it inland, he would help them fight, otherwise, he would and could not help them. When the mandarins demurred at this frankness, he grew so impatient that the interpreter was scared to continue translating. Gordon seized his dictionary, looked up the word "idiocy", and carried it round for each of the council to read. The Chinese later complained to Wade: "However great might be his military ability, his knowledge of the world seemed limited. His conduct has been strange." Wade reported to London: "his judgement is no longer in balance . . . his very devoutness is dangerous."[19]

Time would vindicate Gordon, for the Chinese agreed

[19] Pollock, *Gordon of Khartoum*, p. 272.

to peaceful terms the following year with the Russians at a treaty in Saint Petersburg, and Chang stayed his hand. In his memoirs, Wade would admit that Gordon got it right. Gordon would never see that, and back home in England he was dispirited. Wars against the Ashanti and Abyssinians came and went without a summons. He had leave to use up, so took himself off to Ireland, the source of endless debate in the London newspapers. Writing to a friend from his Cork hotel, he said that from what he had seen, the peasantry in Northwest and Southwest Ireland was as bad as anything he had seen around the world. Under punitive rents, England was allowing the Irish to be kept in conditions in which "we wouldn't keep our cattle". The slave trade, he said, had only been ended when the government had compensated the traders, and he argued that Britain should make £50m available for the Irish to buy back the land, any half measure would "only embitter feelings . . . these people are made as we are . . . they are patient beyond belief . . . but at the same time broken-spirited and desperate."

When his friend forwarded the letter to *The Times*, who published it, an editorial declared it "the heroic method of dealing with Ireland", and a paper in Dublin called Gordon "one of the most remarkable men of our time". When the British prime minister, William Gladstone, was briefed on the stir caused by Gordon's comments, he was assured that the latter was "not clothed in the rightest of minds", though nine years later, a watered down version of the idea would become government policy under The Purchase of Land (Ireland) Act 1885.[20]

Back in England, he stayed mostly with his sister Augusta

[20] Ibid., p. 283.

in Southampton, disdaining invitations to London. With a couple of drinks inside him, he was good and sought-after company, but he was fed up. When the Prince of Wales invited Gordon to dinner, he turned it down, and when the royal equerry suggested that some sort of excuse would be appropriate, Gordon told him to tell the prince that he went to bed at 9:30 P.M. The prince laughed and invited him to lunch, instead, but entertaining royalty with war stories was no substitute for not being taken seriously by the army, which did not know what to do with him. He agreed to take a posting an army friend did not want, which took him to Mauritius, an undemanding command where there was less than a regiment of troops and where he devoted his afternoons to writing about one thing that kept him sane—his Christian faith.

He did not belong to any denomination ("I confess I hate going to church"), considered most clergy too worldly, and yet Gordon was often up at 4:30 A.M. reading his Bible ("it is alive and makes alive"). Cut off for long stretches of his army career from any access to a Sunday church, he had developed some very idiosyncratic doctrines, his positioning of the Garden of Eden in some respects the easiest of them. That theory was based on a single line in Genesis: "A river flowed out of Eden to water the garden, and there it divided and became four rivers."[21] An English clergyman had mentioned to Gordon that the Hebrew *min*, "from" or "out of", used before Eden, could occasionally mean "to". Though no scholar has ever seriously argued that it might apply in this sentence, for Gordon the possibility that the Nile, Euphrates, and Jordan might have flowed *into* Eden was sensational. When he then came across a tree in the

[21] Genesis 2:10.

Seychelles with fruit resembling male and female genitalia, he was convinced he was onto something.

Freudians might choke at this, and while even Gordon's biggest fans have not tended to claim it among his finest moments, it still displayed two qualities that the latter loved. His capacity for enthusiasm and the way he took his faith so seriously, shown in the first line of what he wrote on the matter: "Allow that Genesis is not allegorical, that Eden, its garden, its two trees, did exist on this earth."[22] For Gordon, the Bible contained real history, real people, and the deepest account of reality. At the same time, he was fascinated by the undoubtedly allegorical power of much Scripture. Indeed, he believed that the whole Christian Bible was equivalent to a human life, from birth to death: "It would be nice if we could see where we are, and get warned for our future guidance; say one were in Jacob, then one would be prepared for Egypt and brick-making." This was a mystical, even Rabbinic way of exploring Scripture, and even among those who rolled their eyes, no one seemed to doubt his intentions. Gordon wanted the truth, including the truth about himself, and was prepared to accept unpalatable insights: "we need never go beyond our own selves to find the Pharisee, the Sadducee, the heathen."

The trouble with his one-man church was that, at times, his doctrines vacillated with his moods: "Some of my letters are written by one nature, some by the other. . . . This conflict makes me terribly inconsistent."[23] With maturity, he felt the need to resolve this inconsistency, for he took theology too seriously for it to be left to curiosity or opin-

[22] General Gordon, "The Site of the Garden of Eden", *Strand Magazine* 17, no. 40 (1899): 314.
[23] Gordon, *Letters to His Sister*, p. 98.

ion. It was his life, and he even gave biblical names to the temptations he fought. "Anak" and "Agag" were ambition/newspapers and smoking/brandy, respectively. Though he hated dinner parties, when he did get forced along, "I drink Cognac . . . and talk too much."[24] "The Archers" and "The Doles" were the tendency of spite/bitterness towards others and the depression that sometimes haunted him. Just before sailing for Mauritius in the summer of 1881, Gordon had stayed as the guest of a Midlands clergyman named Rev. Horace Waller. Waller had taken him to task for neglecting Holy Communion in his devotions, and Gordon had duly attended Communion at Waller's parish the next day. It was a revelation, turning his spirituality "upside down", as he put it, and he was now attending Communion regularly on Mauritius. A magistrate named John Ackroyd sometimes used to sit next to him in the Anglican cathedral and recalled how the pew would shake when Gordon was praying.[25]

Prior to his discovery of the importance of Communion, the main focus of Gordon's theology had been what he termed "the indwelling of the Holy Spirit", inspired by a book he had read after returning from China, dark days that had coincided with the death of his father ("a long dreary struggle [looked back on with horror]. . . . I used to walk out to the Chalk, and go into the churchyard and think about my father, and kick the stones about and walk back.")[26] One night, after reading *Christ Mystical* by the seventeenth-century Anglican bishop Joseph Hall, "something broke in

---

[24] Pollock, *Gordon of Khartoum*, p. 210.

[25] Ibid., p. 309.

[26] Charles Chenevix Trench, *The Road to Khartoum* (New York: Carroll and Graf, 1889), p. 56.

my heart, a palpable feeling, and I knew God loved me—
which I never lost."[27]

He had subsequently spoken about "the indwelling" to
anyone who would listen and wrote tracts that he had
printed and that he would hand out to people he met. One of
Gordon's nephews remembered him coming to stay. When
he was playing in the garden after breakfast with his pet
hedgehog, Gordon had appeared, given him some pocket
money, and asked whether God lived in him: "I promptly
said, 'No; he lives up there', indicating the sky. The answer
was adjudged incorrect, but perhaps he was as satisfied with
it as any other, for he was able to tell me God dwelt in me
and looked out of my eyes and was in everything around
me. I gazed at my hedgehog with renewed interest."[28]

Over the years, the ability of this single revelation to
keep the Archers, Doles, Agag, and Anak at bay had been
something of a diminishing return. One friend later recalled
walking in Gravesend while Gordon was handing out tracts
and *at the same time* avoiding stepping on cracks in the pave-
ment out of superstition. Gordon knew his inconsistencies
and probably knew he was slightly cracked. But the faithful
side of him always responded to confusion by going deeper,
which he had already started to do prior to his conversation
with Waller, by reading and rereading *The Imitation of Christ*,
copies of which he would be buying by the half dozen and
giving away for the rest of his life. That book told him to see
spiritually dry seasons, when the indwelling seemed faint,
as chances to grow ("spiritual progress does not consist in
enjoying great delight and consolation");[29] indeed, to see

[27] Nutting, *Gordon*, p. 283.

[28] Pollock, *Gordon of Khartoum*, p. 234.

[29] Thomas à Kempis, *The Imitation of Christ*, trans. Shirley-Price (London:
Penguin, 1952), p. 15.

adversity of all kinds as a blessing, since it allowed true faith to reveal itself.

The Imitation had also been telling him about the importance of Communion, and now the penny had finally dropped. "I cannot tell you how important I think it is", he wrote to his sister. In Mauritius, he concluded it to be nothing less than "medicine" left by Christ, "His dying request" being for us to take it. Moreover, it was proving a decisive new weapon against Anak and Agag, even if it revealed subtler and more insipid failings he had never noticed about himself: "I never could have thought so many holes and corners would have been searched out."[30] The pursuit of holiness "seems scarcely to have begun", which for Gordon was not a daunting prospect, but he was disturbed as to how he had previously missed all this in his Bible. Two lines in the New Testament now jumped out at him. Christ's words in John's Gospel: "He who eats my flesh and drinks my blood abides in me, and I in him";[31] and Saint Paul's words: "For as often as you eat this bread and drink the chalice, you proclaim the Lord's death until he comes."[32]

His fascination with the Garden of Eden story brought the most astounding thought of all, from which his writings on this subject would take their title: In Genesis, God had said "Do not eat" to Adam, regarding the forbidden fruit. Adam had disobeyed and eaten it. At the Last Supper, Jesus says "Take, eat", regarding Communion. Gordon concluded that the Eucharist was nothing less than the antidote to the poison Adam and Eve consumed in Eden. He wrote a new tract called "Thou shalt not eat. Take eat" and laid

[30] Nutting, *Gordon*, p. 173.
[31] John 6:56.
[32] 1 Corinthians 11:26.

his theory out to Mrs. Freese in Gravesend, who accused him of becoming a Catholic.

Some of Gordon's other doctrines were already well wide of Mrs. Freese's Protestantism. For instance, he believed that people knew when you were thinking ill or well of them, even *in absentia*; he believed that if people gave him a keepsake they had used a lot, it was easier to pray for them; he believed that he was able to offer up to heaven his own suffering on behalf of the souls of other people. In the past, Gordon had expressed surprise at the high quality of the Catholics he had met. "Why does the Romish Church thrive with so many errors in it?" he had asked four years earlier: "The Roman Catholics in China were certainly far more self-sacrificing. I went out with some twenty young men who definitely stated that they went out *never* to return, and took leave of their friends as if they were going to their execution. . . . The Roman Catholic Church is in advance of our present day Protestantism."[33] Now he was embracing one of the most controversial doctrines of the Catholic faith —a belief in the mystical and "Real Presence" of Christ in Communion.

While he was pondering all this, and leading Bible classes among the Chinese population in Port Louis, promotion eventually caught up with Gordon, leaving him too senior in rank to be kept in his current post. The Cape government requested he be seconded to them, instead, to which London all too happily agreed, and General Gordon proceeded directly to South Africa from Mauritius.

The colonists' problem there involved the Basuto people, who had sought protection from the Cape after years of skirmishes with Dutch settlers. Rivalry between the Natal and

[33] Gordon, *Letters to His Sister*, p. 134.

Cape governments (both British administrations) as to who should absorb this protectorate had resulted in a confusion that had managed to infuriate everyone, including London, and left the Basuto fulminating.

On arrival in Cape Town, Gordon first went to visit Cetshwayo, the Zulu king then being held in captivity by the British, presenting him with an ivory-headed cane that had been given to Gordon by the Sultan of Zanzibar and assuring the king that he had "always been interested in him" and that he must not lose hope. Cetshwayo responded, said Gordon, "with a deep '*Ah!*' [and] pointed upwards".

Once he had settled, Gordon decided that he liked the Boers ("they are a God-fearing people.")[34] He also liked Masupha, King of Basutoland, whose mountain kingdom he reached a few weeks later and whose accusations of duplicity against the Cape government he had no trouble believing. The Basuto were, Gordon was sure, being "goaded into rebellion by the badness and inefficiency of the magistracy". The Cape government had little use for this kind of open talk, and when Gordon began to suspect that they had sent him to Masupha to provoke the latter into war, a campaign they wanted Gordon to lead, he declared: "Is it likely that I would fight against a man with whom I am life and soul?"[35] In a more measured memo written before his resignation, he recommended that Basutoland be granted autonomy, a notion ridiculed by the Cape government and then put into practise two years later ("the Gordon policy without Gordon", noted *The Cape Times*), which legal nicety would later exempt Lesotho from *apartheid* rule.

Such vindication of his instincts lay in the deep future, and

[34] Ibid., p. 199.
[35] Beatty, *His Country Was the World*, p. 216.

back in England he was uncharacteristically listless: "Earth's joys grow very dim, its glories fade." He was also without money since, according to new army rules, he had not been paid while seconded, which left him momentarily penniless since he had refused payment in the Cape. "Chinese Gordon" still had his admirers, including the owner of P&O shipping, who had given him free travel for life, and the Belgian king, Leopold, who wanted him to go to the Congo on a huge salary. He was sorely tempted, but it would mean resigning his British army commission, something his sense of loyalty still balked at. Instead, in January 1883, with the army still having no role for him, but unwilling to get rid of him, he borrowed some money and sailed for the Holy Land. When the army raised no objection, he stayed there for a year.

It was the first proper holiday he had ever had: "I have lived my life too quickly." He started reading Saint Augustine but made a point of not reading any tourist guidebooks, because he wanted to make his own mind up about the location of all the holy sites, armed only with his Bible and map-making skills. He rented a place in Jaffa ("I ride along the shore every evening, and walk my horse back; there are capital sands")[36] and began wrestling again with doctrine. If only faith mattered, he reasoned, why all the warnings to behave better? Who can yet be sure of salvation? he asked one of the several correspondents who began to receive voluminous streams of his consciousness. "Our names are written in the Book of Life, yet may be blotted out (read Apocalypse iii. 5)."

He had considered living with the monks at Saint Catherine's in the Sinai Desert and visited Mar Saba monastery in

---

[36] Gordon, *Letters to His Sister*, p. 54.

the Kidron valley, but, in the end, he liked the house in Jaffa, where the poultry strutted in and out as he wrote his letters. He found both Jewish and Arab men to be too agitated to become friendly with ("The feature of the people out here is self-exculpation on every subject"),[37] but he liked his Arab landlady, who made sure he did not starve. But no one was less likely to miss a social life than Gordon, and, as he plumbed deeper into the mysteries of faith, he aired old ghosts, notably the death of his sister Emily when he was ten years old: "I remember a deep bitterness. . . . Humanly speaking it changed my life, it was never the same since. I have never known a sorrow like it, in all my life."[38]

Before Emily's death, he had been a rascal, breaking windows with a catapult, spitting into visitors' hats, and ringing doorbells. His father, an army general himself, once described parenting him as "sitting on a powder keg". Even after her death, he was wild, back-termed at cadet school in Woolwich for bullying and insubordination. But there was a conscience emerging, and the frequency with which he was in trouble was partly due to his confessing to every misdemeanor. When his mother decided to forgive one incident so that he could accompany the family on an outing, he insisted on being punished.

There were many things about both God and life in general that he realised he would never understand. He liked a line by the Baptist preacher Charles Spurgeon: "I believe that not a worm is picked up by a bird without direct intervention of God, yet I entirely believe in man's free will; but I cannot and do not pretend to reconcile the two." The same God had made Charlie Gordon both a temple of the

[37] Ibid., p. 279.
[38] Pollock, *Gordon of Khartoum*, p. 33.

Holy Spirit and a lowly worm. Humans were "the master-piece of all creation" but also born to "one continual cru-cifixion", whether they knew it or not. He marvelled at "what God must be, to manage all the things of creation to perfection, the thoughts of each heart, the words and acts of each created being, or insect; it is a stupendous idea. . . . Then think that neither death nor life, nor powers, nor prin-cipalities shall separate us from His love."[39]

He was not the only soul-searching pilgrim in Palestine. There was a retired Royal Navy officer in Jerusalem, walk-ing around with a cross on his back, and there was a house near the Damascus Gate known as "The American Colony", whose inhabitants were awaiting the end of the world. It was rented by a family named the Spaffords, and Gordon would sometimes go and sit on their roof and gaze at the city. Their youngest daughter recalled tiptoeing up the stairs to their roof to spy on him: "He was not very tall and had fair, curly hair, and I remember how blue his eyes were, and the blue double-breasted suit he wore. I did not know General Gordon was famous, only that he was my friend and I loved him."[40] Among Gordon's musings as he gazed out was a passage from Ephesians in which the apostle Paul summed up his mission: "to make all men see what is the plan of the mystery hidden for ages in God who created all things; that through the Church the manifold wisdom of God might now be made known to the principalities and powers in the heavenly places. This was according to the eternal purpose which he has realized in Christ Jesus our Lord."[41]

---

[39] Gordon, *Letters to His Sister*, p. 78.
[40] Pollock, *Gordon of Khartoum*, p. 344.
[41] Ephesians 3:9-11.

This dense passage confused Gordon. What exactly was the church by which the heavenly realms were going to be shown the wisdom of God? What did that mean? Gordon had once written that "each man is a church or a temple of God", but he knew Paul was talking about something collective. Church *per se* had not been part of his thinking before. He had given away most of his possessions, visited the sick and prayed, but he had done it alone. Few biblical scholars read the Bible more than he did, but different passages had taken him in different directions regarding the nature of reality: "Once I did believe that some perished altogether at the end of the world—were annihilated, as having no souls. After this, I believed that the world was made up of incarnated children of God and incarnated children of the evil spirit; and then I came to the belief that *the two are one*."[42] After that, he said, he had believed that all souls were going to be saved and had preexisted with God, which had led him to conclude that humans and animals had reincarnated multiple times. Now he wrote: "I had the heresy of no free will and no eternal punishment. I have come back to the fold and wish I had never said or written a word against either."[43] The more he understood about his isolation, the more he yearned for a church beyond his own moods, opinions, and interpretations, for he saw clearly now that Truth was "a sharp razor-edge; a hair's breadth right or left is error".[44]

Everything was pulling him in one direction. One of the books he had with him in Jerusalem was a pocketbook of Roman Catholic *pensées* edited by the British novelist Charlotte Mary Yonge. It was called *Gold Dust* and contained the

[42] Elton, *General Gordon*, p. 248.
[43] Ibid., p. 320.
[44] Gordon, *Letters to His Sister*, p. 230.

following prayer, which Gordon marked: "O Jesus, gentle and humble of heart, hear me! From the desire of being esteemed, from the desire of being loved, from the desire to be sought, Deliver me, Jesus. From the desire to be mourned, from the desire of praise, from the desire of preference, from the desire of influence, from the desire of approval, from the desire of authority, from the fear of humiliation, from the fear of being despised, from the fear of repulse, from the fear of calumny, from the fear of oblivion, from the fear of ridicule, from the fear of injury, from the fear of suspicion, Deliver me, Jesus."[45]

He said he was attending Communion at whatever church would give it to him, including Catholic and Orthodox churches. Of the sacrament, *Gold Dust* wrote: "Never has human love, in its brightest dreams, been able to form any idea of the sweetness the love of GOD imparts to the soul, and which is brought still nearer to us by the Blessed Sacrament."[46] But Anak was twitching, for on the empty beaches of Jaffa word reached him of a massive rebellion in the Sudan. As a display of popular Islamic anger, the uprising had everyone's attention, and for Gordon there was extra reason to be interested, for he had spent his early forties working in the Sudan and suspected that he had caused it.

The chain of events that had led to that episode in his life had begun in the summer of 1872 with a chance meeting at the British Embassy in Constantinople with an Armenian Christian named Nubar Pasha, who was working for the Ottoman Empire as prime minister to the Khedive of Egypt. Nubar tried to persuade him to take the job of governor of Equatoria, a region recently appropriated by

[45] Adrien Sylvain, *Gold Dust*, ed. Charlotte Yonge (London: J. Masters, ca. 1880), p. 46.
[46] Ibid., p. 50.

the Khedive, south of Sudan and toward the Great Lakes
of Central Africa. Employed by the Khedive, he would replace the explorer Sir Samuel Baker and have legislative responsibility for the colony, together with an army at his dis-
posal made up of Turks, Egyptians, Central Africans, and
an Armenian mercenary force known as the Bashi-Bazouks.
Nubar assured him that the Khedive was committed to end
slave trade, which still flourished in the region. Gordon,
who was bored with the diplomatic job on the Danube he
was doing at the time, wrote to London and obtained permission to be seconded.

Before he knew it, he was in Cairo telling the Khedive
that "not all people worship the gods of gold and silver" and
insisting on taking the job for £2,000 rather than £10,000 per
annum. Equatoria was 3,000 miles south of Cairo, and when
he got there, he had found its administration a shambles, the
Bashi-Bazouks running rather than stopping the slave trade,
and the local tribes either openly hostile or starving to death.
None of the soldiers had been paid for months and were
pillaging to feed themselves, while Baker's account of his
time there appeared to be a work of fiction. Four out of the
twelve European staff Gordon hired died of fever, and the
rest he would eventually send away. Flies, rats, and snakes
teemed about the camp.

Gordon rose to the challenge with grim resolve ("things
go untowardly more in this country than anywhere else
. . . *every, every*thing seems to go wrong.") Inspecting the
country on camel, resolving disputes, forcing money out
of the Khedive to pay the soldiers, blocking and arresting
slave trains on their way north, he began to take a hold of
his mission, inch by inch. When he complained to Cairo
that the slaves he was stopping were being sold at the Khedive's own garrison of Khartoum, the Khedive responded

by sacking the Governor General of Khartoum and extending Gordon's jurisdiction to include the Sudan, a cumulative territory the size of Western Europe. The Khedive was a shrewd man, and his motives for this expanded appointment were decidedly mixed, as Gordon came to realise. Although Cairo did indeed profit from the continued illicit slave trade, the Khedive's bigger concern was the vast debt he owed to European creditors, credit he had partly spent on his own prodigious tastes, but also on the construction of the Suez Canal. The loans accumulated so much interest that it had broken Egypt's budget, hence unpaid soldiers not just in Equatoria, but in the Sudan and Egypt, too, as well as unpaid civil servants, for whom bribes had become a form of subsistence. Needing to renegotiate the debt, the Khedive hoped presenting himself as antislavery would help sway European public opinion and, thus, loose his creditors' hands.

Gordon soon had little illusion regarding the Khedive, but was also increasingly aware of the hypocrisy of the European position, having lent the Khedive money to give it back to them in engineering fees. In the meantime, Gordon set to work: "He closed slave markets, halted caravans, and had slave-merchants publicly hanged. When the slave-traders in the Bahr-al-Ghazal region revolted, he unleashed the cattle-nomads of the steppes against them."[47] Having been alongside him in one scrap, a black sheik told another Muslim how Gordon had lit a cigarette at the height of the battle: "Never in my life did I see such a thing."[48] Gordon had to rub his own eyes when the elders of one tribe appeared for negotiations ceremonially dressed in armour dating to the Crusades.

---

[47] Michael Asher, *Khartoum* (London: Viking, 2005), p. 3.
[48] Elton, *General Gordon*, p. 243.

He remained in his element when fighting, he admitted
to his sister: "I am at present two men: the one violent,
brutal, hard, and in every way despicable; the other would
hurt no one."[49] Khartoum was a fortified entrepot through
which gum, gold, ebony, and ivory passed out of Central
Africa on its way to European and Arab markets. Only in
Khartoum did Gordon realise quite how engrained slavery
was in the territory he was running and how complex the
business of eradicating it would be. He estimated that seven-
eighths of the population were slaves and that two-thirds of
the tax revenue had until recently been generated from it.
The Khedive had therefore been paying his European creditors, which included the British government, with money
generated from the sale of slaves. Now, Gordon's policing of
the routes was forcing slave caravans to make huge bypasses
into the desert, adding to the number of slaves dying on their
way to Lower Egypt and the Red Sea. And to make matters
even less straightforward, those slaves he did free usually
did not wish to return home. Every sheik and chief in the
country had been involved, and half his army. Faced with
these levels of complicity, receiving a stream of correspondence from the antislavery lobby in Britain did not cheer
Gordon: "It is very shocking: have some more salmon";
"I have, I think, stopped their writing by acknowledging
ourselves to be a pillaging horde of brigands and proposing
to them to leave their comfortable homes and come out to
their favourite, 'poor blacks'."[50]

He still hated the trade, though, and decided on a strategy. He would end the charade of everyone carrying on
behind his back and have all slaves registered, with a date

[49] Gordon, *Letters to His Sister*, p. 291.
[50] Chenevix Trench, *Road to Khartoum*, p. 99.

set ten years on for fuller emancipation. While he was in the midst of enforcing this, a telegram arrived in Khartoum requesting Gordon's urgent presence in Cairo. The Khedive wanted Gordon to represent him at an impending meeting in the city with his major creditors, including senior representatives from both the British and French governments and the Rothschild banking family. At the meeting, Gordon argued that it would be in the interest of all of them to suspend interest payments for a year so that Egypt could pay its soldiers and civil servants. It fell on deaf ears: "Everyone laughs at me!"[51]

Undeterred, he sent a telegram from Cairo to the Chair of the Bank of England, making the same point, but the latter replied: "I cannot look at you: the matter is in the hands of Her Majesty's government."[52] When Britain's chief resident advisor to the Khedive, Evelyn Baring, who was in London at the time, heard what Gordon was suggesting, he commented: "[Gordon] is an excellent, simple-hearted, and impractical man, about as much fit for the work he has at hand as I am to be pope."[53] Gordon, who always drank more than he intended to when in Cairo, said he considered well-paid British residents living lavishly off the Egyptians to be immoral: "we have bloodsucked Egypt."[54] Among those at the meetings was Count Ferdinand de Lesseps, chief engineer of the Suez Canal. Charles Gordon, he observed, was "a man of great ability, very intelligent, very honest, and very brave, but he keeps all the Sudan accounts in his pocket, written on small bits of paper. All that he pays out he puts in his right pocket, and all that he receives in his left. He

[51] Beatty, *His Country Was the World*, p. 189.
[52] Ibid., p. 189.
[53] Pollock, *Gordon of Khartoum*, p. 211.
[54] Gordon, *Letters to His Sister*, p. 125.

then makes up two bags, sends them to Cairo, and money is sent back to him. He is not the man to regulate the affairs of Egypt."[55]

Gordon's approach to finances may have lacked sophistication, but he was far from naïve: he was convinced that the only reasons France and Britain had not already exploited the weakness of the Ottoman Empire to assume total control of Egypt was distrust between the two of them and "ninety millions sterling of debt on Egypt".[56] Eventually the Khedive told him to return to Khartoum. Gordon left, relieved but disgusted, and more assured than ever that there was "little difference between white and black men", not meaning it as a particular compliment to either. Still, returning south his faith felt strong ("I have the Shekinah and I do like trusting to Him") and the beguiling panoply of the desert: "the lights and shadows of this land are wonderful."

There never was such a place, he told his sister Augusta, "for knowing yourself". Most of the Sudan was uninhabited, and the Arabs had only moved there in recent decades, to avoid Egyptian taxes. It was transit country, "a man-eater", one called it; flies and scorpions everywhere, and little water either side of the Nile. Some days, Gordon told Augusta, he was sorely tempted to use brandy and laudanum to numb the sheer discomfort of it but knew that would destroy his liver. Regarding alcohol, he could go without it for months and then, when he had a bottle in a hotel room, drink it for breakfast. Smoking he found harder to stop. His resilience astounded Sudanese and Europeans alike, but resilience was not immunity or immortality, and his body was getting ravaged by fever, bites, and exhaustion. On one

[55] Beatty, *His Country Was the World*, p. 189.
[56] Charles George Gordon, *The Journals of Major-Gen. C. G. Gordon, C.B., at Khartoum*, vol. 2, ed. Hake (Leipzig: Bernhard Tauchnitz, 1885), p. 92.

particularly arduous excursion, to settle a border dispute with the King of Abyssinia, he was warned by the king that he could have Gordon killed if he kept contradicting him. Gordon utterly disarmed him by replying that he could think of nothing better. In another letter to Augusta he admitted: "I feel *alone*."[57]

When he resigned, after five years, his ship home had stopped at Naples, where a French passenger took him to see a show at Teatro di San Carlo. When half-naked female dancers appeared on stage, Gordon left, exclaiming: "And you call that civilisation!?"[58] Looking back at the country from the country from which he had come, he said he considered the Sudanese to be "a fine, brave people", admired their hard lives and their Muslim piety, and hoped they would one day rise up against the Ottomans. Now that they had done that, he felt no different: "I feel for the rebels and am proud of their prowess, and our Lord will work good for them out of it."[59]

The size of the uprising had been signalled to the world when the Khedive sent 10,000 troops under a seconded British officer named General Hicks. Hicks' army had been wiped out almost to a man, the victors later marking the spot by building a pyramid of skulls in the desert. Garrison after garrison had fallen to them, under the charismatic leadership of a man known as "the Mahdi", until only Khartoum and a small handful of river garrisons were holding out. The Mahdi, a Sufi "dervish", was said to be planning to invade Egypt once he had taken Khartoum and then march to Mecca, where he would purify Islam of its Ottoman luxuries. Each garrison his men had seized, each cache of field

[57] Gordon, *Letters to His Sister*, p. 151.
[58] Pollock, *Gordon of Khartoum*, p. 233.
[59] Chenevix Trench, *Road to Khartoum*, p. 196.

artillery, rifles, and ammunition that fell into his hands, had swelled his power, reputation, and numbers, until a camp of over 100,000 people had the whole of the Middle East on edge.

Britain's concern was to keep the Suez open, while keeping other European powers from getting involved, but the prospect of filling the vacuum left by the ongoing collapse of Ottoman control in the Sudan was not attractive. For the financially cautious government of Prime Minister William Gladstone, the Sudan appeared barren, unprofitable land that the uprising was not making look any more attractive. The Suez was certainly threatened if it continued, but that could be mitigated by sending troops to the western shores of the Red Sea. Raising a Union flag in the interior was not a conversation Gladstone was prepared to entertain, despite heated arguments to the contrary and the clear unravelling of the Ottoman situation. He did, however, concede the need to show moral leadership in the region regarding the fate of foreigners caught in Khartoum.

These included merchants from all over the Mediterranean, North Africa, India, Europe, and the Middle East, for, even by today's standards, Khartoum had become a thriving place, with four miles of fortified defences as well as the protection of the Blue and White Niles at whose confluence it stood. You could buy Bass Pale Ale and tinned meat in the Greek shops. There was a Catholic mission, hospital, and enough Greeks to have their own quarter and church. On top of this, there were Egyptian clerks and local sheiks, and tens of thousands of former or current slaves either lived there or were in transit with trading caravans. The sound of kettle drums was a constant accompaniment to life in Khartoum. There were professional soldiers, drawn from the Great Lakes to Central Europe, more and more of whom had now come in from abandoned outposts, and most of whom had not been paid for over a year. All these were now jammed inside Khartoum or were trying to get out. Many in Khartoum had travelled to the Mahdi's camp after hearing of Hicks' defeat, leaving their women and children behind in the city. On Fridays, there would still be vast numbers praying together in the city, led by an *ulema* that was declaring the Mahdi to be an imposter. Many Europeans had left on the Nile while they could, while others had got out following the caravan route east to the Red Sea. But for many, Khartoum was their livelihood, and they were clinging on, hoping the British would eventually do something. In the meantime, the city had thick walls, farms within those walls, soldiers, ammunition, and an endless supply of water.

Before the French consul had left this cauldron, he threw a dinner party that was attended by a reporter from *The Times* who had arrived in the city. It was, he said, "a *salon* superior to many in Paris—wax-lights, mirrors, ten servants in livery, cut-glass, silver, and flowers; a dinner thoroughly Parisian turned out by his French *chef*; champagne, hock, claret, etc."[60] Still in his twenties, the reporter was an Irish Catholic named Frank Power, who had described his journey up from Cairo to his mother. One evening on the boat, he had absentmindedly thrown a piece of lemon rind from his drink into the river. Despite crocodiles having already killed a man that day, someone jumped in to get it. That, he said, was the poverty they had been reduced to under the Ottomans. He decided to stay on in the city and see what happened.

Back in London, the riddle of what to do about Khar-

---

[60] Frank Power, *Letters from Khartoum: Written during the Siege* (London, 1885), p. 51 (letter dated 1 December 1883.

toum was proving impossible to solve. If reports that the Mahdi was planning to advance on the city were true, there were as many as 11,000 people who would need evacuation. This was too many to evacuate on the Nile, for no river-boat could handle more than 300 passengers, and even if a flotilla of such boats were led to the Mediterranean, there was a stretch of rapids between Cairo and Khartoum where people walked or travelled by camel, and boats had to be dismantled and put back together on the Upper Nile. It was a headache, but it was not Gordon's headache. On leaving Jerusalem, he had gone to Brussels, agreed terms with the King Leopold to take the Congo job, and returned to England where he resigned his commission. A magazine editor tracked him down at his sister's house and asked him his views on Khartoum. Initially reluctant to be drawn in, he could not stop himself once he had started. He said evacuation was impossible ("Where will you get camels to take them away? Will the Mahdi supply them?") and that the only possible policy was to send troops. The interview was published in the *Pall Mall Gazette* the next day under the headline "SEND GORDON", but Gladstone, now in his seventies, was completely adamant that his government would not be drawn into a war over the uprising, a war that would force them to stay in Sudan. He disliked the Ottoman Empire as much as anyone and argued that the Sudanese were entitled to claim freedom from such governance. Why should the British get in the way? The answer was that otherwise thousands of people were about to get slaughtered in Khartoum.

Frank Power said that when people in Khartoum heard that Gordon was on his way, they queued up to read his telegram. It had been sent from a telegraph station halfway up the Nile and was addressed to the town: "DO NOT BE PANIC-STRICKEN. YE ARE MEN NOT WOMEN. I AM COMING—GORDON." If the fifty-one-year-old had needed convincing to sacrifice a well-paid Congo job in order to be smuggled with one other British officer, Lt. Colonel Stewart, into what many thought was a Sudanese death-trap, that had been nothing compared to the reluctance of William Gladstone to send him. Gordon was precisely the sort of person Gladstone was most suspicious of, and telegrams had gone back and forth between the foreign secretary and Evelyn Baring in Cairo. Baring, remembering Gordon from his previous time in the Sudan, urged London to choose someone else. But Gladstone's suspicion was matched by his parsimony, and eventually there was no one else capable of achieving anything with so little resources, and time was running out. After seeing Gordon on his way upstream, Baring wrote to London: "He is certainly half-cracked, but it is impossible not to be charmed by the simplicity and honesty of his character. . . . I believe he is the best man to send."[61]

The best man in the rebels' camp was a forty-year-old boat-builder's son named Mohammed Ahmed. The Dongola tribe of which he was part had been one of those to have migrated south from Egypt to avoid Ottoman taxes, which had been followed by the deeply unpopular extension of Ottoman presence into the Sudan, followed now by its outlawing of the slave trade, at which the Dongola had excelled. From his mixture of Nubian and Arabic blood, he claimed direct ancestry from the Prophet, and had initially drawn a small group of followers around him on a river island, where his dreams, visions, and prayers convinced him of a destiny to renew all of Islam by destroying the Otto-

---

[61] Chenevix Trench, *Road to Khartoum*, p. 215.

mans. When news of his claims reached Cairo, a contingent of soldiers had been sent to arrest him, but their cumbersome approach was so broadcast that the Mahdi's men had been able to rush the boats and kill them all.

That single incident had begun the spiral that was continuing to widen, with up to 200,000 jihadists and camp followers now around the Mahdi's tent in Kordofan, two to three weeks southwest of Khartoum. There were over fifty different tribes in the Sudan, and it had been no easy thing to bring them together, even with a shared faith spread through centuries of interaction with Arabic Islam. Following the capture of an Ottoman garrison called El Obeid, the Mahdi had taken prisoner a Catholic missionary named Fr. Joseph Ohrwalder. Impressed by Ohrwalder's refusal to convert even on threat of death, the Mahdi had turned him into an unwitting biographer: "His outward appearance was strangely fascinating; he was a man of strong constitution, very dark complexion, and his face always wore a pleasant smile [under which] gleamed a set of singularly white teeth, and between the two upper middle ones was a V-shaped space, which in the Sudan is considered a sign that the owner will be lucky."[62]

Ohrwalder would spend two years observing the Mahdi and said he believed the Mahdi was convinced by his own claims. As to what they were, the priest elucidated: "He called himself Mahdi Khalifate er Rasul (i.e., the successor of the Prophet), while his adherents called him "Sayid" (i.e., Master); Sayidna el Mahdi (i.e., our Master the Mahdi), or Sayidna el Imam (i.e., our Master the head, or one who goes in front). The Mahdi in his every action endeavoured to

[62] Fr. Joseph Ohrwalder, *Ten Years in Captivity in the Mahdi's Camp*, trans. F. R. Wingate (London, 1892), p. 37.

imitate and follow in the exact footsteps of the Prophet."[63]
The rebels' black battle banners, he said, bore the following Arabic vow: "We shall destroy this and create the next
world", as well as what Ohrwalder called "the Moslem
creed" and these words: "Mohammed Ahmed, Successor
of the Prophet". He said he understood the latter claim to
be a direct snub of the Ottoman Sultan of Turkey, who
claimed the same title, and with hatred of whom the rebel
leader used to fuse his ranks. In the Mahdi's charismatic Friday sermons, he never failed to present the Ottoman leader
as the source of not only taxes and injustice, but decadence,
hypocrisy, and corruption.

A man so attuned to the allegorical as Gordon could hardly
have missed the irony of the situation. He was faced with a
mirror or shadow image of himself, beside a biblical river.
"It is an odd river", he had observed the last time he was
here, wishing he had brought his concordance with him so
that he could "try the mystic nature of the Nile."[64] There
would be no time for that, but in Khartoum Frank Power
was staggered at the impact his arrival immediately had on
the town: "When he goes out of doors there are always
crowds of Arab men and women at the gate to kiss his feet,
and twice to-day the furious women, wishing to lift his feet
to kiss them, threw him over. . . . He is Dictator here; the
Mahdi has gone down before him, and to-day sent him a
'salaam', or message of welcome. It is wonderful that one
man could have such an influence on 200,000 people. Numbers of women flock here every day to ask him to touch
their children and to cure them; they call him the 'Father
and the Saviour of the Soudan.'"[65]

---

[63] Ibid.
[64] Gordon, *Letters to His Sister*, p. 74.
[65] Power, *Letters from Khartoum*, p. 97.

Gordon assured Power in private that the same people would lynch him if he tried to leave. In Cairo, he had tried to persuade Baring to let him bring a man named Zubair, a notorious former slaver under house arrest, for he was sure the only way to counter the Mahdi under these circumstances was with like for like. The plan had been rejected because Zubair was too well-known a scalp among the antislavery lobby in London. The next plan, Gordon had decided, was to pay loyal tribes along the river to form an armed escort for an evacuation. But when he sounded out this plan with a gathering of tribal leaders on his way upriver, it had backfired. Realising how weak his position was, they had all gone over to the Mahdi.

British troops had been sent to protect the Red Sea port at Suakin, but none were being allowed to make the trek across the desert to bolster Khartoum. Gordon argued hard by telegram that even one hundred redcoats would change the atmosphere in Khartoum, but that idea had been rejected by Gladstone: "What holes do I not put myself into!" he wrote to his sister: "I believe ambition put me here in this ruin."[66] The Mahdi's salaam to Gordon was followed by a set of dervish clothes and the offer to save his life by his converting to Islam. Gordon declined, but offered the Mahdi governorship of Kordofan, to which the Mahdi replied that all of the Sudan and Egypt would soon be in his hands.

Gordon privately reckoned the Mahdi had "a fair chance" of succeeding, but he was not done yet. The compassionate and military sides of his personality had always had one thing in common, namely, an uncanny ability to put himself in other people's shoes. He also knew the Mahdi would be having his own headaches and that if he was going to stay,

---

[66] Gordon, *Letters to His Sister*, p. 286.

his best strategy lay in making them worse. Ohrwalder describes the Mahdi's army as a vast array of spears, swords, shields, rifles, cavalry, camel-men, and captured artillery batteries, not to mention "camp-followers, baggage-trains, donkeys, herds of cattle and flocks of sheep".[67] Feeding, watering, and sustaining the fervour of what was an unpaid army would be a major concern, and they would eventually run out of ammunition for the captured artillery pieces. Dysentery would be an issue for as long as such a camp remained in one place. Such an army needed plunder, victories, and momentum to survive, so the longer Gordon could stall them, the worse it would get for the Mahdi, who was running out of garrisons to plunder.

In the governor's palace in Khartoum, Gordon was sleeping on a camp cot in his office. There was still telegram communication to Cairo, but it brought no good news. By day, he supervised the strengthening of the ramparts, the armour-plating of riverboats, checking stocks of food, dealing with a myriad of plots and disputes. Gordon did not speak Arabic and had always suspected during his previous sojourn here that he must have been "a Christian dog" in the eyes of most Sudanese. But testimonies by Arabs after the siege suggest some of the warmth toward him was genuine. One caught in Khartoum was a Sherif prince of Mecca, who wrote afterward: "The rich and the poor, the free and the slaves, were alike his children. He was one of those men to whom the verse of the Koran applies: 'The servants of the Merciful are those who walk meekly in the earth, and when the ignorant speak unto them answer Peace! And who pass the night adoring their Lord and standing up to pray unto Him.' Before I knew him I hated the Christians, but Gor-

[67] Asher, *Khartoum*, p. 165.

don has taught me to love them, and I can see more clearly each day that a religion which makes such heroic, faithful, and disinterested men can only be a religion coming from the true God."[68] Power was also observing Gordon closely: "One day of his work and bother would kill another man, yet he is so cheerful at breakfast, lunch and dinner; but I know he suffers fearfully from low spirits. I hear him walking up and down his room all night (it is next to mine). It is only his piety that carries him through."[69]

Gordon had given two books to Power on his arrival in Khartoum, a copy of *The Imitation of Christ* and *The Dream of Gerontius*, the latter of which Power had sent on to his sister in Dublin with Gordon's markings. It was a poem, written by the Catholic convert Saint John Henry Newman, in which the soul of a dying man appears before the throne of God, only to beg his guardian angel to remove him to a place where he can be made pure before spending eternity in such a Holy Presence: "Take me away, / That sooner I may rise, and go above, / And see Him in the truth of everlasting day."[70]

Like addressing Mary in prayer, belief in purgatory had been banned by the Protestant Reformation, the Book of Common Prayer describing it as "a fond thing vainly invented". Gordon had been sent the Newman poem after telling someone how disturbed he had been by watching his father die, a man of some but not great Christian faith. In his conversion to Catholicism, Newman had come to accept that purgatory was the belief of the early Church, and the twentieth-century apologist C. S. Lewis would also

[68] Pollock, *Gordon of Khartoum*, p. 410.

[69] Power, *Letters from Khartoum*, p. 99.

[70] Geoffrey Hodgkins, *The Best of Me: A Gerontius Centenary Companion* (Rickmansworth: Elgar Editions, 1999), p. 54.

accept purgatory ("Our souls demand purgatory, do they not?") with much the same logic as that with which Newman eventually conveyed the Catholic position:

> Most men, to our apprehensions, are too uninformed in religious habits either for heaven or for hell, yet there is no middle state when Christ comes in judgment. In consequence it was obvious to have recourse to the interval before His coming, as a time during which this incompleteness might be remedied; as a season, not of changing the spiritual bent and character of the soul departed, whatever that be, for probation ends with mortal life, but of developing it into a more determinate form, whether of good or of evil.[71]

In his Khartoum journals, which were turning into a unique combination of military logistics, rants, cartoon sketches, and theology, Gordon mused how pain in purgatory could change souls, since it did not always have that effect in the world. With regards to the innocent kindness he had met in some of the Sudanese soldiers now defending him, and the genuine godliness he had recognised in some Arabs, he might also have been more at peace with the line eventually taken by the Second Vatican Council on those who died having never been told of Christ, as opposed to the line taken by strict Protestantism. The former holds that though all salvation is worked through Christ, those "who, through no fault of their own, do not know the Gospel of Christ or his Church, but who nevertheless seek God with a sincere heart, and, moved by grace, try in their actions to do his will as they know it through the

[71] John Henry Newman, *An Essay on the Development of Christian Doctrine* (Harmondsworth: Penguin, 1973), p. 418.

dictates of their conscience—those too may achieve eternal salvation."[72]

In London, Gladstone was not changing his mind. If Gordon could not organise an evacuation, he told Baring, he should get out himself while the river was still clear. Power telegrammed an impassioned article to *The Times*, explaining why "it would be cowardly and shameful to leave Khartoum", but that only served to stiffen Gladstone's resolve not to be manipulated into sending troops, despite public demonstrations in Manchester and London. Power's passion spilled into a letter to his family, where he said that he considered the people of the Sudan to have been so cruelly treated by outsiders that "I will, indeed, forgive the fellow who puts a lance in me, if that is to be my fate."[73] As the vanguard of the Mahdi's camp began to appear behind the palm trees on the western banks, Gordon watched them from the roof of the palace through his Parisian telescope. To keep any sort of supply line going, his steamers would soon be having to run a gauntlet of whatever heavy guns they had, and before long he knew exactly, for the sound of artillery became such a constant in the months that followed that he could eventually tell from listening which gun was firing, from where, and in what direction. The bombardment, which went fifty-four days without ceasing at one point, was both ways, for Gordon not only had artillery of his own, but he had the means to produce 500,000 rifle rounds a month.

The nearby garrison at Sennar was meanwhile holding out under Egyptian officers and had telegram communication

---

[72] *Catechism of the Catholic Church* (London: Geoffrey Chapman, 1995), par. 847.

[73] Power, *Letters from Khartoum*, p. 90.

with Gordon, who knew that his honour would never allow him to abandon Khartoum while soldiers were bravely risking their lives under his command. Finally, the telegraph wire between Cairo and Khartoum was cut. Of all that would ensue, Sir Samuel Baker later wrote: "As soon as I heard Gordon was to go to the Sudan, I knew there would be a fight."[74]

Evelyn Baring, caught between the two most stubborn men of his age and now without a telegraph to Khartoum, thought that Gladstone's policy had turned into "a mere phantasm of the diplomatic and parliamentary mind" and that, as far as Gordon was concerned, the telegraph line had in some ways already become superfluous: "Since Gordon was not a man who paid any attention to instructions, it mattered very little what instructions he was given anyway."[75] As an officer (his resignation of his commission having been reversed), Gordon knew the significance of disobedience. In the journal he was keeping at Khartoum, he wrote: "I own to having been very insubordinate to Her Majesty's Government. . . . I know if *I* was chief I would never employ *myself*, for I am incorrigible."

Having decided to stay regardless of what orders reached him, he launched a series of aggressive sorties by gunboat on the Mahdi's positions, which were spread out along the river. These were successful and at times managed to land and capture cattle, while Gordon oversaw the laying of wires and improvised mines around the fort. Since he knew the enemy's artillery capacity, he had been able to calculate how much ammunition they probably had left from Hicks' arsenal, and to drain the heaviest of that mortar he began draw-

[74] Chenevix Trench, *Road to Khartoum*, p. 240.
[75] Asher, *Khartoum*, p. 98.

ing fire onto a hulk steamer he had floated at the edge of
their range. Although the headache of feeding the massive
civilian population prevented him from enjoying what was
going on, he came close at times ("I think I would like to
be in a real siege").[76] With spies, plots, and communication
running between both camps, he was often unsure whom
to trust. Two Turkish officers were hung, and the prison
kept full with food thieves, but morale somehow was holding, and when a new steamer was cobbled together from
old ones, the town elders told him they wanted to name it
after him, which he politely declined: "I have put most of
you in prison and otherwise bullied you, and I have no fear
of your forgetting me."[77]

They would not on either side. In one of the Sudanese
stories that would build up around the siege, a sniper in
the Mahdi's force claimed that every time he had Gordon
in his sights through his shutters in the palace, which he
never closed, he could not seem to get even close. He took
a *surtug* canoe out into the middle of the river one night
to get a better line: "When I got near to the Palace, I saw
the figure of an angel standing outside the window. When
I fired he caught the bullets and threw them back at me. I
heard them go 'plop!' 'plop!' just like that into the water,
not a yard away from my surtug."[78]

Back home, Gladstone was going berserk. A statesman
known for using words with the control of an Impressionist
painter, emotional but oblique, it was as if Gordon was going out of his way to unsettle him. The Gordon story was
now being reported on almost daily in France and Spain,
as well as Britain, and with so much silence from both

[76] Gordon, *Khartoum Journals*, 2:89.
[77] Ibid., 2:57.
[78] Pollock, *Gordon of Khartoum*, p. 416.

Gordon and Gladstone, reportage began to focus on the campaign to have a relief expedition sent to Khartoum. There were those in the cabinet who sympathized with Gordon. Messages were still being smuggled into Khartoum by highly paid couriers, and one from Gordon was leaked to the press. Gladstone happened to be at a country weekend when he saw Gordon's suggestion of sending gunboats to burn down the river station at Berber before it was captured: "his face hardened and whitened, his eyes burnt . . . with a deep fire as if they would have consumed the paper."[79]

Into this tension occurred what might have otherwise been a minor publishing event. One of Gordon's friends had edited a collection of Gordon's letters from the Holy Land, under the title *Reflections in Palestine*. In Whitehall, people read it with disbelief, Lord Northbrook, former Viceroy of India, declaring it "the book of a madman". Queen Victoria's private secretary, Sir Henry Ponsonby, wrote to Gladstone's secretary: "I don't believe the Christian lunatic has the slightest intention of coming back again."[80] The book revealed what Gordon's friends knew, that his faith was intense and formed the basis of his deepest outlook: "I think our life is one progressive series of finding out Satan. As we grow in grace, we are constantly finding out that he is a traitor; he is continually being unmasked";[81] "I have a strong belief that our mental and other struggles here are the roots of larger forms of movement . . . in other worlds";[82] "The more you are persecuted by your enemies, by your flesh,

[79] Chenevix Trench, *Road to Khartoum*, p. 260.

[80] Pollock, *Gordon of Khartoum*, p. 408.

[81] Gordon, Charles George, *Reflections in Palestine*) (London: Macmillan, 1884), p. 85.

[82] Ibid., p. 108.

the more share you take of the sum total of the Church's suffering."[83]

There was another letter from Palestine, not in the book, in which he had written: "I would give my life for these poor people of the Sudan. How can I help feeling for them? All the time I was there, every night I used to pray that God would lay upon me the burden of their sins and crush me with it instead of those poor sheep. I really wished and longed for it."[84] When Queen Victoria added her voice to the Press' clamouring for a relief expedition, Gladstone finally broke. In September 1884, eight months after Gordon's arrival in Khartoum, news of an incoming expedition reached the town. Gordon immediately sent Stewart and Power downstream to meet the expedition and for Power to get news to the outside world of what was happening. He gave him letters for everyone he could think of, from the pope to the Sultan of Turkey.

Frank Power was Catholic, and in a letter to his family said that Gordon had requested his name be added to Frank's when Masses were being said in Ireland for him: "He is quite Catholic and believes in the real presence in our Holy Communion." It is not completely clear whether in the word "our" Power was talking about Gordon's appreciation of transubstantiation or the bread and wine that Gordon was himself now praying over, which we know from one of his letters he was doing in Khartoum.[85] Power would not be able to clarify, for he was soon dead. It was the Mahdi who informed Gordon by messenger that both Stewart and Power had been slain on the river, and all their letters taken: "We

[83] Ibid., p. 111.
[84] Nutting, *Gordon*, p. 280.
[85] Pollock, *Gordon of Khartoum*, p. 392.

never miss any of your news, nor what is in your innermost thoughts."[86] He urged Gordon to convert and join him, or face inevitable death: "You must surely die." Gordon was in no mood to parley and replied: "It is impossible for me to have any more words with Mohammed Ahmed, only lead." This came with news of a thousand of his best African soldiers being cut down after their officers had grown over-confident in clearing an enemy stronghold between Khartoum and the Blue Nile. Strategically and emotionally eviscerated, he could do little to rally those left, with rations down to two dates a day.

Still the kettle drums played: "Whenever I hear them I feel viciously inclined."[87] The troops left under his command, here and at Sennar, were a mixture of Egyptians (Muslims and Copts), Sudanese Africans, and the "Bashi-Bazouks". Gordon valued the Sudanese Africans most ("if one sticks to them, they will stick to you") and now deployed them to use up the town's supply of rifle rounds to rain continual fire on the enemy. Even now, he did not miss England. "I dwell on the joy of never seeing Great Britain again, with its horrid, wearisome *dinner* parties and miseries. How we can put up with those things passes my imagination! It is perfect bondage. At those dinner parties we are all in masks, saying what we do not believe, eating and drinking things we do not want, and then abusing one another. I would sooner live like a Dervish with the Mahdi."[88]

Hunger was now so bad that soldiers on the ramparts were being thrown on their backs by the recoil of their rifles. Morale had slumped in both camps to the extent that

[86] Gordon, *Khartoum Journals*, 2:236.

[87] Charles George Gordon, *The Journals of Major-Gen. C. G. Gordon, C.B., At Khartoum*, vol. 1, ed. Hake (Leipzig: Bernhard Tauchnitz, 1885), p. 303.

[88] Ibid., p. 268.

defectors were moving in each direction. Some coming in from the rebels brought the news that the Mahdi was going mad and that he had now started drinking alcohol and taking other men's wives. Ohrwalder would later confirm this. Gordon recorded sourly in his journal: "I had hitherto hoped I had to do with a regular fanatic."[89] But he was getting desperate, too, trying to keep the town's morale up by leaking false messages confirming the approach of the British expedition. He was now completely reliant on them arriving, but still adamant that if they came with orders to take him only: "I WILL NOT OBEY IT, BUT WILL STAY HERE, AND FALL WITH THE TOWN."[90]

Gordon's hair had turned white. He did not fear death, he told the journal: "I fear defeat."[91] The first indication that the expedition was actually approaching was when half the Mahdi's force disappeared north to go and fight them. Gordon had been at Khartoum for a year, and now the river was at its lowest, leaving their defences at their most vulnerable.

When wailing started in the enemy camp, he knew the British had prevailed but had no idea how far off they were, and now every minute felt torturous. Men were passing out on the ramparts, and it was impossible to block all the weak points in the defence being exposed by the drop in the river. They were now exposed and could hear the Mahdi's army baying for revenge. Gordon ordered the commander at Sennar to surrender rather than be massacred. Obdurman, the outlying twin fort at Khartoum, then fell to an attack. And that night they came.

[89] Ibid., p. 90.
[90] Ibid., 2:34.
[91] Ibid., 1:79.

Ohrwalder said the Mahdi had given orders for Gordon to be brought to him alive. Forty years later, an Englishman named Henderson working for the Sudan Political Service was talking to some villagers about Rudolph Slatin, a garrison governor who had converted to Islam to save himself during the siege. They were sitting on the banks of the Blue Nile, and the subject turned to Gordon. "I saw him die", said an old man. He went on to describe the breakthrough on the riverbank, the slaughter of "the Copts", and the final arrival at the palace, where they found Gordon standing unarmed at the top of the steps. "We looked at him and he looked at us. Then he tore open his tunic and said 'Strike! Strike hard!' and somebody flung a spear, and it was over." Henderson added: "There was a brief pause and he, or it may have been another, added the words '*Kan shadeed fi deenu*. He was strong in his Faith'."[92]

Father Ohrwalder, who remained in captivity for another seven years, said that for a long time afterward, you could see the blood on the steps. Gordon's head was on a stake, but his ability to affect affairs continued. For as complex, crazed, and as tortured as he could be in real life, in death the simplicity of his soul shone. The boats carrying the British recce arrived two days later and turned around when it saw the Mahdi's black banners flying from the palace roof. Uproar followed when the news reached England. The queen was staying at her house on the Isle of Wight when she was told and marched across the grounds to rouse Sir Henry Ponsonby, screaming "Too late!" when he appeared. Gladstone felt the fury of the public's reaction and resigned after a vote of no confidence.

The long siege had broken the resolve of "the Mahdi"

---

[92] Pollock, *Gordon of Khartoum*, p. 425.

to carry on, and he never left Khartoum, barely leaving his harem while there, and died from "debauchery and disease" a few months later. His successor, Abdullah ("the Khalifa"), fought not only the Mahdi's family, but tribes who left Khartoum to return to their homes. Ohrwalder said that in some districts half the population died, in others the loss of life was even greater. Whole tribes were completely blotted out. A 1947 report estimated that the population of Sudan fell from eight million to two million over the next twelve years.[93] An invasion of Egypt failed; an attack on Abyssinia succeeded, but meanwhile harvests had gone uncollected and a locust plague devoured the country. Villages became so bereft of men, said Ohrwalder, that animals were entering huts and seizing women and children. After ten years in captivity, Ohrwalder eventually made his escape to Egypt.

The Khalifa's end came when a British force, with a young Winston Churchill, defeated him and blew up the Mahdi's mausoleum in belated revenge for Gordon's death. As Gladstone had predicted, Britain was then obliged to stay, administering the country as the lead role in an Anglo-Egyptian protectorate for the next sixty years: "On the whole it was the most successful and altruistic of Britain's colonial ventures, from which Britain gained very little and the Sudanese people a great deal."[94] With its reputation as a tough posting, Sudan attracted the crème de la crème of their generation, as Daoud Abd-Latif, one of post-independent Sudan's leading lights once recalled. Born in 1914, he had "developed a loathing for the British" that softened as he interacted with them for work: "Over time he grew to admire the tenacity

[93] Harley Usill, "Britain's Achievement in the Sudan", *World Affairs* 110, no. 4 (1947): 290–92.
[94] Chenevix Trench, *Road to Khartoum*, p. 294.

and dedication of the District Officers, living alone in remote parts of the country for months on end: '[They] had
a tremendous sense of mission, most of them, a real sense
of mission, and were very idealistic. [They] lived amongst a
people who respected them, and many times, loved them—
and whom they loved.'"[95] This was not "Rule Britannia"
at its worst, and while arrogance, racism, and self-interest
may never have been absent from the British Empire, when
Sudan received independence in 1956, the first president, a
Muslim, thanked the British in his inaugural speech. Schools,
hospitals, roads, a dam remained, as did a Church with staying power, and while the future would prove nightmarish
for many Sudanese, it would never be as nightmarish as Sudan's past.

   The letters from Khartoum indicate that Gordon was sent
a copy of Newman's poem, read it on the journey between
Cairo and Khartoum, and then gave it on his arrival (together
with a copy of *The Imitation of Christ*) to Frank Power. When
Power's sister sent her copy to Newman, the idea grew that
Gordon had been reading and marking the poem, in which a
soul is taken by its guardian angel before God's throne, right
to the end. Copies of Gordon's markings were reverently
made, and, four years after the fall of Khartoum, an English
priest named Fr. Thomas Knight gave a copy of the poem
as a wedding present to a young Catholic composer named
Edward Elgar, who recalled that Fr. Knight had "copied into
its pages every mark inserted by General Gordon in his [Gor-
don's] copy, so that I have the advantage of knowing those
portions of the poem which specially attracted the attention
of the great hero."[96]

[95] Jamal Mahjoub, *A Line in the River* (London: Bloomsbury, 2019), p. 349.
[96] Hodgkins, *The Best of Me*, p. 3.

Inspired by the combination of Newman's poem and its link to the heroic gesture of Gordon in Khartoum, Elgar immediately considered setting the poem to music, but was put off because he feared the poem's explicitly Catholic themes would be unpalatable for the cultural market. Over the years that followed, he instead worked on more ephemeral pieces, which brought him acclaim but not the commercial breakthrough he yearned for, and he was still having to work as a music teacher and organist to make ends meet. Meanwhile, the power of the *Gerontius* project was "soaking in my mind for at least eight years".

When he was offered a premiere slot at Birmingham's prestigious music festival in 1900, he knew he had to throw caution to the wind and produce something that established his name forever. He went back to Fr. Knight's wedding present and resolved to put "my own heart's blood" into it. Writing from a beautiful cottage in the Malvern Hills, as soon as he had finished he knew he had channelled something of extraordinary grace, writing at the bottom of the score: "This is the best of me; for the rest, I ate, and drank, and slept, loved, and hated, like another: my life was as the vapour, and is not; but this I saw and knew: this, if anything of mine, is worth your memory."[97] He dedicated *The Dream of Gerontius* "To the Greater Glory of God".

Composed for orchestra, choir (with as many as 490 singers appearing in early performances), a semi-chorus (an elite choir within a choir), and soloists, the score at one point contains an eight-part chorus; at another, the stringed instruments are following, playing twenty different parts. Victorians were used to epic productions, but it was the "spontaneous and unembarrassed" sincerity of the piece that would

[97] Elgar quoted these lines from *Sesame and Lilies* (1865) by John Ruskin.

astonish people. It was such a new sound, a combination of
vast scale and soulful intimacy, that the first performance in
Birmingham collapsed under the pressure, and it was only
the following year, after a performance in Germany, that
it began to grow in reputation. Incorporating as it did the
Catholic funeral liturgy, it drew the audience into the role
of a Catholic congregation. In one review, entitled "I Go
to Mass", a critic wrote: "I am not of the way of thinking which sends people to Mass, and I am a heretic on the
points of belief which find expression herein, [but] the intensity of feeling, united with a sort of mystical exaltation
which I still feel . . . had its way with me. . . . There was
no hope for me; there could be no going back to earth . . .
the Angel's song completed my conversion."[98] At an early
performance in Chicago, people were said to watch "as in
a trance". It was "a new language", one critic said. After a
performance in New York in 1903, someone wrote to Elgar
saying the first half had ended with tumultuous applause,
while at the finish "thousands filed out almost in silence."
In Germany, where England had previously been known as
"the land with no music", a critic called it "imperishably
beautiful".[99] It is "dangerous" music, wrote a British critic:
"music of the type that makes converts".

For Elgar, however, the failure of the first evening in Birmingham had been such an agony that he had written straight
afterward to his publisher: "I always said God was against
art and I still believe it. . . . I have allowed my heart to open
once—it is now shut against every religious feeling & every
soft, gentle impulse for ever."[100] He was true to his word,
and, as the work grew in influence, he felt increasingly de-

[98] Hodgkins, *The Best of Me*, p. 250.
[99] Ibid., p. 194.
[100] Ibid., p. 7.

tached from the spirit that had inspired it. During a performance in Norwich in 1908, he was seen weeping in the audience. He was drifting into an elite London world of fin de siècle cynicism and the occult and, on his deathbed in 1934, uttered five words to a friend that the latter said were "too tragic" to repeat.[101]

The music now had a life of its own, performed in 1903 at the opening of Westminster Cathedral, the first Catholic cathedral in London since the Reformation. King Edward VII was keen to attend but was warned it would be controversial. At early performances in Anglican cathedrals, the opening words (which address Mary) were changed, but later the change was dropped. After World War II, when the British council was looking for something to symbolise national rebuilding, they funded a large-scale recording of *The Dream of Gerontius* with the Huddersfield Choral Society that is still listened to. When the Beirut diplomatic hostage Terry Waite was given a radio after four and a half years of solitary confinement, he later said that the very first thing he picked up on BBC World Service was "that lovely melody" from the beginning of Elgar's *Gerontius*, coming live from the First Night of the Proms. After his release, when he told his doctor how much the experience had meant to him, the latter said that his daughter had been singing in the chorus at the Royal Albert Hall that night, and he had been there.

In a 2013 BBC programme about the abiding power of Elgar's *Gerontius*, one member of the public said that when his son had been dying of Hodgkin's disease "he asked me what happened after death. I couldn't tell him." He said that a year after his son's death, he went to see a performance of *Gerontius*: "That was the first time I was able to grieve. [It]

[101] Ibid., p. 1.

enhances my faith . . . the music I believe was composed for and with the help of God."[102]

Cynicism would eventually strike back at Gordon's own legacy. Plenty of people had laughed at him throughout his life or doubted his reliability, which was why his return to Khartoum was the first time he had been entrusted with independent command as a general, albeit with a commissioned staff of just one. The most severe posthumous attack came in 1917 from a man who represented a new flourishing of liberal atheism within British culture. Exactly what "liberal" meant or means is hard to understand. Byron had once started a magazine called *The Liberal*. Others used it as both a compliment and a criticism, and it had both political and religious connotations. For Newman, it was "an error overspreading, as a snare, the whole earth. . . . [It] is the doctrine that there is no positive truth in religion, but that one creed is as good as another. . . . It is inconsistent with any recognition of any religion as *true*. . . . There never was a device of the Enemy so cleverly framed and with such promise of success. . . ." But, as he said earlier, " I think it threatens to have a formidable success; though it is not easy to see what will be its ultimate issue."[103]

---

[102] *Soul Music*, BBC Radio 4, 30 July 2013. In the programme, the writer and broadcaster Stephen Johnson said he had once asked a Jesuit why Catholic liturgy for the dead was "so strangely appealing" and that the priest had replied that it was "the idea you can do something for the dead". Another writer, reviewing a performance of *Gerontius* by the London Philharmonic Orchestra in 2011 in *The Guardian*, wrote: "It is hard to explain why *The Dream of Gerontius* manages to have such a powerful effect on someone who rejects every particle of the religious impulses that nourish it." Andrew Clements, *The Guardian*, 28 March 2011.

[103] From Newman's "*Biglietto* Speech", given in Rome on the occasion of being raised to cardinal, on 12 May 1879, and appearing in full in *The Times* the following day.

At Cambridge University in 1903, Lytton Strachey was elected to a semi-secret society called the "Cambridge Conversazione Society", otherwise known as "the Apostles". They would meet on Sunday mornings and perform mock-religious services. "Masses" were held with sardines, and the society's records were kept in a wardrobe known as "the Ark". These included talks given, such as one given by Strachey called "Christ or Caliban?", in which, according to his biographer Michael Holroyd: "Caliban represented freedom from restraint, and Christ the repression of the nineteenth century."[104] There was a taste for sexual rebellion within the Apostles that Strachey particularly relished. He was "obsessed with sodomy", says Holroyd; his correspondence containing "frequent references to buggery and rape" and sufficiently outré to describe one child he met as "most inviting".[105] Although he married (his wife later committed suicide), he considered overcoming all sexual restraint to be his personal mission. His friend Virginia Woolf (who also committed suicide) recalled him once walking into a drawing room where she was talking with her sister. Pointing to a stain on her sister's dress, Strachey asked: "Semen?" In her memoir, *Moments of Being*, Woolf said it was a watershed moment that affected their whole group of friends: "With that one word all barriers of reticence and reserve went down."

Philosophical credibility for this approach to life was provided by G. E. Moore, another member of the Apostles, as well as a professor of Moral Philosophy and Logic at Cambridge. His 1903 book *Principia Ethica* urged a postreligious freedom where friendship and beauty were all that mattered:

---

[104] Michael Holroyd, *Lytton Strachey* (London: Vintage, 1995), p. 79.
[105] Ibid., pp. 105, 85.

"By far the most valuable things, which we can know or imagine, are certain states of consciousness which may be roughly described as the pleasures of human intercourse and the enjoyment of beautiful objects."[106] Strachey wrote to congratulate him: "your book has . . . shattered all writers on ethics from Aristotle and Christ to Herbert Spencer."[107]

As a manifesto for sexual revolution, *Principia* is a surprisingly dull and contorted read, and even Moore would later distance himself from its "qualifying qualifications". Beatrice Webb, a contemporary of them both, considered the Apostles "a pernicious set" and *Principia Ethica* "metaphysical justification for doing what you like".[108] But even if one ascribes Strachey's over-enthusiasm for the book to his impatience at the establishment's hypocritical moral torpor (a diagnosis Gordon would have agreed with), there is a wilful tone of blasphemy in another letter he wrote at this time:

> We can't be content with telling truths—we must tell the whole truth; and the whole truth is the Devil. Voltaire abolished Christianity by believing in god. It's madness of us to dream of making dowagers understand that feelings are good, when we say in the same breath that the best ones are sodomitical. If we were crafty and careful, I dare say we'd pull it off. But why should we take the trouble?

[106] G. E. Moore, *Principia Ethica* (New York: SophiaOmni Press, 2017), p. 159.
[107] Holroyd, *Lytton Strachey*, p. 89.
[108] Ibid., p. 92. Aldous Huxley, social and artistic acquaintance of the Stracheys, wrote in his 1937 book *Ends and Means*: "I had motives for not wanting the world to have a meaning; consequently assumed that it had none, and was able without any difficulty to find satisfying reasons for this assumption. . . . The philosopher who finds no meaning in the world . . . is also concerned to prove that there is no valid reason why he personally should not do as he wants to do . . . the philosophy of meaninglessness was essentially an instrument of liberation, sexually and politically."

On the whole I believe that our time will come about a
hundred years hence, when preparations have been made,
and compromises come to, so that, at the publication of
our letters, everyone will be, finally, converted.[109]

Strachey's correspondence may not be widely read today, but the spirit in which it was written is certainly commonplace. When the Prime Minister of Spain Luis Zapa-
tero was passing a set of laws on sex, reproduction, and
families precisely a century later, he replied to opposition
from the Catholic Church with a mischievous inversion of
Scripture that Strachey might have devised himself: "It is
freedom that makes us true. Not the truth that makes us
free."[110] This was Strachey's modernism, and in the attrac-
tiveness of Charles Gordon he detected a vestigial pull in the
British heart toward a more traditional and chivalric code.
Like Gordon, Strachey was the son of a general, but he was
no knight, and when World War I broke out, and he was
deemed physically too weak to be conscripted, he blamed
the war's continued popularity on a male ideal of the honourable soldier that had been perpetuated by the Victorians.
In March 1917, he embarked on a project to puncture the
reputation for saintliness that surrounded Charles Gordon,
joking to a correspondent: "I really must set to and seriously attack the General." And also: "I'm afraid it would
be fatal to leave my stool until I've captured his first line of
trenches."[111]

"The End of General Gordon" was the last in a quartet of

---

[109] Ibid., p. 92.
[110] Gabriele Kuby, *The Global Sexual Revolution: Destruction of Freedom in the
Name of Freedom*, trans. Kirchner (Kettering: Angelico Press, 2015), p. 259.
The reference is to Jesus' words in John's Gospel, 8:32: "The truth will make
you free."
[111] Holroyd, *Lytton Strachey*, pp. 676, 381.

essays by Strachey published as *Eminent Victorians* in 1918, the sarcasm of the title sustained throughout the book, as was caricature, cynicism, and innuendo. It outsold anything else Strachey ever wrote, resonating with a jaded postwar audience and presenting Gordon as religiously mad, sexually repressed, probably alcoholic, and a stooge of militarism. Its success in ending further idolatry of General Gordon belied the fact that it was a well-written lampoon (and would always be taken as such by historians), invented scenes, flattened Gordon's personality, and could never approach the matter of his celibacy without smirking. As a student of Sigmund Freud and a child of Bohemia, that Christian virtue was prudery or a lie, and in either case anathema.

During Gordon's first period in the Sudan, Baring's assistant in Cairo, Rivers Wilson, had once found himself travelling with Fr. Daniele Comboni, who ran the Roman Catholic missions in Central Africa. Comboni knew Gordon well, the latter having helped him transport Catholic missionaries, and Wilson asked him what he thought the secret of Gordon's influence was in Khartoum. Comboni shocked him by immediately replying: "His chastity".[112] According to Comboni's Catholic understanding of chastity, it was "a fruit of the Holy Spirit", a term broader than celibacy, in that one does not have to be celibate to be chaste. A chaste person is one not enslaved by sexual desire, capable of exercising such restraint within a faithful and sexually active marriage. Of its opposite, promiscuity, Pope Francis

---

[112] Pollock, *Gordon of Khartoum*, p. 216. Gordon had helped Comboni get Catholic missionaries onto the shores of Lake Victoria, including paying for their transport and stopping Protestant missions applying to start up at the same locations. Comboni was personally impressed with him: "This man who meditates on the Bible three hours a day, lives without a woman, like a perfect monk, and prays a lot."

has written: "a person who cannot choose to love for ever can hardly love for even a single day."[113] Or, as Elizabeth Anscombe, the Catholic convert, Cambridge philosopher, and mother of seven memorably insisted: "There is no such thing as a casual, non-significant sexual act; everyone knows this."[114]

Celibacy demands even greater levels of self-control, but those whose faith allows them to attain to it are encouraged to do so by the New Testament: "There are eunuchs who have been so from birth, and there are eunuchs who have been made eunuchs by men, and there are eunuchs who have made themselves eunuchs for the sake of the kingdom of heaven. He who is able to receive this, let him receive it."[115] Christ, who says these words in Matthew's Gospel, was celibate, and the apostle Paul echoed the ideal: "The unmarried man is anxious about the affairs of the Lord, how to please the Lord; but the married man is anxious about wordly affairs, how to please his wife, and his interests are divided. And the unmarried woman. . . ."[116] Though neither Christ nor Paul therefore insisted on celibacy, both lived it as an ideal, and Gordon believed he could follow them, writing once: "Certainly celibacy is a great boon; I feel my presence is not necessary."[117] As a young man, I was as careless as many of my generation in this regard, and none the happier for it. For many years now, I have been celibate and have experienced a clarity of thought I did not think

[113] Pope Francis, Post-Synodal Apostolic Exhortation on Love in the Family *Amoris Laetitia* (19 March 2016), par. 319, quoting Pope John Paul II, apostolic exhortation *Familiaris Consortio* (22 November 1981), par. 11.

[114] Elizabeth Anscombe, *Contraception and Chastity* (London: Catholic Truth Society, 2003).

[115] Matthew 19:12.

[116] 1 Corinthians 7:32–34.

[117] Gordon, *Letters to His Sister*, p. 78.

possible. There are moments of loneliness, but never enough to make me think I cannot prayerfully bear this state. And it is a state, not just the absence of something; what Saint Thérèse of Lisieux calls "a profound silence". From this perspective, Gordon's celibacy appears to me both plausible and commendable.

Of late, Gordon has become a forgotten figure, not well known enough even for satire. In 2005, the writer Mark Urban published a collection of essays on famous British generals. Of Gordon's legacy, he concluded: "Gordon is significant because he represented a perversion of the democratic process." Gordon exploited the media, he continues, and made direct appeals to public opinion: "Soldiers would have to learn those skills, but they would also have to be taught to exercise them in support of the government's aims, not against them."[118] Urban's principle, that democracy is the standard by which to measure an individual's actions, would be qualified by the African Robert Cardinal Sarah, who has argued that former colonial powers adopted democracy and liberty as "goddesses" in the post-independence era, justifying further influence and the insatiable appetite of "King Money".[119] As an African Christian, he views the contemporary promulgation of faith-neutral "global ethics" (and the dissemination of the same as a condition for investment in poorer countries) as a continuation of this strategy, concealing something bigger than greed, something looking to replace the world's faiths and traditions with a dangerously insubstantial set of values, something that sounds like Christ but is not Christ (which, in New Testament Greek, is the

[118] Mark Urban, *Generals* (London: Faber and Faber, 2005), p. 181.
[119] Robert Cardinal Sarah with Nicolas Diat, *The Power of Silence: Against the Dictatorship of Noise*, trans. Michael J. Miller (San Francisco: Ignatius Press, 2017), pp. 157, 171.

meaning of "anti-Christ"). Against such a reading of the times, one anticipated by Newman, democracy *per se* becomes too contingent, and in fact too neutral, to offer a guiding principle or guaranteed ally.

Ethical posturing for purposes of power was already a feature of Victorian democracy, producing such a fog of intentions regarding the Sudan that, even for a loyal servant like Baring, understanding his own government's wishes became almost impossible, as was resisting a suspicion that had occurred long ago to Gordon: that at the centre of the British Empire's administration lay a spinning moral compass. For all his contribution to the confusion of policy in Khartoum, Gordon was not so expedient and refused to leave the city simply because he thought it would be the wrong thing to do. Whatever his reasons for coming to this conclusion, his journal makes it clear that he knew as well as anyone what it meant in terms of military doctrine: "we do not like to be what club men call insubordinate, though, of all insubordinates, the club men are the worst."[120] Both admirers and detractors have argued that by this point Gordon was no longer playing to a human audience. In one of his last letters to his sister, he wrote: "He will not dwell in a proud heart, which I have in excess. [If I get humbled,] you will not mind the humbling for me."[121] In the face of his death, and widespread admiration for his decision, William Gladstone (in what amounted to a reelection campaign) described Gordon as "a hero of heroes" in Parliament. His personal thoughts on the matter remained far more bitter, but a bronze statue erected to the soldier in Trafalgar Square symbolised the official exoneration.

[120] *Khartoum Journals*, 1:208.
[121] Gordon, *Letters to His Sister*, p. 295.

Time would prove less forgiving, or interested, and, after such prominent statues were removed to protect them from air-raids during World War II, Gordon's was quietly relegated to a spot on the Embankment, where it remains. Charlton Heston played General Gordon in the 1966 movie *Khartoum* (Omar Sharif played the Mahdi), and biographies of him have appeared from time to time, correcting Strachey's use of sources, but—with one noteworthy exception—not offering much sense in return of the human being who was Charlie Gordon.[122] Today, his story (once extraordinary even to his enemies) is too seldom mentioned even to draw much satire or scrutiny. To current academic methodologies, as for his Victorian bosses, Gordon presents too many anomalies to be useful, and it is quiet rather than controversy that reigns around that statue. His strangeness thus has at least remained unthwarted, and no part of the Church claims responsibility for his legacy; he might well be delighted with all this, but I still cherish his memory and am glad to have told his story.

More celebrated, and canonised by the Catholic Church, is a Sudanese woman who escaped from Khartoum a few weeks before it fell to the Mahdi. A former slave, she was named Bakhita, "lucky" or "blessed" in Swahili, the name given to her by an owner. Another (she had five owners in all) left her with 114 tattoos. She eventually ended up with an owner in Khartoum, where the acting Italian Consul, Calisto Legnani, freed her (by buying her) and gave her paid employment. Hoping in the success of Gordon's resistance, in order to save what he could of his considerable business interests in the country, Legnani had stayed in Khartoum

---

[122] The exception was John Pollock's 1993 biography *Gordon: The Man behind the Legend* (Constable), reissued in 2005 under the title *Gordon of Khartoum: An Extraordinary Soldier*.

long after others like him had fled. When he finally decided
to bribe his way through the thinner, eastern line of the
siege, Bakhita begged to be taken with him. She remembered their caravan receiving news of Khartoum's fall as it
reached the Red Sea.

Accompanying Legnani on to Italy, she began working
for friends of his as a nanny. When they left her and her
young charge in the care of a Venetian convent, while they
went away on a trip, Bakhita fell in love with the Catholic faith and, on the family's return, asked to be released to
become a nun. The child's mother refused and had to be
reminded by a Church lawyer that Bakhita was no longer a
slave. Once baptised ("the sadness was gone, and she seemed
completely transfigured"), she entered a convent in Schio,
between Lake Garda and the Dolomite mountains, where
she lived for fifty years as Sorella Giuseppina Bakhita.

A great novelty to the people there, the townsfolk at
first called her the "Little Brown Mother" or "Little Black
Mother" and in time grew fond of her. Her duties included
serving meals to the schoolchildren ("as soon as the children saw her they would cling to her habit and not let her
go"), and during the First World War she helped nurse injured Italian troops, several of whom kept in touch with
her for the rest of their lives. Eventually they became proud
of her in Schio, and, once she had mastered the Veneto
dialect, she was sent around the region to speak on behalf
of the African missions. Trams were said to stop when she
was in a town, and, while many may have come out of curiosity, all were said to have left agreeing about her "calmness, peace, and humility". Her admirers included the future
Pope Pius X, a Veneto Catholic from a peasant background
almost as humble as her own, and he asked to meet with
her. As pope, he would write a stirring encyclical, *Pascendi*

Dominici Gregis, in which he called for Catholics to be resolute amid the philosophies of modernism ("the synthesis
of all heresies") and to hold to the "divine deposit" of
Christian revelation, "faithfully guarded and infallibly interpreted" by the Church.[123]

When Bakhita fell ill in 1947, one nun asked her why
God was sending her yet more suffering. Bakhita replied:
"If he does not come to us with a little suffering, to whom
is he supposed to go?" After she died, tremendous crowds
queued in Schio to pay their respects, while "her body remained incredibly soft and warm."[124] One of the first to see
her had been a man up early and desperately trying to find
a job: "He entered, removed his hat, and began to speak
almost out loud, begging Bakhita to help him find work
because he had nowhere else to turn." He put his hat back
on and was given a job later that day at Rossi's, the local
wool mill. As the nuns were about to place the body into
its coffin for the funeral, they had a phone call from Rossi's.
All the workers now wanted to come and pay their respects,
and in they came, genuflecting before the corpse of the nun
they now just called "Mother".

Miracles attributed to the heavenly intercession of Bakhita
started to take place after her death, hundreds in Italy alone,
and the Vatican began a canonical investigation of the evidence. In 1993, John Paul II carried Bakhita's bones back
to the Sudan and celebrated Mass in Khartoum, attended by
300,000 Christians from all denominations, "setting their
hearts ablaze" and bringing attention to their plight. They
needed it, for they were enduring state-sponsored Islamic

[123] Pius X, encyclical letter *Pascendi Dominici Gregis* (8 September 1907), pars.
39, 28.
[124] Roberto Italo Zanini, *Bakhita: From Slave to Saint*, trans. Andrew Matt
(San Francisco: Ignatius Press, 2013), p. 123.

extremism, the Catholic bishop of El Obeid later reporting systematic rape, aerial bombing, minefields, and even the reemergence of the slave trade. He closed his letter, written in 1999, by asking Sudan's first saint, Josephine Bakhita for her prayers: "May she obtain for the Church and for Sudan the gift of justice and peace."[125]

When she was formally canonised, at a Mass in Rome the following year, an Italian journalist visited the Sudan: "Going to Mass in Jabarona or in any of the Catholic chapels scattered throughout Sudan is an unforgettable experience. It is so different from most of our Western Sunday Masses that it can barely be described or understood without seeing it for oneself. Every gesture, every word is imbued with a palpable sense that the faith and trust and courage to meet the challenges of the day, and maybe even those of tomorrow, are gifts that we receive as God's children."[126]

He reported a song about Saint Bakhita being sung in the churches, the last verse of which reads:

> When I come before the tenderness of God,
> I'm certain that I won't be turned away
> because God is so rich in mercy,
> And that's why, slowly, slowly,
> I'll turn to Saint Peter and say:
> You can close the gate—I'm here to stay.[127]

Praise God for that. I cannot but believe that on the great and glorious day when the Lord appears with all his saints, history will declare it was the world that was mad, and not Charlie Gordon.

[125] Ibid., pp. 206–7.
[126] Ibid., p. 211.
[127] Ibid., p. 212.

POSTSCRIPT

The Logical Catholic

In his book *The 21*, Martin Mosebach attempts to understand, from the viewpoint of secularised Europe, how it was possible that twenty-one migrant construction workers (twenty of them Coptic Christians from Egypt; the other a Ghanaian they had befriended) were able to face execution so calmly on a beach in Libya in 2015. He knew the demeanour with which they had died because, like many others, he had watched a recording of their execution, filmed by their jihadist killers. Meant to induce terror, it so impressed Mosebach that he travelled to Egypt to explore a rural, Coptic world in which martyrdom, miracles and unchanged liturgy had been normal life for 1,500 years.

Mosebach defines the Copts as *"homines liturgi"*, people steeped in the rhythms of ancient Christian liturgy; "which in the Western world is now a very rare mode of being human".[1] Even without priests, they had kept up their daily cycle of chants, prayers, and hymns in Libya. Mosebach compares European cathedrals to dinosaur bones left behind by Europe's own *homines liturgi*, now on the verge of complete extinction: "without the associated rite, it is hard to see how such a place of worship could have been [the] kind

[1] Martin Mosebach, *The 21*, trans. Alta L. Price (Walden, N.Y.: Plough, 2019), p. 152. One of the 21 was in fact a West African Christian, but had lived and prayed with his Egyptian companions for months. The Coptic Church has since recognised him as a Coptic martyr.

of 'awe-inspiring place' one gets a glimpse of reading Exodus."[2] He ends his travels back in modern Cairo, wondering whether this extraordinary Christian community, which has survived so much, will survive an age of shopping malls. The Church in Europe knows how serious a question that is, even if, by Mosebach's reasoning, she still possesses the liturgy with which to answer.

Even allowing for their disproportionate heritage and reach, the ability of Catholicism and Orthodoxy to serve as rallying points for resistance under Soviet atheism was of a different order to Protestantism, which was all but wiped out in countries like Poland. In *The Insanity of God*, Nik Ripken (a Protestant missionary trying to make sense of the extreme persecution of the Church) tells of traveling to post-Soviet Russia and being introduced to a Christian who had served seventeen years in prison for refusing to recant his faith. Each morning, the man told Ripken, he would face eastward as was his tradition and sing the same hymn, and every morning the other inmates would hurl abuse at him. One day, having been in repeated trouble for writing verses of Scripture on his wall, he was dragged from his cell by guards to be executed. As they dragged him out, "fifteen hundred hardened criminals stood at attention by their beds. They faced the east and they began to sing. Dimitri told me that it sounded to him like the greatest choir in all human history. Fifteen hundred criminals raised their arms and began to sing [the same hymn] that they had heard Dimitri sing to Jesus every morning for all those years."[3]

The oldest Churches can seem (and in fact are) antiquated, but tradition also gives rooting that reveals its strength un-

[2] Ibid., p. 152.
[3] Nik Ripken with Gregg Lewis, *The Insanity of God* (Nashville: B&H Publishing, 2013), p. 158.

der pressure. It was no coincidence that Hans and Sophie Scholl were drawn to Catholicism under the Nazis, since, by 1944, the witness of much of German Protestantism had been hollowed out. Many churches had joined a State-approved "Positive Church", dutifully omitting Old Testament readings, displaying swastikas inside, and even preaching Hitler's racial theories from their pulpits. The hierarchical nature of the Roman Catholic Church, so easily disparaged in our day, had prevented any such formal association with this puppet church. There were compromises at a diplomatic level, and individual Catholics proud to serve in the Gestapo, but, from as early as 1929, Catholic bishops were leading the public counter-propaganda: "Close your ears and do not join their associations, close your doors and do not let their newspapers into your homes, close your hands and do not support their endeavours in elections."[4] It was such voices Albert Einstein was referring to, in 1940, when he recalled: "Only the Church stood squarely across the path of Hitler's campaign for suppressing the truth. . . . I am forced thus to confess that what I once despised I now praise unreservedly."[5]

Whenever Pope Pius XII spoke out, or allowed others to speak out, Catholics in Nazi Europe were punished in retaliation, but, behind the scenes, much was done. The Israeli consul in postwar Milan would estimate that the Catholic Church saved between 700,000 and 860,000 Jewish people from certain death,[6] and David Dalin, a Jewish historian, has argued that sensationalist history in Europe and the United

[4] John Frain, *The Cross and the Third Reich* (Oxford: Family Publications, 2009), p. 42.

[5] Ibid., p. 311.

[6] David Dalin, *The Myth of Hitler's Pope: How Pope Pius XII Rescued Jews from the Nazis* (New York: Simon and Schuster, 2012), p. 11.

States criticising Pius XII since the 1960s "must be recognized for what it is: an assault on . . . traditional religion. It is astonishing that so little commentary exists about the extreme nature of attacks on the Catholic Church."[7] Pius XII was thanked after the war by the first two presidents of Israel, the World Jewish Congress, the chief rabbis of Palestine, Egypt, France, London, and Rome, and the Israel Philharmonic Orchestra, who stood for a minute's silence when he died. These included people, one presumes, who had known and witnessed what actually happened on the ground in Europe.

Even if World War II can still be said to have destroyed the notion of "Christendom" in Europe, for some souls the faith had never shone brighter; and that they may have been a minority hardly diminished their courage. In Germany, the resistance was summed up in the motto of the failed military coup of 1944, ETIAM SI OMNES, EGO NON— "Even if all others, not I". Formed by senior (and some of them devout) Catholic and Protestant officers, the plot had gained expediency after the disastrous withdrawal from Russia, but, according to its last survivor, Philipp Von Boeselager, it was sparked by Hitler's banning of Christmas services in the German army in 1942.

Certainly, few Germans might have identified with such a motto more than Saint Teresa Benedicta of the Cross. Born Edith Stein, she had converted to Catholicism in 1921, a decision that alienated her from her beloved and devout Jewish mother. By becoming a Carmelite nun, she gave up the chance of a family of her own as well as her role in the philosophical movement of the day, phenomenology, out of which existentialism was emerging. Prewar feminists, for

[7] Ibid., p. 3.

whom she had been a role model as an academic, rejected her after a series of lectures she delivered on Catholic woman-hood, in which she said that men and women had "differ-ing" souls and that women entering previously male pro-fessions should do so in "an authentically feminine way".[8]

Only her sister Rosa, who had also converted, remained at her side, and they were arrested together at a convent in occupied Holland, following anti-Nazi statements by the local Catholic hierarchy. They were taken first to the cen-tral camp at Amersfoorte-Westerbork then to the camp at Westerbork, where Edith wrote to her Carmelite convent asking for woollen stockings, blankets, the next volume of the breviary, as well as a cross, rosary beads, and warm un-derwear for Rosa. She told them: "so far I have been able to pray gloriously."[9] A survivor from the camp recalled seeing her help mothers looking after their children. Those des-tined for Auschwitz, which most of them were, were not registered there if they were killed on arrival, and there is no subsequent record of the sisters.

Her eventual conversion had come at the farmhouse of some friends over two decades earlier, after she had taken a copy of Saint Teresa of Ávila's *Autobiography* from the shelf and stayed up all night reading it. She would never say what it was about the Spanish saint, also of Jewish descent, that convinced her, only that when she finished the book, she an-nounced: "That is the truth." Thereafter, there was nothing lukewarm about Stein's faith, and, six years on, the former atheist was insisting that religion was "not something to be relegated to a quiet corner or for a few festive hours". It

[8] Edith Stein, *Essays on Woman*, trans. Freda Mary Oben (Washington, D.C.: Institute of Carmelite Studies, 2017), p. 50.

[9] Edith Stein, *Self-Portrait in Letters 1916–1942*, ed. and trans. Josephine Koeppel (Washington, D.C.: Institute of Carmelite Studies, 1993), p. 353.

must, she said, "be the root and basis of all life: and that, not merely for a few chosen ones, but for every true Christian (though of these there is still but a 'little flock')."[10]

By the time I read those lines, my protest was over.

[10] Ibid., p. 54.

Epilogue

I see clearly that you are mistaking the road, and that you
will never arrive at the end of your journey. You want to
climb the mountain, whereas God wishes you to descend
it. He is awaiting you in the fruitful valley of humility.[1]

Saint Thérèse of Lisieux

Stand by the roads, and look, and ask for the ancient paths,
where the good way is; and walk in it, and find rest for
your souls.

Jeremiah 6:16

It was not difficult to refrain from idolising my father, as his
historic act of heroism was a happy adjunct to our childhood, rather than a halo. Perhaps that was particularly because we as children knew him later in life, when family
responsibilities had (almost) tamed him, but he had always
been extremely clumsy. As a young officer, he was once
prosecuted for blowing up a railway toilet, having intended
to play a prank on fellow officers disembarking from the
train after a training exercise. He had stolen ("pinched")
an explosive from the exercise for that purpose, but could
not open a window at the critical moment. It was one of the
first times that *The Times* in London ever ran a light-hearted
piece at the foot of its front page, which saved his career,
since the general deciding his military fate found it amusing
and decided not to court-martial him.

[1] Thérèse of Lisieux, *The Story of a Soul: The Autobiography of St. Thérèse
of Lisieux*, trans. Thomas Taylor (London: Burns and Oates, 1912), p. 229.

It would not be the last time he inadvertently entertained newspaper readers. As his firstborn, when I got stuck in my highchair, Dad decided to call the fire brigade to help him, a story the local press ran with along the lines of "Fat Baby Gets Stuck". Nor had the Darlington railway station been his first run-in with the law. During the nationalist uprising in Cyprus, the British army had to fly a barrister out from England to defend him in a civil suit. Since his job included forcing entry into monasteries looking for weapons and flushing snipers out of towns, scope for annoying the locals was presumably large: "We envied the French in Algeria", he would say.

A shy boy, his first report at Sandhurst said he was too quiet, but after a term he developed a taste for adrenalin and gin. In later life, on long car journeys, I would get a few more stories out of him. Driving a military vehicle outside Tripoli in the 1960s, when two Libyan police motorcyclists tried to stop him, he swerved one of them into a ditch and raced back to camp. In the Far East, he once accepted a bet to swim across a bay with sharks in it. It was another world, a world in which adjutant's horses were hoisted into trees and brigadiers had to be pulled out of casinos. It was a world in which he thrived.

When the Belgium colony in the Congo collapsed, my father was sent there in 1960 with the United Nations, attached to the Ghana Army. The Belgians had pulled out so quickly, he told me, that they had left the radios playing in their homes. A chaotic civil war had erupted to replace them, and in the violence that ensued, Dad and his company were ambushed. In the citation for the military cross that he was duly awarded, he was commended for his "supreme leadership and courage", personally removing roadblocks in sight of the enemy and taking out a Bren machine gun po-

sition with hand grenades. After the tour, he rejoined his
regiment in West Germany, via a pilgrimage to both Fatima
and Rome.

Like many fighters, he struggled with peace, which brought
up ghosts from his childhood. He had been born under a
different name in a Dublin orphanage in 1935, where he
spent the first two years of his life. In a letter to the person in England who would adopt him, one of the nuns
there described him as "a little Napoleon, always smiling".
His adoptive father was a troubled soul, part of a generation
who were eligible for conscription in both World War I and
II. He spent almost a decade in uniform, despite not being
a regular. His elder sister, with whom he had adopted Dad,
was a retired psychiatric matron who was also conscripted
into the war. Aged four in 1939, Dad was placed with a
vicar and his wife in Kent, listening to German bombers
flying overhead toward London. At six, he was sent to a
Catholic boarding school in Leicestershire, where the head-
master, a writer named Fr. Claude Leetham, became a men-
tor. The artist Thomas Henry, who illustrated the popular
Just William books, lived close by, and we have a painting of
Dad at the time, showing a fair, curly-haired lad with blue
eyes and a big Irish smile. He did not know he was adopted
until he was eighteen, by which time he was drinking and
on the edge of suicide. Dad wrote to the orphanage to find
his mother, whom he had grown up thinking was dead. She
was alive and eventually asked him to stop contacting her.

The emotions this stirred were channelled into infantry
life and embraced the parts of the army most people hated
the most—the drill, anonymity, and discipline. He became
exceptionally fit, winning a national race between Birmingham and London with a Polish soldier who went on to appear in *The Guinness Book of Records*. The army offered him

an identity matched only by the Catholic Church, to which he was fiercely loyal and to whom at school he had hoped to offer his life as a priest. His father had refused, wanting him to join the army, and they had taken their deadlock to Cardinal Heenan, then archbishop of Leeds, who said: "We'll get him in the end."

As his letters to Fr. Leetham show, in his early days in the army he still thought the Catholic priesthood would be his eventual lot, and he defended the Church's unpopular position on both abortion and contraception, without which he must have imagined he would not have been born. In an unpublished letter to *The Guardian*, he said that these practices were "depriving the right to existence of an immortal soul, a future citizen of heaven". In a letter to his aunt, after he had settled into army life, he thanked her for adopting him and for what he described as his "Roman Catholicism and sense of destiny".

That sense of destiny included his vocation to the priesthood, but when his army friends started to get married and have children, he became confused. He fell in love with a girl but hesitated to propose, and then she married someone else. After that, the wish to marry gripped him, and he made the decision after the Second Vatican Council to be ordained as an Anglican: "The Pope opened a window, and I flew out", was all he said on the matter. After marrying my mother, he went back into the army as an Anglican chaplain, where people enjoyed the "Padre" with the Irish smile and a military cross to boot. He was never what you would call an over-thinking theologian, once describing heaven as "like one long NAAFI break", and was happy to end a sermon with a Bob Hope joke. God was God, duty was duty, miracles were miracles, and anyone who questioned these things had probably not read Part One Orders. It was years before I realised the genius of this outlook.

It was a humbling era of shrinkage for the post-Imperial British army, but Dad never seemed to mind, forsaking as he already had some of his own destiny to be a family man. He could be heartfelt. Preaching to a regimental association in 2007, he referred to the recent death of a soldier in Afghanistan:

> Now we come to a mystery which all of us must face in one way or another. As some of you know, we lost our daughter within the last twelve months and we've had to think about this a lot. Amongst other things of course, we are conscious of how many people have to cope with all sorts of sufferings. You may be suffering now. [This soldier's family] certainly is. We belong to a support group in Exeter and are humbled and amazed how many people cope. As all of us, all humanity, are in this together, I have got to say to those in the regiment who are not members of the regular congregation here that the Christian church has a lot to pass on about this matter. The answer lies in the next world and is all to do with God.

My sister's death had devastated him, but still the Church was there for him, in the warmth of the local Anglican parish and hours of Hebrew and Greek study. His grief also saw the resurfacing of his Catholic roots, starting with a devotion to Saint Thérèse of Lisieux, whose intercession he could be heard imploring, sometimes with sobs, for months after the funeral and to whose convent in Normandy my brother and I would take him on pilgrimage. He was still funny, even in his grief, and one morning, at a bed and breakfast while on that pilgrimage, I came down to find him dressed in his clerical shirt, holding himself up on the back of a chair, his trousers falling down, repeating to a bunch of bewildered French guests: "*Mon fils va payer.*" It would be tragic had he not laughed to the point of weeping at lunch that day in Lisieux when I described the scene to my brother. We had not seen him so happy in years—maybe that was Saint Thérèse. When I went to Ireland with him, we were taken out to lunch by people who had known his mother. I remember sitting in a fish restaurant in Kinsale with him, while they discussed who they thought his father might have been.

He was clever in a non-academic way and often turned out to be right, which could be annoying, but was after all impressive. He had questions, but even his questions revealed a fundamentally straightforward spirit: he once bought a book called *Will I See My Dog in Heaven?* After strokes began to wreck his speech and mobility, he spent more and more time studying his Bible, hours a day, with a highlighter like a tourist with a guidebook. By then, he had started suffering from bad dreams and was on medication for depression, so the Word and Saint Thérèse were no pastimes for him, but swords against the chaos. Saint John's Gospel was his favourite, and he had given the vicar two passages from it to be read at his funeral: "Eternal life is this: to know you, the only true God. And Jesus Christ whom you have sent." In both passages, Jesus referred to God as "Father". That was important. In a note in his Jerusalem Bible above the other reading he had written the words: "hunger for scripture".

When I told him that I had decided to resign my orders as an Anglican chaplain in order to be received into the Roman Catholic Church, he declared his resolve to follow me. In the end he beat me to it, a bedside occasion that pretty much defines gentleness in my memory. The nightmares had by then gone, he had come off the depression pills, and the smile was still there, rarer but brighter than ever. I could see that he was ready for death, that peace had won the battle for his soul, faith had scored its victory. The last time I visited him, I lay down on the bed next to him and prayed with some rosary beads, and he joined in on the amens. There are a lot of amens in the rosary, and I can still hear his voice, broken by strokes, but resolute: "Amen." "Amen." "Amen." When I kissed him goodbye, he said something I could not catch, so I asked him to repeat it: "Thank you, especially for the prayers."

I was received into the Catholic Church a few weeks later. Awaiting Confirmation and Mass in an empty cathedral on the south coast, I thought about the confession I had just then made, in which, aside from all the grubby things that flesh is heir to, I had confessed self-importance. It was such a relief to have confessed this ridiculous sin that it occurred to me that I should have confessed my anxiety, too, my ability to worry endlessly about the details of my life. Worrying about worry is hard to stop once you have started, and I looked in despair at the tabernacle of the Blessed Sacrament, thinking I had ruined the moment, when heard a voice as clear as a bell: "Don't worry, you're not that important."

The first time I noticed the song of ascents, I had driven down to the House of Lords from Yorkshire to attend a reception about the persecuted Church, being hosted by a Pakistani Christian I had met. As I made my way back through the central lobby with an elderly English evangelist, we met a group of London-based Christians who came to pray each time Parliament was in session. They were from all over the world, and mostly not born here—Christians from Europe, Africa, Asia, and South America were praying for my nation's soul. Deeply moved, I left them talking and went over to look at the mosaic on the floor. "NISI DOMINUS AEDIFICAVERIT DOMUM, IN VANUM LABORAVERUNT QUI AEDIFICANT eam" ("Unless the Lord builds the house, those who build it labor in vain" [Psalm 127]). It was from one of fifteen psalms in the Bible that in Hebrew bear the title "Song of Ascents". Like so much about the ancient world, no one today categorically knows what that title means, though a popular notion is that they were psalms sung by pilgrims as they entered Jerusalem, climbing the steps toward the Temple on the last part of their journey to celebrate the annual festivals. The Hebrew for festival is *hag*, similar to the Arabic *haj*, carrying the meaning of a *turning* to God.

One man who had done as much as anyone to bring me back to God was an African named Richard Khutela. Of all the unusual people I have met, he possibly takes the prize. Formally a chief, he had fought with the ANC's MK underground army during the apartheid years, trained as a doctor in Soviet Russia, and experienced imprisonment on death row. He also played the piano and appreciated the West for its choral tradition. He had never ended up on the political (or medical) gravy train, and I never probed why, for he was a friend rather than an interviewee. What I knew was that after a life in which he had embraced Communism, science, and Africanism, he had ended up returning to the faith of his youth. "I'm quite evangelical", he warned me when we met. And he was, in part because I kept peppering him with questions about God.

One day, he told me this story. He had been being riding as a passenger in someone's car when they went past a town on the coast where the driver had grown up. The town was built around a large lagoon obscured now by property developments, but during the driver's childhood, farmland had run all the way to the lagoon, and he and his mother and sister had lived down there in a laborer's cottage. Each evening before dusk, he and his sister would run over to a tree and wait for a fish eagle to launch itself across the water and go hunting. Each evening it would do this, and they would wait until it flew back with its prey. One day, because their mother was crying, they stayed inside, instead. They had no money, she told them, and there was no food in the house except some old potatoes. As they prayed with her, they heard a noise outside, and the children ran out. On the ground in front of them was a fish, dropped by the eagle, and that night they ate fish and chips.

You can shrug the story off as whimsical. You can question my telling of it, or Richard's, or his friend's. You can look through mythology to find a trope of folk tales involving God, birds, and fish. You could examine it as a socio-political text and do any number of things before you ever asked yourself whether it might have been an actual miracle. And that is understandable, for if you accepted one, then why not a million? And even if you did that, you could still ask what they ate the next night. For me, it is a story told by one person to another, with no explanation or evidence beyond the sincerity of the teller. When I looked at Richard, he seemed as happily confounded by it as I was. I had seen that look before, since being baffled had always been as likely to raise a grin as a frown on my father's face. It was the smile, paradoxically, that made you take them both seriously, until that smile became your own.

The light of Christ that I began to follow soon afterward promised to be both a lamp to my feet and a revealer of every sin, delusion, and absurdity I carry; it has not stopped burning. Richard Khutela died in South Africa a few years after telling me this story. May the souls of all the faithful departed, through the mercy of God, rest in peace. Amen.